YEARBOOK IN
EARLY CHILDHOOD EDUCATION

Bernard Spodek • Olivia N. Saracho
EDITORS

YEARBOOK IN EARLY CHILDHOOD EDUCATION

Editorial Advisory Board

The *Yearbook in Early Childhood Education* is a series of annual publications. Each volume addresses a timely topic of major significance in the field of early childhood education, and contains chapters that present and interpret current knowledge of aspects of that topic, written by experts in the field. Key issues—including concerns about educational equity, multiculturalism, the needs of diverse populations of children and families, and the ethical dimensions of the field—are woven into the organization of each of the volumes.

YEARBOOK
IN
EARLY CHILDHOOD EDUCATION
VOLUME 7

ISSUES IN EARLY CHILDHOOD EDUCATIONAL ASSESSMENT AND EVALUATION

Bernard Spodek • Olivia N. Saracho

EDITORS

TEACHERS
COLLEGE
PRESS

Teachers College, Columbia University
New York • London

Published by Teachers College Press, 1234 Amsterdam Avenue, New York, NY 10027

Library of Congress Cataloging-in-Publication Data

Issues in early childhood educational assessment and evaluation /
    Bernard Spodek and Olivia N. Saracho, editors.
        p.   cm. — (Yearbook in early childhood education ; v. 7)
    Includes bibliographical references and index.
    ISBN 0-8077-3579-5 (cloth)
    1. Early childhood education — United States — Evaluation.   2. Early
childhood education — Great Britain — Evaluation.   3. Educational
tests and measurements.   I. Spodek, Bernard.   II. Saracho, Olivia
N.   III. Series.
    LB1139.25.I87   1997
    372.21 — dc20   96-24894

ISBN 0-8077-3579-5 (cloth)

Printed on acid-free paper
Manufactured in the United States of America

04   03   02   01   00   99   98   97   8   7   6   5   4   3   2   1

Contents

Introduction

Olivia N. Saracho and Bernard Spodek

The concern for evaluation in early childhood education has grown rapidly over the past few years. Not too long ago the idea of evaluation — especially the evaluation of children — was alien to the beliefs of prekindergarten teachers. Over a decade ago one could not find a textbook on evaluation in early childhood education. Today over a half dozen textbooks on evaluating young children are available. Teachers, parents, and policy makers are all increasingly concerned about evaluation in early childhood education.

The conventional wisdom that removed the concern for evaluation in early childhood education was that good teachers of young children intuitively knew what was appropriate for young children and could match the activities provided to the needs of the children in their classes. To formally evaluate these programs was unnecessary. In addition, the value of an early childhood program, especially at the prekindergarten level, was in providing children with good, wholesome experiences. Since teachers were not concerned about the outcomes of these experiences, they would be unnecessarily imposed upon if formal evaluations were made. Additionally, it was feared that evaluation in early childhood education would lead to increased program structure.

There are a number of reasons for the heightened interest today in evaluation in early childhood education. Increasing amounts of public funds are being spent on early childhood education programs. Policy makers and the general public are concerned that these funds not be wasted and that the programs supported be worthwhile, both for the community at large as well as for the children enrolled in these programs. Additionally, as increasing numbers of children are enrolled in both public and private early childhood programs, teachers, parents, and policy makers wish to learn how these programs are functioning and about the outcomes of these programs.

Evaluation requires that we make a judgment of worth about some aspect of education. Making that judgment is usually a twofold process.

1

First we collect information about what we wish to evaluate. Then we use that information to make an assessment. The information we collect may vary. Programs may be evaluated, for example, based on their philosophies or on whether the activities provided to young children meet certain criteria. In such an evaluation, an analysis of program assumptions or an observation of program activities might provide the appropriate basis for a judgment of value, while information about program outcomes would be irrelevant. If, on the other hand, a program is to be evaluated as to its effectiveness, then information on outcomes — achievement data, for example — would need to be collected.

CONSIDERING EVALUATION IN EARLY CHILDHOOD EDUCATION

In addressing evaluation in early childhood education we need to be concerned with what is being evaluated, how it is being evaluated, who is doing the evaluation, and what purposes are being served by the evaluation.

What Should Be Evaluated?

There are a number of different aspects of early childhood education that are evaluated. The nature of the program itself may be assessed. Some programs are implementations of specific curriculum models. The basic assumptions and theories underlying the model might be analyzed in the abstract, and how well the implementation reflects the models in reality might be judged. In addition, information can be collected on the effectiveness of a program model. The former would require only the analysis of documents and the observation of practice. The latter evaluation might be short term — looking at how children function at the end of a period of schooling, or long term — identifying program effects 3, 5, or many more years later.

Early childhood classroom settings also might be evaluated independent of the curriculum models they represent. In evaluating settings, classrooms are observed and information typically is collected on a checklist or rating scale. The Harms and Clifford *Early Childhood Environment Rating Scale* (1980) is an example of a scale used to rate classroom settings. Other approaches to evaluating classrooms also are available (see Harms & Clifford, 1993).

Educational materials and equipment used in early childhood classrooms may be evaluated using a variety of criteria. A number of different

guidelines have been developed to do this. The Educational Products Information Exchange (1973) developed a *Criterion Checklist* for evaluating
educational materials, including looking at the producer, the material's
administrative requirements, curricular requirements, pedagogical requirements, and other elements. Other guidelines also have been developed over time (see Spodek, 1985).

Teachers in early childhood programs may be evaluated. Information
could be collected on teacher planning as well as teachers' interactions in
classrooms. Although teachers often are evaluated by administrators and
others, this is seldom done systematically.

Finally, children in early childhood classrooms are evaluated. Prior
to entrance into a formal program children are judged as to whether they
are developing normally. If a disability is found, then the child will be
recommended for an early childhood special education program. Children
without identifiable disabilities also may be recommended for admission
to prekindergarten programs for children considered to be at risk for future educational failure. This assessment of risk may be the result of a
judgment made on developmental screening; the child may not be seen as
having a disability, but may be considered to be developmentally delayed.
The judgment also may be made based on demographic factors, such as
family economic conditions, prevalent language, or single parent or teenage parent. Thus, an assessment is made of both the child's current development and the conditions under which the child is developing.

Children later are evaluated in regard to their achievement in school.
Achievement may be defined broadly or narrowly. At times academic
achievement alone is assessed. At other times children's ability to adjust or
their social competence may be assessed. This evaluation can be used to
assess the effectiveness of programs or to determine the child's individual
progress in school. What is evaluated reflects what the evaluators and
their audiences want to know about education as well as what they think
is important about children and their programs.

How to Evaluate?

In discussing what should be evaluated, reference has been made to different approaches to gathering data. Checklists, rating scales, or direct observation can be used to collect information on how classrooms function or to
assess children's achievement. Standardized tests may give different results
from observations of performance in a natural setting or from collecting
and analyzing pupil products. The use of standardized tests with young
children has been seriously questioned.

Who Will Evaluate?

Often the issue raised is whether individuals closest to the programs and the children enrolled — teachers and parents — should conduct evaluations or whether outsiders should do it. Parents and teachers may be seen as biased in favor of their programs and children and thus might skew an evaluation. In order to maintain a degree of objectivity, outsiders, often experts in evaluation, may be called upon to conduct an evaluation. There are trade-offs in using one form of evaluation as opposed to another. In gaining objectivity, evaluators may be losing authenticity.

Why Evaluate?

This question is probably the most important. All evaluation serves some purpose. However, different purposes are served by different evaluations.

Often evaluation is used to improve education. The information gained about the program can be used to modify it. Similarly, the information we collect about children can allow us to better match the experiences we provide with their ability to learn from those experiences. It is always important that the purpose of an evaluation be made explicit before the evaluation process begins.

A BRIEF OVERVIEW

This volume reviews two kinds of evaluation in early childhood education: evaluation of programs and evaluation of children. The first four chapters are devoted to issues of program evaluation. In Chapter 1 Bruce Fuller, Susan D. Holloway, and Laurie Bozzi review recent evaluations of early childhood programs from the viewpoints of policy makers, teachers and providers, and parents. They discuss the implications of these three sets of perspectives for the design of early childhood program evaluations. In their review, they focus primarily on center-based, child-care programs, although they incorporate some of the studies of Head Start.

In Chapter 2 Herbert J. Walberg and Arthur J. Reynolds review research on the evaluation of long-term outcomes of early childhood programs. They present a nine-factor model of educational productivity that provides a framework for explaining long-term effects of these programs. This type of research is relatively new, and there are few studies that have followed children over a long period of time. However, there are important questions that can be answered from this research, and the answers can help us better understand early childhood programs and their consequences.

Lawrence J. Schweinhart and Ann S. Epstein suggest in Chapter 3 that we need to look at evaluation of early childhood programs within the framework of the program models that are used. In addition, Schweinhart and Epstein report that not all teachers consciously implement a particular program model.

Although most chapters in this book refer to early childhood education in the United States, Chapter 4 by Tony Bertram and Christine Pascal deals with the evaluation of early childhood programs in Great Britain. The concern for quality in the early childhood programs there has led to the development of a collaborative model of evaluation of early childhood programs from which early childhood educators in the United States can learn a great deal.

The next four chapters in this volume deal with the evaluation of children in early childhood programs. The use of standardized tests to evaluate young children's learning has raised controversy in early childhood education. In Chapter 5 William L. Goodwin and Laura D. Goodwin review concerns about the use of standardized measures in early childhood education. They present principles for the appropriate use of standardized measures and provide examples of standardized measures that can be used with young children.

There are a number of alternative ways to evaluate learning in young children other than standardized measures. In Chapter 6 Doris Bergen discusses the use of observational techniques for evaluating learning in young children. She discusses the common features of observational techniques and describes the various procedures that can be used.

Dominic F. Gullo in Chapter 7 discusses using pupil products for student evaluation. He identifies the problems in the use of pupil products for evaluating children, then discusses these products in the light of those problems. He provides general principles that can guide the use of pupil products in the assessment process and addresses questions regarding the analysis of pupil products for assessment. He also discusses the procedures to be used in assessing pupil products.

Most forms of evaluation used in early childhood programs relate to academic readiness and achievement or to intellectual development. Yet the development of social competence is an important goal of early childhood education. In Chapter 8 Sally Atkins-Burnett, Julie Nicholson, and Samuel J. Meisels review the research on the assessment of social competence in young children. They define social competence, describe its importance for young children, and summarize the various measures available for assessing social competence in young children.

The field of early childhood education has long viewed parents as important to the process of early childhood education. Parents need to be considered in relation to the evaluation of children's learning. Alice Sterling Honig in Chapter 9 discusses the role of parents in the evaluative process. She also discusses what educators can do to help parents better understand the process of evaluation in early childhood education.

In the final chapter in this volume, Bernard Spodek and Olivia N. Saracho look at the future uses of evaluation in early childhood education. They discuss ways that evaluation has been used in the past and some of the problems that have been identified. They see an increasing use of evaluation in early childhood education and discuss how assessment can be used to improve programs and practices in the field.

REFERENCES

Educational Products Information Exchange. (1973). *Report 54: Improving materials selection procedures: A basic "how to" handbook.* New York: Epie.

Harms, T., & Clifford, R. M. (1980). *Early Childhood Environment Rating Scale.* New York: Teachers College Press.

Harms, T., & Clifford, R. M. (1993). Studying educational settings. In B. Spodek (Ed.), *Handbook of research on the education of young children* (pp. 477–492). New York: Macmillan.

Spodek, B. (1985). *Teaching in the early years* (3rd ed.). Englewood Cliffs, NJ: Prentice-Hall.

CHAPTER 1

Evaluating Child Care and Preschools: Advancing the Interests of Government, Teachers, or Parents?

Bruce Fuller, Susan D. Holloway, and Laurie Bozzi

Rising political interest in young children and the family has sparked a flurry of child-care evaluation initiatives. The old debate over whether exposure to child care yields positive or negative effects for children has given way to a wider panoply of questions: Is the supply of child-care organizations sufficient and equitably distributed across communities, rich and poor? What is the current state of child-care quality? How do professionals and parents residing in diverse communities vary in their conceptions of "quality"? To what extent does child care "empower" impoverished parents to enter the work force and become self-sufficient?

These resurgent concerns — whether heard in the speeches of political leaders or seen in academic journals — are intriguing and at times point constructively to policy alternatives. At other times the rhetoric stings, intended more to blame the poor than to assist families with positive incentives and enabling services. Over the past decade important initiatives have sprouted from this bewildering mix of polemics and evidence: rapid expansion of Head Start, followed by rising concern over sharp variability in its quality; enactment of the national child-care block grant program, followed by debate over how to balance expansion of supply with quality improvements; and passage of ambitious welfare reforms that are creating greater demand for scarce child-care spaces.

Crafting a broad and stable "public interest" in expanding early childhood programs has proven to be a difficult and uncertain project. However, rising political heat spurs the more rapid baking of public policy. Decision-makers ask more frequently about the actual effects of alternative policy mechanisms and costly programs. Child-care activists mobilize evaluation evidence, which stimulates fresh policy action. Activists and researchers alike play crucial roles in *legitimating* government's involvement in family and child development programs. Evaluators quietly confront the issue of whether to support favored institutions or, more dispassionately, to provide rigorous evidence on program effects: what interventions work or don't work, and why?

THE POLITICAL FOUNDATIONS OF PROGRAM EVALUATION

This brings us to the heart of our argument: *Evaluations in the child-care and preschool field now aim primarily to inform policy makers, focusing on the varied interests of government.* We do not interpret this tacit agenda of researchers or evaluators in a dark light, as a negative exercise. We do argue, however, that it is a limiting way of defining evaluation research. Two additional ways of organizing child-care evaluations have taken root in recent years, although they are still sprouting just at the surface of this intellectual soil. Assessments of how *teachers and providers* view the quality and character of preschool organizations have begun to emerge, and evidence — from survey and ethnographic studies — is accumulating on how *parents* define and understand the quality of their providers. Evaluators, in making research design decisions, implicitly decide whose voices will be heard and amplified, and whose interests are paramount.

We all have the interests of young children in mind, but the interests of policy makers or professional elites do not always converge with diverse local interests of providers and parents. For example, one important national study of family day-care quality recently proclaimed: "Although there is debate about what is most essential to quality . . . there seems to be a consensus among those most directly involved — parents and providers" (Galinsky, Howes, Kontos, & Shinn, 1994, p. 25). A rather surprising statement, given that professional organizations have become increasingly sensitive to ways in which definitions of child-care quality and "proper socialization" held by many ethnic minority parents depart from upper-middle-class Anglo norms. Many parents from non-Anglo groups, particularly Latinos, even shy away from placing their youngsters in formal preschools (discussed below). Similarly, empirical and philosophical debate has arisen over whether didactic or "developmentally appropriate" preschool practices result in positive child outcomes (e.g., Stipek, 1993). Galinsky and colleagues (1994) focus on global characteristics, claiming that we agree on the importance of the provider–child interaction. However, what kind of social relations are culturally expected?

We all carry in our heads implicit models for how our favorite policy or program should be boosting young children's development. Certainly, universal definitions of quality are important, and pleas for more provider training or smaller group sizes can be defended on empirical grounds. The problem is that conceptions of "development" usually must be narrowed to mobilize political support for preschool initiatives. Intellectual costs are incurred when we narrow the range of developmental outcomes to be studied, or implicitly assume that central actors can manipulate the policy apparatus to boost the "right kind" of preschool supply or the "appropriate" types of classroom practices. We risk ignoring the pluralistic socialization agendas exercised by parents and providers.

We are *not* arguing that policy makers and their scholarly advisers should stop attempting to mobilize political support or cease investigating how policy touches the local effects of preschools. We are, however, centering this review on one key point: Evaluators of child-care programs make choices as to whether they are speaking to the interests of government, providers, or parents. Evaluations conducted within the policy context always contain political judgments. Those who utilize evaluations— from preschool directors to White House staffers—should become more cognizant of the *political foundations* of research designs. Whose institutional interests are being served? Evaluation findings inevitably lead to judgments about which types of preschool programs should receive funding or how quality can best be raised. This lies at the heart of empirically informed politics. It leads to embracing or repudiating certain financing streams (Head Start, independent provider contracts, or vouchers), regulatory agencies, and ideologies pertaining to how quality can be improved. Indeed, evaluation designs serve to legitimate or critically reflect upon how each of these three constituencies *sees* the socialization and growth of children, as well as the organizations that advance particularistic conceptions of child development.

The remainder of this chapter is organized in four sections. First, we review recent evaluations that primarily serve *policy makers*, delving into issues of whether the supply of child care and preschools is sufficient, as well as whether access and quality are equally distributed. Second, we examine initial work that sheds light on early childhood *teachers and providers*, describing some of their work-life issues and how they assess the "quality" of their settings. Third, we turn to empirical research on how *parents* assess the quality and character of preschool organizations. This form of evaluation research is linked to survey studies of parents' choices and access to different types of child care. Researchers have been digging more deeply to learn qualitatively how parents from diverse ethnic and class backgrounds actually define the quality of their child-care arrangements and emphasize quite different conceptions of "child development." Finally, we discuss implications for how these three perspectives require more innovative evaluation designs. Throughout, our review focuses mainly on center-based programs providing full-day child care to pre-school-aged children. We incorporate some of the literature on family day care and Head Start, but generally do not cover informal child-care arrangements or care for school-aged children.

We emphasize two starting assumptions. We see nothing wrong about conducting evaluations that speak to particular interests or organizational levels. Nor do we assume that the interests of government, providers, and parents are always in conflict. For example, the provision of equally accessible preschool programs that are affordable, high in quality, and diverse in character is an objective that is shared across many members of the three groups. Our argument is that evaluators — and readers of evaluations — must think more carefully about how research designs reinforce or question what forms of child socialization and "development" match the aims of particular families. We must specify *conditions* under which assumed child outcomes, and programmatic remedies, are valid for the population being studied. The broader literature on program evaluation is replete with examples of how the *framing* of the evaluation and research question constrains whose views are brought into the light of day and how much variation is observed (e.g., Cronbach et al., 1980), a point early childhood evaluators are just beginning to face.

EVALUATION FOR POLICY MAKERS

Evaluation evidence amplifies the voice of certain actors — usually residents of professional organizations who support, utilize, or conduct evaluation research. We might call these actors *centralized activists*. We begin with the important evaluation findings that flow from this milieu. Then, we ask about the limitations and risks of this professional discourse, particularly when it inadvertently mutes the more diverse voices of teachers, providers, and parents.

Priority Evaluation Issues

Policy-centered evaluations have focused on the interrelated questions of access and quality: *Is the supply of child care sufficient? Are child-care and preschool organizations distributed equitably, or does access to quality care remain tied to family income and neighborhood resources?* The demand for child care services and formal preschooling has grown enormously over the past 3 decades. In 1990, among mothers with children under age 5, 54% were employed outside the home (Hofferth, Brayfield, Deich, & Holcomb, 1991). These families included 9.3 million preschool-aged children who required care by some combination of parents, kin members, family day-care providers, or center-based programs. Actors in and around government ask whether the supply of child-care options is sufficient and distributed evenly across families — households that differ sharply in terms of their economic resources, ethnic composition, and preferences for how to care for and socialize their young children. The institutional arrangement of child care in the United States represents a mixed market of providers, supported through private fees and government subsidies. Various organizational factors may constrain the family's capacity to select particular types of child care: fee levels, distance and transportation costs, worries about overall "quality," including divergent conceptions of what constitutes "high-quality" activities and social rules found within the provider's setting.

Empirical Findings

Questions about the adequacy of child-care and preschool supply are beginning to receive careful empirical attention. The most recent national survey of center-based programs, conducted in 1990, revealed underutilized capacity: The number of licensed slots for children was found to exceed actual enrollments. An estimated 4.2 million child slots were available within licensed centers that served 4 million youngsters (Kisker, Hofferth, Phillips, & Farquhar, 1991). Drawing from sample data on family day-care homes, an estimated 860,000 slots were available with licensed providers that served 700,000 children. Child-care shortages or restricted options may persist in some states and local areas, however. Siegel and Loman (1991) found that several inner-city Chicago neighborhoods had *no* formal child-care provider, despite high proportions of households headed by poor single parents. A shortage of slots also may plague parents with infants or children who have special needs.

Are Child-Care Providers Distributed Equally Across Communities? Government is recurrently interested in whether diverse families have equal access to different types of child care and preschooling. Since the 1960s, federal policy and state initiatives in urban states have aimed to broaden access for low-income parents, especially access to center-based programs, including expansion of Head Start and community-based preschools. Recent evaluations have begun to assess the extent to which these policy and financing initiatives have helped to equalize supply and basic access. One initial study of centers and families in five cities concluded that children from working-class and middle-income families appeared to participate at lower rates than youngsters from either low- or high-income households (Whitebook, Howes, & Phillips, 1989). Nationwide *family-level* data, however, reveal that this U-shaped pattern of participation in center-based programs depends largely on family ethnicity, as detailed below. It remains unclear whether uneven distribution of organizational supply constrains access to centers, or whether particular ethnic and social-class groups prefer informal types of child care.

Organization-level or aggregate data also have been analyzed to examine inequities in supply and access. Analyzing data on all preschools and centers operating in 100 counties nationwide, Fuller and Liang (1993, 1996) found sharp inequalities in supply per capita across regions of the country and between affluent versus low-wealth counties. Among the 25 most affluent counties, one center-based class was available for every 45 children ages 3–5. In the lowest-wealth counties, one preschool class was available for every 77 children. These county-level variations in supply were most strongly related to mean family income observed in the local areas, presence of single-parent households, and population growth, after accounting for the suppressing effect of prices or fee levels. Importantly, counties with a higher preschool supply also showed higher levels of quality; these variables are not inversely related, as opponents of stronger quality regulation have claimed (Edwards, Fuller, & Liang, in press).

A major issue in evaluating supply inequalities is how to define a local community in ways that match parents' own conception of the local area within which they search for child care. Counties may not be meaningful units when they are large and internally heterogeneous in terms of child-care supply and quality. To address this issue Fuller and Liang (in press) studied the per capita distribution of preschools among zip code areas in

Massachusetts, a state with relatively high supply overall. This study revealed that per capita supply was over one-third greater in affluent communities, relative to poor inner-city areas. A somewhat lower supply of preschools was observed for zip code areas dominated by middle-income families, reminiscent of the curvilinear pattern of family-level participation rates observed earlier.

Family-Level Views of Access, Cost, and Ethnic Differences. Survey research has helped to move below organization-level dynamics, to evaluate how individual families select a particular provider from among available options. Ethnic variations in preschool selection are particularly intriguing. Low-income Black families, for instance, about half of which are headed by single mothers, have a higher propensity to use center-based programs than do other ethnic groups. Yet the percentage of White households using center-based programs is roughly equal across all income levels. Enrollment rates for Latino families are lower than for African-American and White families across all income levels. The gap in center-based care use between Black and Latino parents (with employed mothers) equals 23%. Independent of ethnicity, affluent families consistently utilize preschool programs at higher rates than all other families, whether studied with aggregate community or household-level data (Fuller, Holloway, & Liang, 1995).

How parents select certain forms of nonparental care is a process that we are just beginning to understand. Policy makers, of course, are interested in material constraints that lead to unequal access. The growth of subsidies and consistent targeting of low-income families has worked for the most part, notwithstanding remaining shortages in some inner-city and rural areas, and among many working-class families. One study has found that parents tend to prefer center-based programs, when they are affordable, over less formal alternatives (Hofferth & Wissoker, 1992), not taking into account ethnic differences. Debate remains over the causes of Latino families' lower propensity to select center-based programs. Initial work shows that Latina mothers are more likely to share child-care responsibilities with fathers, have closer access to grandparents, and often shy away from what some see as impersonal preschool institutions (Fuller, Eggers-Piérola, Liang, Holloway, & Rambaud, 1996).

Is Quality Distributed Equally Across Communities? While specific inequalities in availability clearly persist, preschool quality appears to be more fairly distributed across diverse communities. The targeting of subsidies and programs over the past 3 decades appears to have been largely successful (from Head Start to targeted child-care vouchers for low-income parents). Drawing on two independent studies of center quality, one research group found that quality is highest in affluent suburban communities (Phillips, Voran, Kisker, Howes, & Whitebook, 1994). They studied both "structural" indicators of quality (child to staff ratios, provider training levels) and more specific indicators of classroom activities, including provider warmth and child–provider interactions. Heterogeneity in quality was observed among preschools and centers serving low-income families. Most notably, Head Start and public school centers were found to be lower in quality relative to independent nonprofit centers in terms of structural dimensions (group size and child to staff ratios). These evaluators also found that middle-class families had the highest propensity to participate in lower-quality centers, often selecting for-profit centers (this confirms earlier work by Coelen, Glantz, & Calore, 1979).

Evidence is less clear that central regulation of quality holds intended effects. One natural experiment—Florida's lowering of allowable child to staff ratios and boosting of provider training requirements in 1992—has been evaluated. These regulatory changes are associated with the hiring of more-highly trained teachers and aides, and with positive teacher practices and child development outcomes (Howes, Smith, & Galinsky, 1995). It is not clear to what extent particular kinds of parents may have self-selected into centers falling under the new regulations, nor are the processes clear by which these policy changes led to positive outcomes. When California experimented with incremental increases in child to staff ratios, no negative effects on teacher practices or child outcomes were observed (Love, Ryer, & Faddis, 1992).

Authors of another recent study of quality concluded that "states with more demanding licensing standards have fewer poor-quality centers" (Helburn, Howes, Bryant, & Kagan, 1995, p. 4). This associational fact often is confused with the causal claim that more intense regulation has resulted in higher quality. State-level variability in regulatory intensity covaries with aggregate levels of family income, maternal employment, and resulting demand for child-care programs. That is, the same affluent urban states that have stricter regulation also have stronger demand for child care among a larger set of affluent families. When one controls on aggregate state-level patterns of family demand, the effects of regulatory intensity diminish considerably. The most effective policy may be to link quality standards tightly to targeted subsidies, as do most state provider contracts and parental voucher programs (Fuller, Raudenbush, Wei, & Holloway, 1993; Helburn, Morris, Culkin, Kagan, & Rustici, 1995). Also, state regulation may be effective in remedying situations in which minimal health and safety standards are not being met. (Phillipsen, Cryer, & Howes, 1995).

The Limits of Evaluation for Policy Makers

This line of work is making clear contributions to our understanding of child-care supply and quality, particularly in illuminating regional inequalities. But, first, most of this research focuses on centers and formal preschools, at the expense of family day care and informal arrangements (an area opened up recently by Kontos, Howes, Shinn, & Galinsky, 1995). Second, large surveys implicitly have placed a premium on universal indicators of provider quality. Conventional indicators of quality are handy for policy makers and help to mobilize political support, two virtuous attributes. Yet they may fail to capture teachers' and parents' definitions.

Third, these policy evaluations theoretically are underdeveloped, often confounding *organization-level* versus *family-level* mechanisms that lead to greater supply of or demand for child care. When the Congress expands Head Start, we can see supply-driven gains in child-care spaces. When affluent parents decide to buy a slot in the market of child-care organizations, however, family-level processes are driving expressed demand. Because the child-care market is segmented institutionally — with private and government financing streams — it is difficult to disentangle organizational from family-level processes (Barnett, 1993). The issue of how different families select child-care providers *under different organizational conditions* is crucial if we are to isolate the value-added effects of centers. The tandem issue is how alternative policy actions penetrate into centers to influence supply and quality. We are just beginning to understand the discrete local effects of child-care tax credits, vouchers, and direct provider subsidies, after taking into account contextual factors that independently boost quality (Gormley, 1995).

EVALUATION FOR TEACHERS AND PROVIDERS

Early childhood teachers shape youngsters' experiences and learning day to day. Yet little evaluation activity has focused on the quality of their work lives, how they define quality, and their reactions to the myriad policies and training programs directed at them. In contrast, educational researchers focusing on K–12 schooling have generated much empirical research on how the behaviors, beliefs, and organizational contexts of teachers influence learning and socialization outcomes.

Priority Evaluation Issues

We begin by reviewing two questions specifically related to teachers that evaluators have begun to examine. For simplicity we use the term *teacher* to include teachers in preschools or child-care centers as well as providers in home-based settings.

First, *what is the quality of teachers' working conditions and how is variation linked to child-level outcomes?* Working conditions presumably are related to high staff turnover in many center-based and home-based settings, and turnover is viewed as an intermediate variable that in turn influences children's attachment to teachers and other developmental outcomes. Assessing the character and quality of working conditions is difficult, given the diversity of settings and organizations in which providers labor (Phillips & Whitebook, 1986). The National Child Care Staffing Study (Whitebook et al., 1989) broke new ground in trying to better understand this diversity of working conditions in center-based programs. Recent work within home-based and kin-care settings has extended knowledge of working conditions outside center-based programs (Kontos et al., 1995).

Second, *how do teachers define quality and the learning agenda for young children?* Researchers usually assume that their preferred indicators of quality are shared by teachers. However, this remains a large empirical question.

Empirical Findings

Working Conditions. Recent studies reveal great variability in the wages, preparation, and day-to-day working conditions of teachers in preschools and center-based programs. Using a sample drawn from five urban areas, Whitebook and colleagues (1989) estimated average annual staff turnover to be 41%. A nationally representative sample including only teachers estimated much lower turnover rates, averaging 25% annually (Kisker et al., 1991). In programs with some turnover, however, the overall rate was estimated to be 50%.

Turnover is likely due, in part, to low wages, poor benefits, and unsupportive work environments (Phillips, Howes, & Whitebook, 1991; Whitebook et al., 1989). In their nationwide study Kisker and colleagues (1991) estimated hourly wages at $7.49 an hour for teachers (excluding aides and assistants). Despite the steady growth of child-care and preschool revenues nationwide from subsidies and parental fees, teacher salaries have remained remarkably static over the past 15 years (Blau, 1992). Fewer than half of preschool teachers are estimated to receive health insurance (Kisker et al., 1991).

Many teachers display strong commitment despite facing mediocre to poor material conditions. Many work additional hours each week without compensation, and teachers report purchasing classroom materials and supplies out of their own pocket (Whitebook, Howes, Darrah, & Friedman, 1982). Despite high turnover rates in some centers, many teachers and aides report high levels of intrinsic satisfaction coming from their work (Kontos & Stremmel, 1988; Phillips et al., 1991). This paradoxical finding highlights the fact that we know very little about the process of provider burnout. How working conditions and the nature of this work lead to exit from the field — for both preschools and home-based providers — is a question that requires more careful study. While empirical links have been established between material working conditions, turnover, and teacher–child relationships, we know few details about how teachers themselves assess these dynamics.

Teachers' Beliefs About Child Development and Socialization. The professional research literature — consumed by policy makers — is replete with the assumption that teachers need to learn more, ideally through preservice or inservice training programs. Teachers often are viewed as the object of quality standards, regulations, and training schemes. Little is known, with the exception of a few small qualitative studies (e.g., Ayers, 1989; Yonemura, 1986; Zinsser, 1991) about what teachers think about quality, child development, and teaching (Ayers, 1989; Spodek, 1988).

How diverse are teachers' conceptions of quality and child development aims, and do they match those expressed by professional researchers? A handful of studies have attempted to illustrate the role of ethnicity and professional training in shaping teachers' beliefs about quality. Qualitative work by Lubeck (1985), for example, compared a Head Start classroom staffed by African-American teachers with a middle-income, tuition-funded preschool staffed by Anglo teachers. She illuminated differences in child-rearing strategies and goals, with the Black teachers emphasizing more directive forms of control, respect for adult authority, and structured tasks. Cultural differences in teachers' views of socialization also were described by Jipson (1991), who gauged the reactions of 30 teachers from diverse ethnic backgrounds and training histories to the guidelines of the National Association for the Education of Young Children (NAEYC) related to "developmentally appropriate" practices (Bredekamp, 1987). Many of the teachers expressed the view that the guidelines did not adequately respond to the diverse cultures and contexts that they regularly faced, and felt that the guidelines confined their professional judgment and discretion, contributing to the de-skilling of their work.

Training is related to teachers' perceptions of quality and their attributions about child behavior and growth. One study found that teachers who had less training in early childhood education, and those with less schooling in general, were more likely to view children as responsible for their own misbehavior (Scott-Little & Holloway, 1994). Teachers who cast the blame on children rather than parents, teachers, or other environmental factors were more likely to endorse a forceful, stern, and disapproving response to instances of misbehavior.

Johnson-Beykont (1995) looked at links between teachers' training levels and their perceptions of the NAEYC guidelines, interviewing 37 teachers in four sites serving low-income children. He found that most of the teachers in his study endorsed a balance of structured learning opportunities and time for child-initiated activities. Those with more training reported a less favorable opinion of teacher-structured activities, although some were convinced that more highly structured activities were beneficial than the mix endorsed by the NAEYC, especially for low-income children. Many reported conflicts with supervisors over the issue of teaching letters and numbers. In a mistaken interpretation of developmentally appropriate practice, some directors banned all teaching of letters and numbers even to those children expressing an interest in learning to read or write; this rigid, bureaucratic response was a source of frustration to teachers. A smaller number of teachers also experienced tension with supervisors over appropriate methods for disciplining children, often feeling that more respect for adult authority should be incorporated into the preschool's socialization goals.

To what extent do teachers' definitions of quality converge with, or depart from, parents' conceptions? An ongoing concern within early childhood has been the extent to which providers' socialization beliefs and practices are congruent with those of parents. The issue of continuity has been raised particularly in regard to low-income families or those from ethnic minorities, although little consensus has emerged as to when continuity is desirable and when it is detrimental to children's development (Powell, 1989). A detailed picture of mothers' and teachers' views about goals, control strategies, and teaching strategies can be found in a longitudinal study of 34 teachers and 67 mothers conducted by Hess, Dickson, Price, and Leong (1979). They found that mothers expected mastery of developmental tasks at an earlier age than teachers; yet teachers were more direct, demanding, and explicit in their teaching style than were parents. Mothers also reported justifying disciplinary acts to their children by referring to their own authority, whereas teachers more often reported invoking rules to back up their attempts to control children. Mothers expected compliance on their own terms, whereas teachers were more flexible in their degree of expected compliance.

A similar study by Kuhns, Holloway, and Scott-Little (1992) provides some explanation for the apparent tendency of mothers to endorse a restrictive and demanding attitude toward children. Those researchers asked 40 mothers and 40 caregivers to respond to a series of hypothetical incidents in which a child committed a norm violation or failed to behave altruistically. Teachers tended to attribute failures to be altruistic to factors controllable by the *adult*, whereas mothers considered norm violations to be controllable by the *child*. Compared with teachers, mothers became more angry, believed it more important to respond, and were more likely to use power assertion and induction in response to children's failures to be altruistic. Mothers also reacted with more anger and with more power assertion to norm violations than did teachers. Such findings link back to policy evaluations in pointing to *how* teacher and provider training influence child outcomes.

In sum, we are just beginning to grasp the diverse ways in which teachers and providers conceive of quality and their underlying assumptions about how to structure children's settings. The earlier focus on working conditions remains important, especially in mobilizing and refining policy action. Yet again, if the field is serious about improving quality in ways that build from teachers' own conceptions, much remains to be learned about the diverse connotations attached to "quality."

EVALUATION FOR PARENTS

Priority Evaluation Issues

What Do Parents Want from Their Child-Care Arrangements? Initial evaluations point to the importance to a family's particular economic *and* cultural contexts in shaping their criteria for selecting and evaluating child-care settings. Priorities and qualitative criteria may be wide-ranging, including concrete features such as cost, location with respect to home and work, convenience, and flexibility in hours of operation. Additionally, a parent might consider compatibility with teachers and providers, as well as whether they seem warm, attentive, and in agreement with the parent's conception of how the child should be socialized and learn.

A small number of studies have attempted to assess parents' evaluations of child-care settings. We know very little about how parents from different ethnic and cultural groups conceptualize the role of preschools in their particular socialization. Are parents in substantial agreement with each other, or are they split along ethnic and social-class lines? Some researchers herald "consensus" (e.g., Galinsky et al., 1994), while others emphasize diversity (e.g., Bowman, 1992). We examine these studies next.

Empirical Findings

Convenience and Affordability. Studies of middle-class families find that criteria pertaining to program characteristics are more important to parents in selecting or evaluating their child-care arrangements than are logistical considerations like cost, hours, and location (Holloway & Fuller, 1992; Kisker, Maynard, Gordon, & Strain, 1989; Powell, 1994). For example, McCall, Tittnich, and Snyder (1994) found that 47% of parents mentioned quality-related issues in explaining their choices; convenience or proximity to home was mentioned by 36%. Yet, surveys treat parental choice of child care as if it were a single decision that involved ranking a number of criteria, whereas it is likely to involve a dynamic process in which a series of trade-offs are made. Prosser and McGroder (1992) argue convincingly that surveys cannot reveal whether parents "maximize quality given cost and convenience limitations . . . or select the least costly among convenient and high-quality options" (p. 49).

Low-income parents may be more likely than middle-class families to make decisions based on cost, hours, and convenience (Gravett, Rogers, & Thompson, 1987). When a low-income single parent works irregular hours or has a child with special needs, the current system of child care may prove entirely inadequate (Polakow, 1993). Qualitative studies reveal that many low-income parents also are concerned with the quality of care and that their definitions of "quality" are somewhat bounded by ethnic or cultural norms (Holloway, Fuller, Rambaud, & Eggers-Piérola, 1995).

Supportive Relationships with Teachers and Providers. Parents in one large survey ranked "provider's communication with parents about their children" as the second most important feature contributing to quality of family day care (Galinsky et al., 1994). Furthermore, participation in a child-care setting that stresses parental involvement has been associated with greater feelings of mastery and satisfaction among low-income mothers (Parker, Piotrkowski, & Peasy, 1987). Research suggests that the parent–provider relationship often is not a positive one. Preschool staff often develop negative perceptions of single mothers, parents who come from different social-class backgrounds, and parents who display differing child-rearing values from those of the teachers (Kontos & Wells, 1986; Zinsser, 1991).

Affective Climate. Among elements of quality that directly influence the child, the provider's affect may be especially important to parents.

Parents seem quite attentive to teachers' affect with their children. Willer and colleagues (1991), for instance, found that 60% of parents mentioned some aspect of caregiving quality (particularly a warm and loving caregiver) as the most important factor determining their choice of preschool or care provider. Parents using family day care seem particularly attentive to the caregiver's warmth and "homelike" behavior (Galinsky et al., 1994).

It seems logical that parents' feeling of trust is greater with regard to providers they feel they know well or are similar to. However, direct evidence for the importance of similarity of provider to parent is mixed. On one hand, Kontos (1993) found no evidence that parents selected family day-care providers who were similar to themselves in terms of socioeconomic status, child-rearing preferences, or social support. However, qualitative work suggests that parents feel more comfortable with providers who are similar to themselves (Zinsser, 1991). Parents may not attribute their feeling of comfort to similarity based on shared cultural values, but it is likely these factors play an important role. Fuller and colleagues (in press) report qualitative evidence that Latina mothers may avoid formal preschools in part because they feel caregivers in such settings lack the warmth and sensitivity they feel are essential to good child care. Atkinson (1987) found that perceived similarity between teachers' beliefs and mothers' beliefs was a highly rated criterion.

Cognitive Stimulation. Survey evidence confirms that parents believe that child-care settings should prepare children to succeed in school (Maynard, Kisker, & Kerachsky, 1990; Willer et al., 1991), although their definitions of cognitive skill development may diverge sharply from professional conceptions of developmentally appropriate practices (Bredekamp, 1987). Parents are likely to be more favorable to a skill-oriented approach than are teachers (who themselves are more skill oriented than those in policy and academic positions). Many middle- and upper-income parents endorse teacher-structured programs (Hyson, 1991), and those in low-income and ethnic minority groups are even more likely to favor such programs, as well as to engage in rote learning activities at home (Corsaro & Rosier, 1992; Joffe, 1977; Stipek, Milburn, Clements, & Daniels, 1992). Programs that augment a "developmental" philosophy with some didactic activities may be acceptable to many parents, provided they are not perceived as contradicting traditional views about authority relations and appear linked to school readiness (Holloway et al., 1995; Stipek, 1993).

Improving Evaluation Designs

Why do studies of parental evaluation of child care appear so contradictory? How can we design better studies in this unexplored territory? First, there has been a failure in the literature to anticipate wide diversity in parental criteria and to document and understand the underlying structural characteristics that are associated with that diversity. As we have seen, parents' criteria are affected by their educational, economic, and cultural backgrounds. Confusion arises when findings from various income groups are pooled. Investigation of child-care preferences by parents belonging to major ethnic groups, such as Latinos, has been cursory at best, in spite of evidence that they are averse to preschools and center-based programs in many cases (Fuller et al., in press; Powell, Zambrana, & Silva-Palacios, 1990).

To improve evaluation designs we can look to the family-support literature that documents evaluations in which program participants define the evaluation questions in conjunction with the evaluators (Powell, 1994). Emerging qualitative work with parents also might lead to more culture-specific indicators of valued child outcomes and antecedent socialization practices that parents believe lead to these situational outcomes.

A related area of research deals with the global question of whether parents are satisfied with their child-care arrangements. Survey evidence presents a starkly ambiguous picture. Most surveys, when asking broad questions about satisfaction, find high reported levels (e.g., Helburn et al., 1995; Holloway & Fuller, 1992). However, when parents are asked about their desire to change preschools or child-care providers, a significant proportion report an interest in doing so (Fuqua & Labensohn, 1986; Kisker et al., 1989). One common type of desired change is to move a child from home-based to center-based care (e.g., Willer et al., 1991).

Finally, future research should investigate the effects on parents of the degree of support (or hostility and criticism) prevailing in their children's child-care setting. While recent writing on home visiting programs has tended to consider the effects of professionals imposing a foreign value system on parents (Behrman, 1993), this view has been aired less often in writings on preschooling and child care.

CONCLUSION: EVALUATION IN WHOSE INTEREST?

Evaluation studies illuminate quite different facets of the early childhood enterprise, depending on whether the researcher begins from the viewpoint of policy maker, teacher, or parent. Policy makers commission most of the formal evaluation studies of child-care and preschool organizations. The issues addressed are articulated by policy makers. Deep affection for generalizable results dictates broad surveys and simple measures of quality. Political mobilization rests on images linked to availability, cost, and the distribution of quality organizations. The best organized interest groups are linked to, and largely financed by, formal provider *organizations*. All these political forces and institutional realities are, in some respects, beneficial.

These beginning points for how policy makers and their scholarly advisers define the issues, the legitimacy of different types of providers, and universal conceptions of quality also serve to narrow how we construct evaluation studies. If we were to begin with how diverse teachers or parents see early childhood organizations and less formal arrangements — especially their pluralistic definitions of quality settings — we would first pinpoint a wider array of intended child-level outcomes. This would likely teach us more about how parents or teachers in highly variable communities think about how they want their children to develop, cognitively and socially.

We are not arguing that there exists one optimal way of doing evaluation studies. Nor are we assuming that the three evaluation approaches are mutually exclusive. We do want to emphasize that if evaluators respond to the issues and problem definitions of policy makers only, we will continue to learn comparatively little about how parents and teachers see the variegated settings in which an increasing number of children are growing up.

Acknowledgment. Appreciation is expressed to the Spencer Foundation for supporting portions of this work.

REFERENCES

Atkinson, A. M. (1987). A comparison of mothers' and providers' preferences and evaluations of day care center services. *Child and Youth Care Quarterly, 16,* 35–47.

Ayers, W. (1989). *The good preschool teacher: Six teachers reflect on their lives.* New York: Teachers College Press.

Barnett, S. (1993). New wine in old bottles: Increasing the coherence of early childhood care and education policy. *Early Childhood Research Quarterly, 8,* 519–558.

Behrman, R. (Ed.). (1993). *The future of home visiting* (Vol. 3, No. 3). Palo Alto: Center for the Future of Children, Packard Foundation.

Blau, D. (1992). The child care labor market. *Journal of Human Resources, 27,* 9–39.

Bowman, B. T. (1992). Child development and its implications for day care. In A. Booth (Ed.), *Child care in the 1990s: Trends and consequences* (pp. 95–100). Hillsdale, NJ: Erlbaum.

Bredekamp, S. (Ed.). (1987). *Developmentally appropriate practice in early childhood programs serving children from birth through age 8.* Washington, DC: National Association for the Education of Young Children.

Coelen, C., Glantz, F., & Calore, D. (1979). *Day care centers in the United States: A national profile, 1976–1977.* Cambridge, MA: Abt Books.

Corsaro, W. A., & Rosier, K. B. (1992). Documenting productive-reproductive processes in children's lives: Transition narratives of a Black family living in poverty. In W. A. Corsaro & P. J. Miller (Eds.), *Interpretive approaches to children's socialization: New directions for child development* (No. 58). San Francisco: Jossey-Bass.

Cronbach, L. J., Ambron, S. R., Dornbusch, S. M., Hess, R. D., Hornik, R. C., Phillips, D. C., Walker, D. F., & Weiner, S. S. (1980). *Toward reform of program evaluation.* San Francisco: Jossey-Bass.

Edwards, J., Fuller, B., & Liang, X. (1996). Explaining inequality in preschooling: Local variation in family demand and organized supply. *Economics of Education Review, 15.*

Fuller, B., Eggers-Piérola, C., Liang, X., Holloway, S., & Rambaud, M. (1996). Rich culture, poor families: Why do Latino families forego preschools? *Teachers College Record, 97,* 400–418.

Fuller, B., Holloway, S., & Liang, X. (1995). Which families choose nonparental child care and centers? The influence of ethnicity, family structure, and parental practices. Unpublished manuscript, Harvard University.

Fuller, B., & Liang, X. (1993). *The unfair search for child care: Working moms, poverty, and the unequal supply of preschools across America* (Report to the Packard Foundation). Cambridge, MA: Harvard University.

Fuller, B., & Liang, X. (1996). Market failure? Estimating inequality in preschool availability. *Educational Evaluation and Policy Analysis, 18,* 31–49.

Fuller, B., Raudenbush, S., Wei, L., & Holloway, S. (1993). Can government raise child care quality? The influence of family demand, poverty, and policy. *Educational Evaluation and Policy Analysis, 15,* 255–278.

Fuqua, R. W., & Labensohn, D. (1986). Parents as consumers of child care. *Family Relations, 35,* 295–303.

Galinsky, E., Howes, C., Kontos, S., & Shinn, M. (1994). *The study of children in family child care and relative care.* New York: Families and Work Institute.

Gormley, Jr., W. (1995). *Everybody's children: Child care as a public problem.* Washington, DC: Brookings.

Gravett, M., Rogers, C. S., & Thompson, L. (1987). Child care decisions among female heads of households with school-age children. *Early Childhood Research Quarterly, 2,* 67–81.

Helburn, S., Howes, C., Bryant, D., & Kagan, S. (1995). *Cost, quality, and child outcomes in child care centers: Executive summary.* Denver: University of Colorado.

Helburn, S., Morris, J., Culkin, M., Kagan, S., & Rustici, J. (1995). Within sector comparisons and the impact of government spending. In S. Helburn (Ed.), *Cost, quality, and child outcomes in child care centers: Technical report* (pp. 221–256). Denver: University of Colorado.

Hess, R. D., Dickson, W. P., Price, G. G., & Leong, D. J. (1979). Some contrasts between mothers and preschool teachers in interaction with their four-year-old children. *American Educational Research Journal, 16*, 307–316.

Hofferth, S., Brayfield, A., Deich, S., & Holcomb, P. (1991). *National child care survey, 1990*. Washington, DC: Urban Institute Press.

Hofferth, S., & Wissoker, D. (1992). Price, quality, and income in child care choice. *Journal of Human Resources, 27*, 70–111.

Holloway, S. D., & Fuller, B. (1992). The great child-care experiment: What are the lessons for school improvement? *Educational Researcher, 21*, 12–19.

Holloway, S. D., Fuller, B., Rambaud, M., & Eggers-Piérola, C. (1995, March). *It's more than ABC's and 123's: Low-income mothers' views about preparing their children for school*. Paper presented at the biennial meeting of the Society for Research in Child Development, Indianapolis.

Howes, C., Smith, E., & Galinsky, E. (1995). *The Florida child care quality improvement study*. New York: Families and Work Institute.

Hyson, M. C. (1991). Building the hothouse: How mothers construct academic environments. In L. Rescoral, M. C. Hyson, & K. Hirsh-Pasek (Eds.), *Academic instruction in early childhood: Challenge or pressure? New directions for child development* (No. 53) (pp. 31–37). San Francisco: Jossey-Bass.

Jipson, J. (1991). Developmentally appropriate practice: Culture, curriculum, connections. *Early Education and Development, 2*, 120–136.

Joffe, C. (1977). *Friendly intruders: Child care professionals and family life*. Berkeley: University of California Press.

Johnson-Beykont, B. (1995). *Teaching the basics in preschool*. Unpublished manuscript, Harvard University, Graduate School of Education.

Kisker, E., Hofferth, S., Phillips, D., & Farquhar, E. (1991). *A profile of child care settings: Early education and care in 1990* (Vol. 1). Princeton, NJ: Mathematica Policy Research.

Kisker, E. E., Maynard, R., Gordon, A., & Strain, M. (1989). *The child care challenge: What parents need and what is available in three metropolitan areas*. Princeton, NJ: Mathematica Policy Research.

Kontos, S. (1993, March). The ecology of family day care. Paper presented at the meeting of the Society for Research in Child Development, New Orleans.

Kontos, S., Howes, C., Shinn, M., & Galinsky, E. (1995). *Quality in family child care and relative care*. New York: Teachers College Press.

Kontos, S., & Stremmel, A. J. (1988). Caregivers' perceptions of working conditions in a child care environment. *Early Childhood Research Quarterly, 3*, 77–90.

Kontos, S., & Wells, W. (1986). Attitudes of caregivers and the day care experiences of families. *Early Childhood Research Quarterly, 1*, 47–67.

Kuhns, C. L., Holloway, S. D., & Scott-Little, M. C. (1992). Mothers' and child-care providers' cognitive, affective, and behavioral responses to children's misbehavior. *Early Education and Development, 3*, 232–243.

Love, J., Ryer, P., & Faddis, B. (1992). *Caring environments: Program quality in California's Publicly Funded Child Development Programs*. Portsmouth, NH: RMC Research Corporation.

Lubeck, S. (1985). *Sandbox society*. London & Philadelphia: Falmer Press.

Maynard, R., Kisker, E. E., & Kerachsky, S. (1990). The minority female single parent demonstration: Child care challenges for low-income families (Working paper in the series *Into the working world*). New York: Rockefeller Foundation.

McCall, R. B., Tittnich, E., & Snyder, P. (1994). Supply and demand in early childhood services. *Journal of Applied Developmental Psychology, 15*, 619–640.

Parker, F. L., Piotrkowski, C. S., & Peasy, L. (1987). Head Start as a social support for mothers: The psychological benefits of involvement. *American Journal of Orthopsychiatry, 57*, 220–223.

Phillips, D., Howes, C., & Whitebook, M. (1991). Child care as an adult work environment. *Journal of Social Issues, 47*(2), 49–70.

Phillips, D., Voran, M., Kisker, E., Howes, C., & Whitebook, M. (1994). Child care for children in poverty: Opportunity or inequity? *Child Development, 65*, 472–492.

Phillips, D., & Whitebook, M. (1986). Who are child care workers: The search for answers. *Young Children, 41*(4), 14–20.

Phillipsen, L., Cryer, D., & Howes, C. (1995). Classroom process and classroom structure. In S. Helburn (Ed.), *Cost, quality, and child outcomes in child care centers: Technical report* (pp. 125–158). Denver: University of Colorado.

Polakow, V. (1993). *Lives on the edge: Single mothers and their children in the other America*. Chicago: University of Chicago Press.

Powell, D. R. (1989). *Families and early childhood programs* (Research Monographs of the National Association for the Education of Young Children, Vol. 3). Washington, DC: NAEYC.

Powell, D. R. (1994). Evaluating family support programs: Are we making progress? In S. L. Kagan & B. Weissbourd (Eds.), *Putting families first: America's family support movement and the challenge of change* (pp. 441–470). San Francisco: Jossey-Bass.

Powell, D. R., Zambrana, R., & Silva-Palacios, V. (1990). Designing culturally responsive parent education: A comparison of low-income Mexican and Mexican-American mothers' preferences. *Family Relations, 39*, 298–304.

Prosser, W. R., & McGroder, S. M. (1992). The supply of and demand for child care: Measurement and analytic issues. In A. Booth (Ed.), *Child care in the 1990s: Trends and consequences* (pp. 42–55). Hillsdale, NJ: Erlbaum.

Scott-Little, M. C., & Holloway, S. D. (1994). Caregivers' attributions about children's misbehavior in child care centers. *Journal of Applied Developmental Psychology, 15*, 241–253.

Siegel, G., & Loman, A. (1991). *Child care and AFDC recipients in Illinois: Patterns, problems, and needs*. St. Louis: Institute of Applied Research.

Spodek, B. (1988). Implicit theories of early childhood teachers: Foundations for professional behavior. In B. Spodek, O. N. Saracho, & D. L. Peters (Eds.), *Professionalism and the early childhood practitioner* (pp. 161–172). New York: Teachers College Press.

Stipek, D. (1993). Is child-centered early childhood education really better? In S. Reifel (Ed.), *Advances in early education and day care: Perspectives on developmentally appropriate practice* (Vol. 5). Greenwich, CT: JAI Press.

Stipek, D., Milburn, S., Clements, D., & Daniels, D. H. (1992). Parental beliefs about appropriate education for young children. *Journal of Applied Developmental Psychology, 13,* 293–310.

Whitebook, M., Howes, C., Darrah, R., & Friedman, J. (1982). Caring for the caregivers: Staff burnout in child care. In L. G. Katz (Ed.), *Current topics in early childhood education* (Vol. 4, pp. 211–235). Norwood, NJ: Ablex.

Whitebook, M., Howes, C., & Phillips, D. (1989). *Who cares? Child care teachers and the quality of care in America* (Child care employee project).

Willer, B., Hofferth, S. L., Kisker, E. E., Divine-Hawkins, P., Farquhar, E., & Glantz, F. B. (1991). *The demand and supply of child care in 1990.* Washington, DC: National Association for the Education of Young Children.

Yonemura, M. V. (1986). *A teacher at work: Professional development and the early childhood educator.* New York: Teachers College Press.

Zinsser, C. (1991). *Raised in east urban: Child care changes in a working class community.* New York: Teachers College Press.

CHAPTER 2

Longitudinal Evaluation
of Program Effectiveness

Herbert J. Walberg and Arthur J. Reynolds

This chapter documents the relevance of longitudinal research for evaluating the impact of early childhood programs and educational experiences. A major theme is that prospective longitudinal studies of the effects of early childhood programs are needed more than ever, especially of large-scale established programs. A second but equally important theme is that for early childhood programs to be effective, they must have a direct impact on the social and psychological factors that promote learning.

IMPORTANCE OF LONGITUDINAL STUDIES

To gain a broad perspective on the possible benefits of longitudinal studies, this paper draws together some findings from studies of the influences of education and psychological environments on learning and development. Our intention is to provide factual background for a synoptic view of learning and human development over the life-span. Since other chapters focus on other aspects of evaluation, we consider studies from preschool through early adulthood and try to draw some lessons for policy and future longitudinal studies.

It seems worth saying at the outset that no single study or method can be viewed as definitive. If many well-designed and well-executed studies point in the same direction, however, then a reasonable amount of confidence can be placed in their conclusions. For many psychologists, the term *well-designed studies* means experiments with random assignment of subjects to treatment and control groups to eliminate causal uncertainties. Few long-term educational studies meet this criterion. Experiments, however, are hardly foolproof since they usually fail the sociological criterion of broad generalizability. Nearly all experiments are restricted to idiosyncratic rather than random national samples; and they often employ better-executed treatments than are found in ordinary practice. Nor are one-shot surveys panaceas. Inducing causality from cross-sectional surveys is suspect since a conclusion that "A causes B" may ignore reverse causation and third causes of both A and B.

Longitudinal studies can offer distinct advantages: Some causal uncertainty may be eliminated by agreeing that later events do not cause earlier events, and that later psychological traits and states do not cause earlier ones. Valid and comprehensive measures of earlier and later personal attributes and intervening conditions may allow rough estimates of causal influences. Moreover, longitudinal studies allow more probing tests of programs since they take time to exert their impact and often do so in complex ways. Still, designing such analyses requires difficult choices such as large samples versus intensive measurements, and random versus program samples. Despite great effort and expense, moreover, subjects, especially from highly mobile impoverished populations, will be lost in increasingly larger numbers over long time periods.

The lesson to be gained is that only those findings that emerge strongly and repeatedly from multiple studies employing different methods can be trusted. Syntheses of previous research, theory building, and secondary analyses of existing data can all help in this effort. Longitudinal studies, however, do have a special place: Other things being equal, they afford a better opportunity than cross-sectional studies to probe causality, and a better chance than most experiments to generalize widely. Carried out over long periods, moreover, they reveal not only immediate effects such as learning, but long-range adult outcomes such as occupational success, civic participation, and avocational accomplishments.

The benefits of longitudinal studies may be best seen in specific findings. They may be striking enough to change personal practices, cause interventions to be reconsidered, and challenge stereotypes. Consider three recent illustrations.

Many social analysts assume that the poor families live in big northern cities and engender generation after generation of poverty. Longitudinal research belies this stereotype. Duncan's (1984) longitudinal analysis of approximately 5,000 American families showed substantial social mobility. For example, of families in the top or bottom 20% of income in 1971, only about half remained in these classifications in 1978. Between 1969 and 1978, 25% of the families fell below official poverty lines in at least one year, but less than 3% remained below in 8 of the 10 years. Even these persistently poor belied stereotypes: two-thirds lived in southern states; one-third were elderly; and only a fifth lived in large cities. Level of education was a minor influence in determining changes in wealth or poverty. Most decisive were voluntary changes in family structure — marriage or divorce, a birth, or a child leaving home. Job-related changes such as layoffs, and physical disabilities were second in importance.

Another remarkable example is Werner and Smith's (1982) research reported in *Vulnerable But Invincible*, a 30-year study of 698 at-risk infants born on the Hawaiian island of Kauai. It shows how some children triumph over physical disadvantages and deprived childhoods. Despite prenatal and perinatal stress; discordant and impoverished home lives; and uneducated, alcoholic, and mentally disturbed parents, some went on to develop healthy personalities, stable careers, and strong interpersonal relations. Some were even hospitalized and separated from their families for extended periods; many infants and toddlers had mothers who worked full time and had no access to stable child care. Some were babies of single or teenage parents with no other adult in household; others were migrant and refugee children without permanent roots in community. Resilient children were protected by consistent nurturing that encouraged trust in its availability. At least one person in their lives buffered stress by accepting them unconditionally, regardless of temperamental idiosyncracies or physical or mental handicaps. Grandparents, older siblings, and teachers provided such bonds in cases in which parents were incapacitated or unavailable. Such informal ties to kin and community were more powerful than government-provided services.

Finally, Schweinhart, Barnes, and Weikart (1993) reported 24-year, follow-up results of the High/Scope Perry Preschool program in Ypsilanti, Michigan. Beginning in 1962, 123 Black children were randomly assigned to preschool and no-preschool groups, and longitudinal assessment continued up to age 27. Although preschool participants exhibited better intellectual aptitude and school performance, the most striking findings of the study were that preschool graduates were significantly more likely than no-preschool participants to be employed in adulthood, to graduate from high school, to go to college, to avoid detention or arrest, and to engage in socially responsible behavior. These differences came about through a complex interplay of postprogram educational experiences initiated by the cognitive advantage gained in preschool. Findings also suggest the limits of 1 or 2 years of preschool education in altering life course outcomes.

Despite the positive effects of preschool participation, one-third of Perry graduates dropped out of high school, 41% were not employed, and 31% had been detained or arrested during youth and adulthood.

BENEFITS OF LONGITUDINAL STUDIES
OF EARLY CHILDHOOD PROGRAMS

In the past decade, state and federal governments have invested heavily in preschool education and other early childhood programs. The first national goal of educational reform states that all children will begin school ready to learn. The extent to which this goal is achieved depends in large part on the documented effects of early childhood programs and experiences. Utilizing longitudinal research in education and human development over the life course, we discuss three major benefits of longitudinal studies: (1) determining the direct and indirect effects of early childhood programs on children's developmental outcomes over the life course, (2) identifying the mechanisms through which program experiences affect children's development, and (3) implementing a theory-driven approach to program evaluation.

Effects of Early Childhood Programs

Since the founding of Head Start in 1965, hundreds of studies have been conducted on the effects of early childhood intervention programs for economically disadvantaged children (Barnett, 1992, 1994; McKey et al., 1985; White, 1985). Although findings uniformly indicate that a wide variety of programs yield short-term effects on scholastic aptitude and achievement, longer-term effects have been more difficult to establish, especially for large-scale programs initiated by local, state, and federal governments. Most of the evidence for program effects into the high school years comes from studies of model programs (Consortium for Longitudinal Studies, 1983; Haskins, 1989; Schweinhart et al., 1993). Among these findings are that program participants have higher school achievement in early adolescence, lower incidence of grade retention and special education placement, and lower incidence of dropping out of high school than no-program participants. While the internal validity of studies of model programs is relatively high, the external validity (generalizability) of findings to other programs, samples, and time periods is relatively low. For example, in contrast to modal programs, model programs often enjoy more financial and human resources in which to implement their services (Reynolds, 1994; Zigler & Muenchow, 1992).

There are many explanations for the lack of evidence for the longer-term effects of large-scale programs. Among them are low program quality due to lack of resources or to poor implementation, use of research designs of convenience, use of a narrow range of measured outcomes in evaluations, and failure to consider the influence of postprogram environments on program impact. However, a less acknowledged reason is the relative absence of longitudinal studies beyond 3 or 4 years. White (1985) noted this dearth of follow-up studies in his meta-analysis of 329 early intervention programs. Haskins (1989) stated that "it is surprising after 20 years, we still do not have good long-term studies of Head Start. The American public spends more than $1 billion per year [now about $4 billion] on Head Start, and yet we have little credible evidence of positive outcomes that we know . . . are possible" (p. 280).

More recently, Barnett (1992, 1994) summarized the effects of additional large-scale studies, which by and large revealed findings similar to studies of model programs. Although the large-scale studies included larger and more representative samples than studies of model programs, many appeared to have low internal validity, which precluded valid interpretations about effectiveness. Among the problems were noncomparability of groups, unexplored selection biases, selective attrition, failure to include retained children in analyses, unverified program implementation, use of retrospective designs, and overreliance on school records and standardized tests. Importantly, most of these problems may contribute to underestimation of program effects rather than overestimation of effects.

Some recent research on large-scale programs tries to avoid some of the pitfalls in longitudinal research such as selective attrition, use of retrospective designs, and noncomparability of groups. Reynolds and colleagues (Reynolds, 1994; Reynolds & Bezruczko, 1993; Reynolds, Bezruczko, Mavrogenes, & Hagemann, 1994) initiated the Chicago Longitudinal Study of Children at Risk, a prospective investigation of the effects of the Chicago Child Parent Centers. This large-scale program is administered in 20 sites and, like many Head Start-type programs, provides comprehensive child development services for cognitive and social development as well as parent involvement activities. Unlike Head Start, children have the opportunity to participate in preschool plus follow-on intervention (preschool to third grade).

Follow-up analyses with a cohort of about 1,200 children through seventh grade has maintained 80% sample recovery with no selective attrition and have taken selection bias into account through investigating program variations and utilizing latent-variable psychometric and econometric analyses, as well as measuring multiple outcomes (e.g., Reynolds, 1994; Reynolds & Temple, 1995). Findings through sixth and seventh grades have indicated that (1) preschool participation (any vs. none) is significantly associated with higher reading and math achievement and with lower incidence of grade retention and special education placement (Reynolds, 1995), (2) a second year of preschool does not significantly add to the longer-term effects of the first year (Reynolds, 1995), and (3) participation in extended early childhood programs up to second or third grade adds significantly to the effect of earlier intervention for reading achievement, math achievement, and incidence of grade retention (Reynolds, 1994).

Certainly, additional longitudinal studies of large-scale programs are needed. Two foci of research appear especially important. One is determination of the optimal timing and duration of participation in early childhood programs. Among economically disadvantaged children, how much more effective is 4 or 5 years of participation compared with 1 or 2 years? Is early entry into programs better than later entry and by how much? A second important research question continues to be identification of the factors that mediate or help transmit the effects of early childhood programs. A mediating factor is one that explains the relationship between program participation and the outcome factor of interest, thus is believed to be the "active ingredient" in program effectiveness. With few exceptions (e.g., Berrueta-Clement, Schweinhart, Barnett, Epstein, & Weikart, 1984; Reynolds, 1992), outcome evaluation has predominated, and process evaluation of program effectiveness has been de-emphasized.

The research designs implemented (and needed) to address these and other questions are likely to be different from many previous studies. Unlike those of the 1960s and 1970s, contemporary early childhood programs have, by and large, proven their effectiveness to many stakeholders. Consequently, experimental designs will be very difficult to implement and keep intact. Indeed, they often are viewed as unethical; denying program participation to eligible children for research purposes is illegal in Head Start and many similar programs. The field of evaluation research has changed as well. Alternatives to the experimental model of evaluation, such as naturalistic inquiry, case study methods, and stakeholder-service approaches, are now more accepted (Cook & Shadish, 1994). Experimental and quasi-experimental designs alone are ill-suited to address hypotheses about causal mediation or the specific processes that brought about program impact. Another alternative is the theory-driven evaluation, and we turn to this perspective next.

Program Theory in Evaluation

Program theory is a conception of how and why a program works. Although it is often implicit in evaluation by the assumptions a researcher makes, program theory generally refers to the explicit formulation of the way a program operates. Bickman (1987) defined program theory as "the construction of a plausible and sensible model of how a program is supposed to work" (p. 5). Accordingly, program theory is specified in relation to purposes and means as defined by planners and evaluators in order to clarify what can be expected from the program and as a guide to selecting measures to assess the inputs, processes, and outcomes.

Theory-driven evaluation is a logical evolution in the field away from a strict reliance on method-driven evaluation. Experiments and quasi-experiments, being dominated by issues of internal validity, cannot answer by themselves how and why programs work. As Cook and Shadish (1986) noted, evaluators have learned "that analyses of implementation and causal mediation are crucial in evaluation for they promote explanation, and explanation may be crucial for the transfer of evaluation findings to new settings and populations" (p. 226).

Although many benefits of theory-driven evaluation have been identified (Bickman, 1987; Chen, 1990; Reynolds & Walberg, 1994), four of them appear particularly useful for early childhood education. First, a theory-driven perspective forces evaluators to specify the postprogram processes through which programs are expected to show effects. These hypothesized pathways can then be tested in confirmatory analysis. This approach can promote strong causal inference about program effectiveness. Second, theory-driven evaluation encourages more appropriate selection of outcome measures. On the basis of theory and previous research, primary outcomes can be identified that are most likely to be affected by the program. Secondary outcomes also can be defined as well as possible unanticipated outcomes of programs. More thoughtful consideration of outcome variables can optimize detection of program effects. A third benefit of theory-driven evaluation is that evaluators can better determine the source of no-effect findings. Such findings can be the result of theory failure, program implementation failure, or failure of the research procedures (e.g., insensitive measures or methodological problems). Without such distinctions, programs could be discarded wrongly, because of poor implementation or because of an insensitive research design rather than an inherent weakness in the program. Finally, theory-driven evaluation can improve the formative use of evaluation findings, mainly because key factors of implementation and intervening factors are specified in advance and can direct attention to program improvement and knowledge transfer. For example, if motivation rather than cognition is found to be the key mechanism of change in compensatory preschool interventions, then program improvement and dissemination efforts would be better directed toward factors that specifically affect motivation.

Research-Based Theory for Evaluation of Educational Productivity

Although program theory in evaluation can derive from many sources, the research knowledge base provides the best source for knowledge integration. In this vein, a vast literature of more than 8,000 psychological studies of the past half century contains estimates of the quantitative correlations and effects of the proximate factors that bear directly on student achievement. During the past decade these studies have been quantitatively synthesized (see Walberg, 1984a, for detailed description). The estimates show that nine psychological factors produce much larger and more consistent effects than class size, staff salaries, expenditures per student, and other crude indicators of quality.

The nine factors appear to require optimization to increase affective, behavioral, and cognitive learning. Potent, consistent, and widely generalizable, these factors fall into three groups:

- Student aptitude
    1. Ability or prior achievement as measured by the usual standardized tests
    2. Development as indexed by chronological age or stage
    3. Motivation or self-concept as indicated by personality tests or the student's willingness to persevere intensively on learning tasks
- Instruction
    4. The amount of time students spend in learning
    5. The quality of the instructional experience, including psychological and curricular aspects
- Environmental factors
    6. The home
    7. Classroom social group
    8. The peer group outside school
    9. Minimum leisure-time television viewing

The first five aspects of student aptitude and instruction are prominent in the educational models of Benjamin S. Bloom, Jerome Bruner, John B. Carroll, Robert Glaser, and others (see Walberg, 1981, 1984b, for a comparative analyses). Each appears necessary for learning in school; without at least a small amount of each, the student may learn little. Large amounts of instruction and high degrees of ability, for example, may count for little if students are unmotivated or instruction is unsuitable.

These five essential factors, however, are only partly alterable by educators since, for example, the curriculum in terms of length of time devoted to various subjects and activities is somewhat determined by diverse economic, political, and social forces. Ability and motivation, moreover, are influenced by parents, by prior learning, and by students' contributions. Thus, educators are unlikely to raise achievement substantially by just their own efforts.

The psychological climate of the classroom group; enduring affection and academic stimulation in the home; an out-of-school peer group with learning interests, goals, and activities — these influence learning both directly and indirectly. Students learn from them directly. These factors, moreover, indirectly benefit learning by raising student ability, motivation, and responsiveness to instruction. In addition, about 10 (not the more typical 30) hours of television viewing a week seems optimal for learning, perhaps because more television time displaces homework and other educationally and developmentally constructive activities outside school.

The major causal influences flow from aptitude, instruction, and psychological environment to learning, although these factors also influence one another. Early achievement appears to raise not only the stock but the rate of learning. Called "the Matthew effect" after the "rich-getting-richer" passage of the Bible, the phenomenon appears fairly pervasive; children who start well at academic work and other endeavors gain at a faster rate and thereby gain increasingly larger advantages as they grow older. It seems that early success may increase motivation and also attract parental and teaching attention to the possibility of developing high talent and accomplishment. Complex reciprocal causation or mutual enhancement of ability, motivation, instruction, and stimulating environments over the early life course probably accounts for the Matthew effect (Walberg & Tsai, 1983).

The first five essential factors appear to substitute, compensate, or trade off for one another at diminishing rates of return. Immense quantities of time, for example, may be needed to bring about a moderate amount of learning if motivation, ability, or instructional quality is minimal. Thus, no single essential factor overwhelms the others; all appear important.

Quantitative syntheses of thousands of experimental and quasi-experimental studies suggest that these generalizable factors are the chief influences on cognitive, affective, and behavioral learning (Walberg, 1983, 1984a). Many of these studies provide strong causal inferences since they are generally true experiments with random assignment, or quasi-experiments with pretests to measure longitudinal gains so as to equate treatment and control groups.

Linking Educational Productivity to Early Childhood Evaluation

In evaluating the effects of early childhood programs, the educational productivity model enables one to posit several mechanisms through which programs are effective. The basic assumption of the productivity model is that interventions will be effective only to the extent that they affect the nine aptitude, instructional, and environmental factors of learning. These are testable propositions, and they could be a major focus of research in early childhood evaluation.

One hypothesis about the mechanisms through which early intervention programs affect later outcomes would be early cognitive achievement or cognitive advantage. This mechanism is clearly subsumed under the broadly construed aptitude domain of the productivity model. This hypothesis has been used to explain the long-term effects of the High/Scope Perry Preschool Program (Berrueta-Clement et al., 1984; Schweinhart et al., 1993; Schweinhart & Weikart, 1980). In this view, the immediate positive effect of preschool on cognitive development at school entry initiates a positive cycle of scholastic development and commitment that culminates in improved adolescent and adult outcomes such as higher rates of high school completion and lower rates of juvenile delinquency. Thus, this early cognitive advantage gained from the program leads to a series of positive transactions throughout the schooling process that result in better adjustment outcomes.

This process is illustrated in a longitudinal study by Reynolds (1992) of the mediated effects of preschool participation on 391 low-income minority children. As shown by the standardized regression coefficients in Figure 2.1, preschool participation positively influenced grade 3 school achievement (standardized reading and math achievement) by first affecting cognitive readiness at school entry, a standardized composite measure of developmental preparedness. Cognitive readiness was associated with higher teacher ratings of classroom adjustment in grade 1, and lower incidence of grade retention in grades 1 and 2. Thus preschool participation contributes significantly to later school achievement through influencing postprogram social and psychological factors.

Meta-analyses of the Consortium for Longitudinal Studies (Royce, Darlington, & Murray, 1983) also support the mediating effects of cognitive and scholastic factors in later adjustment outcomes. This cumulative process is similar to the fan-spread hypothesis or Matthew effect (Merton, 1968; Walberg & Tsai, 1983), whereby initial advantages multiply over time and culminate in better adjustment outcomes.

Another hypothesis about the mechanisms through which early child-

Figure 2.1. Mediated effects of preschool participation through grade 3.

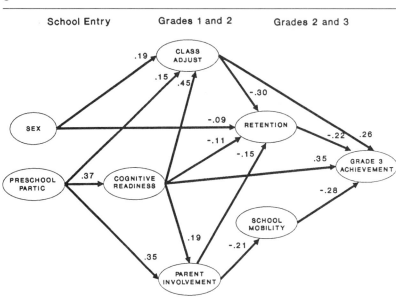

hood programs produce longer-term effects concerns the home environment dimension of the productivity model. A family or home environment hypothesis would predict that longer-term effects of interventions will occur to the extent that the family environment has been improved. The central tenet is that because early intervention programs often involve parents, family processes must be affected to produce longer-term effects on child outcomes. These may include the attitudinal and behavioral measures of parent–child interactions, parent attitudes, school involvement, and educational experiences. This transmission process initially was proposed by Bronfenbrenner (1975) as an explanation of fading effects of preschool intervention programs. With the exception of White, Taylor, and Moss (1992), reviews of research have found that early intervention programs are more effective if they involve parents (Gray & Wandersman, 1980; Seitz, 1990).

Although cognitive advantage and family support hypotheses are plausible explanations for how early childhood programs exert longer-term effects, the educational productivity model suggests that other hypotheses are possible. For example, a motivation hypothesis could replace the one on cognitive advantage above; hypotheses on instructional quality or quantity could replace the family support hypothesis. The motivation hypothesis — that early childhood intervention is effective because it enhances children's motivation to learn — is plausible and empirically supported (Zigler, Abelson, Trickett, & Seitz, 1982; Zigler & Butterfield, 1968).

Obviously, much work is needed in this research area, and the nine-factor productivity model provides an important organizing framework. The theory-driven evaluation perspective has many advantages for research on the effects of early childhood programs. As with examining the direct impact of early childhood programs on child outcomes, longitudinal data are essential in testing mechanisms of effects in the theory-based perspective.

FACTORS INFLUENCING LIFETIME SUCCESS

It may be assumed that the first 4 to 6 years of schooling are necessary to acquire literacy, numeracy, and some basic knowledge and skills needed to function in modern society. Beyond this, of what use is further education? The usual view is that additional education promotes acquisition of knowledge and skills useful in the pursuit of subsequent education, work, and leisure. In accord with this view, it is clear that people with more education do better in these respects, although it is less clear that education is the cause of their success.

Long-Term Effects of Education

One of the few longitudinal studies yielding stringent estimates of the long-term effects of education, with social background and early intelligence statistically controlled, was conducted in Sweden. In 1961, Harnqvist (1984) surveyed about 12,000, or 10 percent, of the Swedes born in 1948, and in 1980 followed up random samples of them with mail and interview surveys. Education, as compared with parental social class and measured intelligence, showed pervasive effects on adult characteristics of men and women. Those with greater amounts of education liked school more than others; but even early school leavers saw the need for more education for the present generation of children. Those with more education more often described their job as providing opportunities for new knowledge, and they reported they had more influence on their own working conditions than did others.

Cultural activities such as reading literature and going to theaters and concerts were more frequent among the more educated. By contrast, entertainment activities such as reading weekly magazines and viewing television and sports events were more frequent among the less educated. The more educated had more frequent contacts with co-workers; the less educated more often saw family and relatives. Highly educated men reported higher skills in cooking and lower skills in car repair, and having better information about how to appeal decisions and less about seeking economic support from society. In one-hour interviews, the more educated men used more words and proportionately more different and longer words. The less educated required far more prompts and interventions to complete the interviews. Such pervasive education effects on life activities and verbal competence seem likely to be found in other countries.

The Terman Study

The most famous longitudinal study in American psychology was begun by Terman (1925) and is still continuing (Tomlinson-Keasey & Little, 1990). The Terman data on gifted children span a sizable fraction of the twentieth century. The study followed a group of bright American children, periodically assessing personality characteristics, social attitudes, and mental capabilities to ascertain changes due to developmental or environmental factors. An advantage of this study is that IQ is almost controlled (participants were limited to those with IQs over 135) thus making other influences such as home environment and personality variables more apparent.

For his study Terman defined the gifted child as one whose IQ score is 135 or higher, which is found in only about one in 200 of the school population. The age range of the 643 grade school students was approximately 4–14 years, with a median age between 9 and 10. Later, 378 high school students were added to the study. Some birthdays were as early as 1908–1918. In 1996 survivors could be as old as 88.

The testing protocol included the Stanford-Binet Intelligence tests, Stanford Achievement tests, a General Information test, tests of interests, and medical examinations. Field workers made home visits for parent interviews and assessment of the home environment.

In 1928, students and parents again were interviewed and questionnaires were completed. In 1936, 1950, 1955, 1960, 1972, and 1986 questionnaires were mailed to the students. As the students married, their spouses were included to a limited degree.

The farsightedness of Terman is seen in his choice of variables. His thoughtfully prepared study includes measures of personality factors, social behaviors, and instructional factors, as well as measures of home environment such as the number of books in the home, parental marital happiness, and the amount of time spent reading.

Gifted children were found to have more hobbies than other children. Terman suggests that the close relationship between IQ and reading scores is because gifted children are such voracious readers. Gifted girls were found to score higher on masculine tests than average girls and were less interested in girlish activities. Gifted children were found to score above average on measures of emotional stability (Woodworth-Cady test).

To obtain a clearer view of factors that might influence the career achievement of the gifted, another dimension was added to the study in 1940. The data of the upper 25%, the "A" group, and the lower 25%, the "C" group, were compared in an effort to study the impact of factors other than intelligence on adult outcome. Terman defined success as how well children would use their superior intellect.

Using this approach Terman found a difference in parent educational levels. Twice as many "A" parents as "C" parents were college graduates. "A" fathers were more likely to be professional. Divorce or separation was more common among "C" families than "A" families. There was no difference in academic achievement during the elementary school years but a clear difference during high school. Of the "A"s, 97% entered college, and 90% of them graduated; 68% of the "C" group enrolled in college, and 37% graduated. Terman reports that data collected from the case histories and trait ratings by parents and teachers in 1922 further differentiated the "A" and "C" groups in adulthood. These observations are consistent with Freud's assertion of the long-term effect of childhood experiences. Terman's findings are supported by studies of early life experiences of eminent men (Walberg, 1981).

A modern multivariate analysis also showed significant relations of early traits and conditions to later adult accomplishments (Tomlinson-Keasey & Little, 1990). However, the sizes of the relations were very small. None of the early personality traits correlated higher than .14 with adult adjustment and occupational achievement. Intellectual skill correlated weakly and positively with occupational achievement but negatively with adult personal adjustment. Early family harmony, however, correlated about .3 with adult personal adjustment.

Socioeconomic Status and Other Attainments

A vast literature bears upon the intergenerational effect of parents' socioeconomic status (SES) on their children's academic development and life success. Many ambitious surveys and secondary analyses by economists and sociologists such as Featherman, Griliches, Hauser, Jencks, Lazear, Taubman, and others bear upon this question (see recent reviews by the economist Michaels, 1982, and the sociologist Sewell, 1981). Other studies have examined the influences of parents' education on the cognitive development and health status of their children.

Current reviews conclude that student learning is consistently associated with levels of parent education. It may prove difficult, however, to synthesize quantitatively the unique effects of parental SES in the context of rival causes as revealed in multivariate analyses because the constructs and their measures vary widely among investigations, thereby reducing the comparability of the causal weightings. These differences are attributable to differences in operationalization and in a priori theory (taken implicitly as a set of untested assumptions rather than hypotheses) on which investigators have achieved little consensus.

The SES influences on academic learning, moreover, may operate in several ways that are difficult to separate: Taking, for example, parental education as an index of SES, knowledge of child rearing, as well as higher income — conferred in part by more parental education — may contribute both to parenting capacity and effects on children's learning. More highly educated parents, for example, may themselves provide superior direct services to their children as a result of their knowledge; but they also may purchase, as a consequence of their higher income, superior child-rearing goods and services.

One question, however, that can now be answered concerns the simple association of parental SES and children's learning. White (1976) collected 636 correlation coefficients of parental education, occupation, and income with ability and academic achievement from 101 published and unpublished studies. In White's synthesis, the average correlations of learning with parental income, occupation level, and education are 0.31, 0.20, and 0.19, respectively. (The correlations may be over- or underestimated because of restriction of range in sampling, unreliability of measures, and other reasons.)

That income correlates the highest of the three may suggest that wealthy parents may confer more decisive advantages than highly educated parents by purchasing time-saving household goods such as dishwashers and thereby being able to spend more time with their children, buying intellectually enhancing toys and books for them, or hiring parent-surrogate services, such as day care and tutors, to nurture them. Little should be made of these speculations, however, since the SES correlations are all small and differ only slightly from one another.

Both the mean and standard deviation of all SES–learning correlations are 0.25, so that, on average, SES accounts for 6% of the variance in learning. Thus, contrary to the great importance given to parental SES by some educational sociologists, its association with learning is surprisingly weak; SES may constrain learning and social ascendancy far less than many believe.

Education, Success, and Happiness

If education by itself does not decisively influence adult success as measured by various indexes, neither do SES and other aspects of social background. Walberg and Weinstein (1984) analyzed the statistical dependencies of adult outcomes on 25 indexes of social background (including age and sex of the respondent and parental characteristics), diplomas and degrees, and a vocabulary test obtained on about 2,000 men and women in the General Social Survey.

All independent variables in combination accounted for only small amounts of estimated variance in adult outcomes, ranging from 3% of the variance in happiness to 43% in occupational prestige. Family background, diplomas and degrees, and verbal competence together accounted for less than 13% of the variance in self-reported income, health, and happiness. Among the combinations of predictors and outcomes, diplomas and degrees uniquely accounted for the largest amount of variance in occupational prestige; but this amount was a trivial 2.3%.

These findings seem typical of recent associations of educational and other measured formative effects on various adult outcomes. Only one of these, however, has been quantitatively synthesized. Witter, Okun, Stock, and Haring's (1984) collection of 176 zero-order correlations of self-rated well-being from 90 studies showed that amount and quality of education accounted for only about 1%–3% of the variance in indexes of life satisfaction and happiness. When the association was controlled for occupational prestige, the variance estimates were even smaller; the association apparently has remained constant for the past half century.

It appears at best that social background, education, and verbal competence in combination give adults slight to moderate advantages on indicators of adult success. Their separate influences, however, are weak — perhaps nil — and difficult to detect. Although they remain systematically and statistically undocumented, many other factors, such as accidental opportunities and personal initiative and perseverance, may play far larger roles.

CONCLUSION

This chapter highlighted the importance of longitudinal studies in understanding the effects of early childhood programs as well as other early educational experiences. It is evident that longitudinal studies of the effects of large-scale early childhood interventions are rare but are essential for informing researchers and the public about what can be expected from preschool and other early childhood programs. These studies are especially critical in (1) documenting the causal mechanisms by which early childhood programs promote effectiveness and (2) enhancing the capacity to undertake theory-driven evaluations of program impact. The research-based theory of the nine-factor model of educational productivity was discussed as a framework for explaining how early childhood programs may achieve their postulated longer-term effects. Some research supports the relevance of early cognitive advantage in promoting program effects, while other research suggests the centrality of the home environment. However, this research is just getting underway.

We can be far less sure about how these and other determinants in the first decade influence adult accomplishments, partly because success in education hardly guarantees success in careers and other adult endeavors. More studies, better conceived and executed, might illuminate many pressing questions. They are certainly worth doing. Studies beginning in early childhood and addressing issues of program effectiveness can provide a foundation for addressing these questions.

REFERENCES

Barnett, W. S. (1992). Benefits of compensatory preschool education. *Journal of Human Resources, 27,* 279–312.

Barnett, W. S. (1994, October). *Long-term effects of early childhood care and education on disadvantaged children's cognitive development and school success.* Paper presented at the Eighth Rutgers Invitational Symposium on Education: New Directions for Policy and Research in Early Childhood Care and Education, New Brunswick, NJ.

Berrueta-Clement, J. R., Schweinhart, L. J., Barnett, W. S., Epstein, A. S., & Weikart, D. P. (1984). *Changed lives: The effects of the Perry Preschool Program on youths through age 19.* Ypsilanti, MI: High/Scope Press.

Bickman, L. (1987). *The functions of program theory.* In L. Bickman (Ed.), *Using program theory in evaluation* (pp. 5–18). San Francisco: Jossey-Bass.

Bronfenbrenner, U. (1975). Is early intervention effective? In M. Guttentag & E. Struening (Eds.), *Handbook of evaluation research* (Vol. 2, pp. 519–603). Beverly Hills, CA: Sage.

Chen, H. T. (1990). *Theory-driven evaluations.* Beverly Hills, CA: Sage.

Consortium for Longitudinal Studies. (1983). *As the twig is bent — Lasting effects of preschool programs.* Hillsdale, NJ: Erlbaum.

Cook, T. D., & Shadish, W. R. (1986). Program evaluation: The worldly science. *Annual Review of Psychology, 37,* 193–232.

Cook, T. D., & Shadish, W. R. (1994). Social experiments: Some developments over the past fifteen years. *Annual Review of Psychology, 45,* 545–580.

Duncan, G. J. (1984). *Years of poverty, years of plenty.* Ann Arbor, MI: Institute for Social Research.

Gray, S. W., & Wandersman, L. P. (1980). The methodology of home-based intervention studies: Problems and promising strategies. *Child Development, 51,* 993–1009.

Harnqvist, K. (1984). *An empirical study of long-term effects of education.* Paper presented at the First International Conference on Education in the '90s, Tel Aviv, Israel.

Haskins, R. (1989). Beyond metaphor: The efficacy of early childhood education. *American Psychologist, 44,* 274–282.

McKey, R. H., Condelli, L., Ganson, H., Barrett, B. J., McConkey, C., & Plantz, M. C. (1985). *The impact of Head Start on children, families, and communities* (DHHS Publication No. OHDS 85-31193). Washington, DC: U. S. Government Printing Office.

Merton, R. K. (1968). The Matthew effect in science. *Science, 175,* 56–63.

Michaels, R. T. (1982). Measuring non-monetary benefits of education: A survey. In W. W. McMahon & T. G. Geske (Eds.), *Financing education.* Urbana: University of Illinois Press.

Ornish, D. (1990). *Program for reversing heart disease.* New York: Random House.

Reynolds, A. J. (1992). Mediated effects of preschool intervention. *Early Education and Development, 3,* 139–164.

Reynolds, A. J. (1994). Effects of a preschool plus follow-on intervention for children at risk. *Developmental Psychology, 30,* 787–804.

Reynolds, A. J. (1995). One year of preschool intervention or two: Does it matter? *Early Childhood Research Quarterly, 10,* 1-31.

Reynolds, A. J., & Bezruczko, N. (1993). Early schooling of children at risk through fourth grade. *Merrill-Palmer Quarterly, 39,* 457–480.

Reynolds, A. J., Bezruczko, N., Mavrogenes, N. A., & Hagemann, M. (1994, April). *User's guide: Longitudinal study of children at risk. A study of children in the Chicago Public Schools* (Version 3). Chicago: Chicago Public Schools, Department of Research, Evaluation and Planning.

Reynolds, A. J., & Temple, J. A. (1995). Quasi-experimental estimates of the effects of a preschool intervention: Psychometric and econometric comparisons. *Evaluation Review, 19,* 347–373.

Reynolds, A. J., & Walberg, H. J. (1994). Theory-based evaluation. In T. Husen & T. N. Postlethwaite (Eds.), *International Encyclopedia of Education* (pp. 6378-6384). New York: Pergamon Press.

Royce, J. M., Darlington, R. B., & Murray, H. W. (1983). Pooled analyses: Findings across studies. In Consortium for Longitudinal Studies, *As the twig is bent — Lasting effects of preschool programs* (pp. 411–459). Hillsdale, NJ: Erlbaum.

Schweinhart, L. J., Barnes, H. V., & Weikart, D. P. with Barnett, W. S., & Epstein, A. S. (1993). *Significant benefits: The High/Scope Perry Preschool study through age 27.* Ypsilanti, MI: High/Scope Press.

Schweinhart, L. J., & Weikart, D. P. (1980). *Young children grow up: The effects of the Perry Preschool Program on Youths through age 15.* Ypsilanti, MI: High/Scope Press.

Seitz, V. (1990). Intervention programs for impoverished children: A comparison of educational and family support models. *Annals of Child Development, 7,* 73–103.

Sewell, W. H. (1981). Notes on educational, occupational, and economic achievement in American society. *Phi Delta Kappan, 77,* 322–325.

Terman, L. M. (1925). *Genetic studies of genius: Mental and physical traits of a thousand gifted children* (Vol. 1). Stanford: Stanford University Press.

Tomlinson-Keasey, C., & Little, T. D. (1990). Predicting educational attainment, occupational achievement, intellectual skill, and personal adjustment among gifted men and women. *Journal of Educational Psychology, 82,* 442–445.

Walberg, H. J. (1981). A psychological theory of educational productivity. In F. H. Farley & N. Gordon (Eds.), *Psychology and education* (pp. 81–110). Chicago: National Society for the Study of Education.

Walberg, H. J. (1983). Scientific literacy and economic productivity in international perspective. *Daedalus, 112*(2), 1–28.

Walberg, H. J. (1984a). Improving the productivity of America's schools. *Educational Leadership, 41*(3), 19–26.

Walberg, H. J. (1984b, May). *National abilities and economic growth.* Paper presented at meeting of the American Association for the Advancement of Science, New York.

Walberg, H. J., & Tsai, S.-L. (1983). Matthew effects in education. *American Educational Research Journal, 20,* 359–374.

Walberg, H. J., & Weinstein, T. (1984). Adult outcomes of connections, certification, and verbal competence. *Journal of Educational Research, 77,* 207–212.

Werner, E. E., & Smith, R. S. (1982). *Vulnerable but invincible.* New York: McGraw-Hill.

White, K. R. (1976). *The relationship between socioeconomic status and academic achievement.* Unpublished dissertation, University of Colorado, Boulder.

White, K. R. (1985). Efficacy of early intervention. *Journal of Special Education, 19,* 401–416.

White, K. R., Taylor, M. J., & Moss, V. D. (1992). Does research support claims about the benefits of involving parents in early intervention programs? *Review of Educational Research, 62,* 91–125.

Witter, R. A., Okun, M. A., Stock, W. A., & Haring, M. J. (1984). Education and subjective well being: A meta-analysis. *Educational Evaluation and Policy Analysis, 6,* 165–173.

Zigler, E., Abelson, W., Trickett, P. K., & Seitz, V. (1982). Is an intervention program necessary in order to improve economically disadvantaged children's IQ scores. *Child Development, 53,* 340–348.

Zigler, E., & Butterfield, E. C. (1968). Motivational aspects of change in IQ test performance of culturally deprived nursery school children. *Child Development, 39,* 1–14.

Zigler, E., & Muenchow, S. (1992). *Head Start: The inside story of America's most successful educational experiment.* New York: Basic Books.

CHAPTER 3

Curriculum and Evaluation in Early Childhood Programs

Lawrence J. Schweinhart and Ann S. Epstein

Curriculum and evaluation are educational tools. *Education* may be defined as activities in which teachers intentionally lead students to learning. Because education is intentional, it involves curriculum and evaluation. *Curriculum* is a plan of intended lessons, and *evaluation* is a comparison of observed learning with intended lessons. Curriculum focuses on intended education, while evaluation focuses on observed education. It is only logical to evaluate the success of educational activities in light of the curriculum. In contrast to both teacher-centered education and custodial care, good early childhood programs provide learner-centered education, in which teachers create settings and circumstances for student learning.

Early childhood curriculum and evaluation have three levels — general principles that apply to all early childhood programs; various curriculum models used as frameworks for practice in various programs; and specific practices that flow either from general principles and specific curriculum models or from eclectic choices. This chapter presents comparisons of the documentation, validation, and dissemination of six widely used early childhood curriculum models — the Bank Street approach, the Creative Curriculum, Direct Instruction, the Kamii–DeVries constructivist approach, the High/Scope educational approach, and the Montessori method. A recent survey indicates that one-third of early childhood leaders use principal curriculum models as frameworks for their programs, causing concern about the validity of the curriculum practices of those who do not.

TEACHER-CENTERED VERSUS
LEARNER-CENTERED EDUCATION

Distinctions between teacher-centered education, learner-centered education, and custodial care are basic to early childhood education, curriculum, and evaluation. Early childhood education programs operate not only in school and Head Start classrooms, but also in child-care centers and homes. Some early childhood caregivers do not see themselves as teachers in educational programs because they equate education with teacher-centered education, in which teachers communicate lessons to groups of students. Teachers also can engage in learner-centered education, in which they lead students to learning by designing settings and creating circumstances in which students learn lessons on their own or with individual assistance from teachers. Early childhood programs that take a learner-centered approach are educational. Without either teacher- or learner-centered education, early childhood programs are merely custodial.

The distinction between teacher-centered and learner-centered education applies as well to curriculum and evaluation (Schweinhart, 1993; Schweinhart & Weikart, 1988). A teacher-centered curriculum is a set of lessons that a teacher intends to communicate to a group of students. A learner-centered curriculum is a set of lessons that a teacher intends for students to learn in teacher-created settings or circumstances. Similarly, a teacher- or tester-centered evaluation compares students' observed learning with what a teacher intended to communicate to them; like the educational setting, the evaluation setting is determined by the teacher. A learner-centered evaluation compares students' observed learning with what a teacher intended for them to learn in teacher-created settings or circumstances; like the educational setting, the evaluation setting arises from the interaction between teacher-created circumstances and learner-generated behavior.

Some lessons can occur only in learner-centered education, wherein children develop their abilities in initiative-taking, relating to others in various ways, artistic expression, and athletics. Because teacher-centered lessons must be delivered to students who listen, observe, and perhaps respond in kind, they are limited to what can be communicated — verbal messages or actions to be imitated.

Because many teachers of older students equate education with teacher-centered education, the inclusion of learner-centered education in the definition of education is in constant peril. The same danger holds for evaluation. However, in early childhood programs that are educational, curriculum and evaluation need not be teacher centered. Indeed, programs for young children ought to engage in curriculum and evaluation that are learner centered.

SOURCES OF EDUCATIONAL INTENTIONS

The immediate source of education is teachers' educational intentions. In teacher-centered education, teachers *intend* to communicate lessons. In learner-centered education, they *intend* to create the settings or circumstances for student learning. Teachers develop their educational intentions according to their understanding of the curriculum and purposes of early childhood education. They develop this understanding from their own educational experience in the context of educational ideas communicated to them by others.

Teachers' educational ideas can come from many sources. Virtually everyone has had educational experience, at least as a student, and so everyone has educational ideas. Teachers also get educational ideas from their education courses, their observation of other teachers, and their previous teaching experience, including student teaching. They get ideas from observing and interacting with children and parents. They test these ideas against their existing educational ideas and decide what to attend to and what to ignore, what to remember and what to forget. Then they decide if and how they will use their educational ideas in operating their programs. If they decide to make their program educational, they formulate a curriculum of broad educational intentions as goals and specific educational intentions for specific activities. From time to time, they conduct evaluations of what students are learning as compared with what they intend for students to be learning.

LEVELS OF CURRICULUM AND EVALUATION THINKING

As noted earlier, early childhood educators engage in curriculum and evaluation thinking at three levels — general principles, curriculum models, and specific practices. These levels are not mutually exclusive and, in fact, often operate simultaneously.

At the level of *general principles*, early childhood educators either assume or strive for widespread consensus on curriculum and evaluation principles that should apply in every early childhood program. Assumed general principles might be called simply "good practice." Some early

childhood education textbooks implicitly take this position without identifying it as such (e.g., Hendrick, 1988). In recent years, the National
Association for the Education of Young Children (NAEYC) has strived to
recognize and achieve widespread consensus for general curriculum and
evaluation principles called developmentally appropriate practice (Bredekamp, 1987). Critics have challenged the claim that there is consensus on
developmentally appropriate practice, particularly raising questions about
whether the approach is sufficiently sensitive to individual and cultural
differences (e.g., Mallory & New, 1994). A NAEYC panel is struggling to
accommodate the approach to the criticism. What is predictable is that
authoritative claims of consensus about the practice of early childhood
education elicit critics who challenge this consensus.

At the level of *curriculum models*, early childhood educators may
each adopt a specific curriculum model as their own from various curriculum models available. The number of early childhood curriculum models
increased dramatically in the 1970s, when the federal government began
to support their development and dissemination in Planned Variation
Head Start in the preschool years and Follow Through in the primary
grades. The models level has the political advantage over the general
principles level in that it tolerates and even encourages diversity. Early
childhood educators can easily combine the two levels in their thinking
by applying general principles, such as the principles of developmentally
appropriate practice, in their selection of acceptable curriculum models.
Epstein, Schweinhart, and McAdoo (1996) took this approach in their
book *Models of Early Childhood Education* by using developmentally appropriate practice as part of their criteria for comparing curriculum models.

At the level of *specific practices*, early childhood educators adopt
discrete activities or actions, such as providing blocks in the classroom,
encouraging children to make choices, or using a particular assessment
tool. Specific practices may flow from general principles, curriculum models, or both. If they do not flow from these sources, the educational approach is called *eclectic*, selecting what appear to be best practices from a
variety of sources, without a guiding framework.

While some teachers practice eclecticism *without* an explicit rationale, others do so *because of* an explicit theoretical rationale. The rationale
is essentially that curriculum models constrain the autonomy of teachers
by specifying practices to which they must adhere (e.g., Goffin, 1993).
Instead, the rationale goes, teachers should be well grounded in early
childhood development and education so that they can make their own,
eclectic decisions about early childhood educational practice. The Bank
Street College of Education professes this position and protests when its
educational approach is identified as a curriculum model (Epstein et al.,

1996; Goffin, 1993). In fact, many people who hold this position evidence a clear preference of learner-centered education and developmentally appropriate practice over teacher-centered education. It might be said that they accept such general principles as a broad framework for their professed eclecticism.

Similarly, early childhood educators who have adopted curriculum models may use them either as exclusive sources of their educational practices or as guiding frameworks for their selection of practices from various other sources, even other curriculum models. For example, some early childhood educators claim the High/Scope Curriculum as their principal curriculum model, but also employ the Creative Curriculum as a supplemental curriculum model because they consider its educational practices consistent with their principal approach.

Because evaluation compares observed learning with intended lessons, and curriculum is a plan of intended lessons, everything just said about curriculum also applies to evaluation. Evaluation plans should take into account teachers' general curriculum principles, the curriculum model(s) they use, and their specific practices. If teachers espouse developmentally appropriate practice, their evaluations should fit developmentally appropriate practice. If teachers espouse specific curriculum models, their evaluations should fit these curriculum models. If teachers' practices are eclectic, then their evaluations should be eclectic. However, evaluations of purely eclectic programs can never be generalized to other eclectic programs because, by definition, every eclectic program is one of a kind.

At the same time, valid and reliable evaluations depend on the use of valid and reliable assessment tools. Existing assessment tools that have demonstrated their validity and reliability have for the most part assessed teacher-centered rather than learner-centered education, teaching that only communicates information rather than teaching that creates settings and circumstances for student learning. Most early childhood curriculum models have been in existence for only 3 decades or so and have stood in contrast to the major tradition of teacher-centered education. Before then, evaluation was not the central concern that it is today. Hence, tools that assess these varieties of learner-centered education have not yet developed the track record of reliability and validity achieved by assessment tools for teacher-centered education, but the future of early childhood program evaluation lies in learner-centered assessment tools.

CURRICULUM MODELS

Curriculum models espouse positions on a variety of educational ideas and practices, in some of which they agree and in some of which they differ from each other. This chapter began with distinctions between teacher-centered curriculum, learner-centered curriculum, and custodial care programs that have no curriculum. Beyond these distinctions, further curriculum distinctions can be made.

Kohlberg and Mayer (1972) distinguished three educational ideologies, each with its underlying psychological theory. The romantic tradition, supported by maturationist theory, sets great stock in waiting for children to be ready for various lessons. The cultural transmission tradition, supported by associationistic learning theory, assumes that children can learn any lesson at any time if it is sequenced in learnable steps. The progressive tradition, supported by cognitive-developmental or interactionist theory, sees children's learning as occurring within their stages of cognitive development. Curriculum models based on associationistic learning theory present variations of teacher-centered curriculum. Curriculum models based on maturationist or cognitive-developmental theory present variations of learner-centered curriculum.

Weikart (1972) distinguished curriculum models on two dimensions—whether teachers initiate or respond to activities and whether students initiate or respond to activities. In teacher-centered education, teachers initiate and students respond to activities; in learner-centered education, students initiate activities and teachers either initiate or respond to activities; in custodial programs that have no curriculum, teachers and students both merely respond to activities. The key to learner-centered curriculum is that students initiate learning activities. Weikart's further distinction among learner-centered curriculum models is in the degree of initiative taken by teachers. In a romantic/maturationist curriculum model, teachers simply respond to student-initiated activities; in a progressive/cognitive-developmental model, teachers not only respond to student-initiated activities, but also initiate activities themselves.

Description

To assist potential users in selecting a curriculum model, Epstein and others (1996) reviewed and compared six widely used early childhood curriculum and training models. In doing so, they built on the work of several authors and editors over the past 2 decades (DeVries & Kohlberg, 1987; Evans, 1975; Goffin, 1993; Roopnarine & Johnson, 1993). They reviewed the following models.

- Bank Street College of Education's Developmental-Interaction approach
- The Creative Curriculum developed by Diane Trister Dodge at Teaching Strategies, Inc.

- The Direct Instruction model developed by Carl Bereiter and Sieg-fried Engelmann
- The High/Scope educational approach developed under the guid-ance of David Weikart at the High/Scope Educational Research Foundation
- The Kamii–DeVries constructivist approach developed by Con-stance Kamii and Rheta DeVries
- The Montessori method based on the work of Maria Montessori

The *Bank Street Developmental-Interaction approach* (Biber, 1984; Zimiles, 1993) is named for Bank Street College of Education in New York City, which was founded in 1916 and today offers graduate degrees in education. Influenced by the educational thinking of John Dewey, Lucy Sprague Mitchell framed its central tenet of development of the whole child through active learning. From 1928 onward, Barbara Biber used psychodynamic theory to shape the approach. Bank Street later framed a curriculum model for the federal Follow Through primary-grade project. Bank Street encourages teachers to use their own judgment about educa-tional practices in light of their understanding and observation of chil-dren's development.

The *Creative Curriculum* of Teaching Strategies, Inc. (Dodge, 1988; Dodge & Colker, 1992) was developed by Diane Trister Dodge, based on her experience working with early childhood teachers. The approach helps teachers make their practices consistent with their goals for children by rearranging their classrooms to support teachers' developmentally appro-priate practice and children's active learning, which is directed toward social competence. Teachers arrange the learning environment into 10 interest areas: art, blocks, cooking, computers, house corner, library cor-ner, music and movement, the outdoors, sand and water, and table toys. Dodge first presented the Creative Curriculum in 1979, field tested it in three Head Start programs in 1986–87, and expanded it in 1988 and again in 1992, founding Teaching Strategies, Inc., for this purpose. Although the Creative Curriculum acknowledges that support by trainers is desir-able, teachers learn this model primarily through self-instruction rather than training.

The *Direct Instruction model* (Bereiter & Engelmann, 1966) began with the preschool program devoted to scripted learning operated by Carl Bereiter and Siegfried Engelmann at the University of Illinois–Urbana in the mid-1960s, then expanded to primary-grade Follow Through pro-grams and "DISTAR" materials published by Science Research Associates. Direct Instruction focuses on academics, specifically the content of intelli-gence and achievement tests. In Direct Instruction, teachers lead small groups of children in precisely planned 20-minute question-and-answer lessons in language, mathematics, and reading. The classroom includes distinct areas, one for each of the three types of lessons, all free of distracting materials. The developers have found that Direct Instruction suits elementary school teachers better than it suits preschool teachers. In fact, the model seeks to perfect teachers' teacher-centered education rather than convert teachers to learner-centered education.

The *High/Scope Curriculum* (Hohmann, Banet, & Weikart, 1979; Hohmann & Weikart, 1995) was developed in the 1960s and 1970s by High/Scope Educational Research Foundation staff led by David Weikart. Based on Piaget's constructivist theory of child development, the High/Scope Curriculum has broadened its initial focus on disadvantaged preschool children to encompass all children and every type of early childhood setting. In this approach, children are active learners; their classrooms are arranged with discrete, well-equipped interest areas. Each day, children plan, do, and review their own activities, engage in group activities, and spend time outdoors. Teachers facilitate intellectual, social, and physical *key experiences* in children's development. The High/Scope Foundation has trained over 1,200 certified teacher trainers and tens of thousands of teachers (Epstein, 1993).

The *Kamii–DeVries constructivist perspective* (DeVries & Kohlberg, 1987; Kamii & DeVries, 1980, 1993) was developed by Constance Kamii and Rheta DeVries. It is based on the Piagetian, constructivist principle that children develop their knowledge, intelligence, morality, and personality from their interactions with the world within a logico-mathematical framework. Children learn through mental action, which usually involves physical activity. The teacher is assumed to be child centered and well grounded in traditional early childhood education. Teachers using this approach prepare the setting for active learning, stay in touch with what children are thinking from moment to moment, respond to children from their theoretical perspective, and help children extend their ideas.

The *Montessori method* (Lindauer, 1993; Montessori, 1964) was developed by Maria Montessori (1870–1952), an Italian physician who originally worked with poor children with disabilities. Montessori teachers carefully prepare program settings, filling them with Montessori materials, each of which encourages children to learn a specific, predetermined concept or skill—developing their senses, academic abilities, practical life skills, and character. Teachers show children how to use the materials correctly, then let them select their own materials and activities, expecting them to return the materials to their assigned places when they have finished using them. The Montessori method is the world's oldest early childhood curriculum model and is used today by Montessori teachers throughout the world.

Using the teacher-centered/learner-centered distinction, Direct Instruction is teacher centered, while the other curriculum models are more or less learner centered. In the terms of Kohlberg and Mayer (1972), Direct Instruction is a cultural transmission approach, and the other five curriculum models are progressive to varying extents. None of today's curriculum models takes a completely romantic approach, but this approach has influenced the Bank Street Developmental-Interaction approach, the Creative Curriculum, and the Montessori method; the High/ Scope Curriculum and the Kamii–DeVries constructivist approach are fully in the progressive tradition.

Further distinctions give each of these six curriculum models their unique identities. The Bank Street Developmental Interaction approach encourages teachers to be highly responsive to children's choices. The Creative Curriculum focuses on arranging the learning environment into 10 interest areas. Direct Instruction features high-paced, scripted question-and-answer sessions between teachers and small groups. The High/Scope Curriculum emphasizes a daily routine in which children plan, carry out, and review their own activities. In the Kamii–DeVries constructivist approach, teachers involve children in group games to foster their cognitive development. The Montessori approach sets great stock in Montessori materials, each specifically designed to teach children certain lessons.

Comparison

Epstein and others (1996) reviewed the documentation, validation, and dissemination status of these six early childhood curriculum models (see Table 3.1). They based their review not only on published data, but also on extensive materials and feedback supplied by the model developers or present-day representatives. From the perspective of the curriculum model user, documentation means available materials, validation means assurance that the curriculum model is effective, and dissemination means available training and study materials. *Documentation* clarifies the definition of the model's curriculum and training goals, objectives, practices, content, and processes and enables them to be communicated and used by others. *Validation* provides the evidence of how well a model works, how well it achieves its goals and objectives, and whether its claims of effectiveness can be trusted. *Dissemination* is the process and the result of communicating the model to others through documentation and training; it involves the model's generalizability to diverse populations and settings. One of the best arguments for using a model is to take advantage of its validated claims of effectiveness. Thus, successful dissemination ought to, but does not necessarily, require successful validation.

As shown in Table 3.1, all six models scored high on *documentation*

Table 3.1. Documentation, validation, and dissemination of curriculum models.

Criterion	Bank Street	Creative Curriculum	Direct Instruction	High/Scope	Kamii-DeVries	Montessori
Documentation						
Limitations in children's program	**High** —	**High** —	**High** Not comprehensive or developmentally appropriate by NAEYC standards	**High** —	**High** —	**High** —
Limitations in adult training	—	Little theoretical rationale	Does not encourage reflection & sharing	—	Little observation & feedback	—
Validation						
Measures of children	**Medium** Yes	**Low** Yes, no psychometric evidence	**Medium** Yes	**High** Yes	**Medium** Under development	**Medium** No
Measures of adults	No	Yes, no psychometric evidences	Under development	Yes	Under development	Under development
Evidence of effectiveness of curriculum for children	Yes, short term for K–3	No	Mixed, short & long term	Yes, short & long term	Yes, short term	Some, short & long term
Evidence of effectiveness of adult training	No	No	Yes	Yes	No	No
Dissemination						
Primary mode	**High** Higher education	**High** Publications	**Medium** Publications	**High** Field-based association	**Medium** Higher education	**High** Field-based association
Limitations	—	—	Lacks implementation record	—	Primarily in Missouri	—
Cost in money & time	High	Low	Low	Medium	Medium	High
Principal use by NAEYC members	0.7%	5.1%	0.4%	10.4%	2.8%	2.7%

because of their thorough efforts to document their approaches to working with children and training teachers. However, some of the models did have limitations in the thoroughness or appropriateness of their documentation. The Direct Instruction approach is purposely neither comprehensive nor developmentally appropriate by NAEYC's criteria. Three models do not use the full range of effective adult learning strategies: Kamii–DeVries provides little on observation and feedback; the Creative Curriculum is light in its presentation of theoretical rationale; and Direct Instruction does not encourage reflection and sharing during training.

As shown in Table 3.1, High/Scope scored high in *validation*; Montessori, Bank Street, Kamii–DeVries, and Direct Instruction scored medium; and the Creative Curriculum scored low. Validation scores were based on the availability of reliable and valid model-specific assessment tools and evidence for the effectiveness of the curriculum and training models.

Table 3.2 presents the tools that are available for each curriculum model for assessing children's development and adults' program implementation. While these assessment tools were designed to support the goals, objectives, and processes of specific curriculum models, they can be used by anyone who finds them compatible with his or her own educational intentions.

High/Scope is the only approach that offers psychometrically acceptable measures of both children and teaching. Using the High/Scope Child Observation Record (Schweinhart, McNair, Barnes, & Larner, 1991), the teacher or other observer uses anecdotal notes to rate children's development along 30 dimensions. Using the High/Scope Program Implementation Profile (Epstein, 1993), the observer rates teachers' program implementation along various dimensions. Bank Street has a psychometrically acceptable measure of children, the widely used Behavior Ratings and Analysis of Communication in Education (BRACE) (Bowman et al., 1976). The Kamii–DeVries approach has measures of children and teaching under development, particularly through Missouri's Project Construct. The Montessori approach has no measures of children's development, but the Montessori Association of Colleges for Teacher Education is assessing the psychometric characteristics of a measure of teacher candidate competencies. The Creative Curriculum and Direct Instruction offer model-specific measures without evidence of reliability or validity, although Direct Instruction does rely on standardized achievement tests with known psychometric characteristics.

As summarized by Epstein and others (1996), the evidence for the effectiveness of curriculum models and their training systems is as follows.

- The High/Scope educational approach has considerable evidence of the effectiveness of its curriculum (Schweinhart, Barnes, & Weik-

Table 3.2. Curriculum model assessment tools.

Model	Children	Teaching
Bank Street	*Behavior Ratings and Analysis of Communication in Education*[1]	Follow Through checklists & rating scales[2]
Creative Curriculum	Child Development and Learning Checklist	Teacher Knowledge Assessment; Teacher Competency Assessment
Direct Instruction	*Standardized achievement tests*; criterion-referenced tests for each lesson	Teacher observation criteria in draft implementation manual
High/Scope	*High/Scope Child Observation Record*[3]	*High/Scope Program Implementation Profile*[4]
Kamii–DeVries	DeVries' Child Evaluation Form; Project Construct child assessment measures*	Project Construct Teacher Evaluation Guides*
Montessori	——	MACTE[5] teacher candidate competencies*

Note. Italicized assessment tools have evidence of reliability and validity; assessment tools followed by an asterisk have such evidence under investigation; unmarked assessment tools have no such evidence.

[1] Bowman, Mayer, Wolotsky, Gilkeson, Williams, & Pecheone, 1976.

[2] Smithberg, 1977.

[3] Schweinhart, McNair, Barnes, & Larner, 1991.

[4] Epstein, 1993.

[5] Montessori Association of Colleges for Teacher Education.

art, with Barnett & Epstein, 1993; Schweinhart, Weikart, & Larner, 1986) *and* its training system (Epstein, 1993).

- Montessori has some evidence of reaching its goals for children (Boehnlein, 1988; Karnes, Schwedel, & Williams, 1983; Miller & Bizzell, 1983).
- The Bank Street approach has evidence of its effectiveness with

primary-grade children (Bowman et al., 1976; Gilkeson, Smith-berg, Bowman, & Rhine, 1981).

- The Kamii–DeVries model has demonstrated short-term positive effects in some areas of child development (DeVries, Haney, & Zan, 1991; Golub & Kolen, 1976).
- Much evidence has been collected on Direct Instruction, not all of it positive, with intellectual and language effects of preschool programs diminishing in the primary grades, no evidence of positive social-emotional effects, and some evidence of negative effects on social conduct (Burts et al., 1992; Gersten & Keating, 1987; Schweinhart et al., 1986; Hyson, Van Trieste, & Rauch, 1989; Karnes et al., 1983).
- The Creative Curriculum does not yet have evidence of its effectiveness with either children or adults.

It should come as no surprise that model developers themselves often have conducted the evaluations of the effectiveness of their own curriculum models. After all, they have the greatest stake in the accuracy of their claims about the curriculum model's effectiveness. Indeed, it is questionable whether a curriculum model should be disseminated without evidence of its effectiveness. Certainly, model developers will ensure and insist on evaluations that are consistent with, and sensitive to, the goals, objectives, and processes of their curriculum model. On the other hand, the vested interest of model developers in the success of their curriculum models does constitute an apparent if not actual impediment to impartial evaluation. The dilemma is highlighted by the first national evaluation of the Follow Through early elementary project in the 1970s, in which "impartial" national evaluators identified the unique objectives of various models, then tried to measure all of them using the same teacher-centered assessment format.

As shown in Table 3.1, Montessori, Bank Street, High/Scope, and the Creative Curriculum scored high in *dissemination*, while Kamii–DeVries and Direct Instruction scored medium. Direct Instruction scored only medium because, although the curriculum materials have been sold widely, the model lacks implementation records. Kamii–DeVries so far has been used only in Missouri and a few other places. High/Scope, Direct Instruction, Montessori, and the Creative Curriculum appear to have excellent or reasonable capacity for dissemination. High/Scope and Montessori, which have field-based associations supported by face-to-face training, cost more than the Creative Curriculum and Direct Instruction. The Creative Curriculum and Direct Instruction, which are primarily publication-based without face-to-face training, cost less than High/Scope and Montessori, but evidence of their effectiveness without face-to-face training is lacking.

The two higher education approaches, Bank Street and Kamii–DeVries, are more costly than the other models and training in either model lasts 2 years.

A SURVEY OF CURRICULUM MODEL AWARENESS AND USE

To further examine the extent of dissemination of these curriculum models in the United States, Epstein and others (1996) at High/Scope conducted a survey concerning model awareness and use by NAEYC members, the association judged by the authors to best represent the population of U.S. early childhood educators. They anonymously mailed questionnaires to a random sample of NAEYC members, asking that completed questionnaires be returned to the funder, the Charles Stewart Mott Foundation, so as not to identify the survey with the High/Scope Educational Research Foundation, one of the curriculum model developers. Of the 2,000 questionnaires mailed, 671 were returned, 34% of the total.

The survey respondents were *leaders of the nation's early childhood programs*: 42% were directors, 25% were head teachers, and 25% were teachers. Of the programs provided by the respondents, 33% were in nonprofit child-care centers, 25% were in public schools, 16% were in private schools, 8% were in Head Start agencies, 6% were in for-profit, child-care centers, 3% were in college laboratory schools or campus child-care centers, and 6% were in family and group child-care homes. The respondents were well educated: 83% had a bachelor's degree or more, including 41% with a master's degree or doctorate and another 21% with some graduate school.

Noting that developmentally appropriate practice was not to be considered a curriculum model but rather a set of guidelines for various early childhood curriculum models, the questionnaire asked respondents about their awareness and use of the six early childhood curriculum models mentioned previously: Bank Street, Creative Curriculum, Direct Instruction, Kamii–DeVries, High/Scope, and Montessori. An additional 22% of the respondents identified a diverse array of other models: 6% reported that they had developed their own curriculum model; 2% each named Whole Language, Circle of Childhood, or Reggio Emilia; fewer than 1% named another curriculum model.

AWARENESS AND EXAMINATION

As shown in Table 3.3, virtually all respondents (99%) had *heard of* at least one of these curriculum models—with 95% of the respondents

Table 3.3. Percentage of respondents reporting curriculum model use and awareness (N = 671). (From *Models of Early Childhood Education* by Epstein, Schweinhart, and McAdoo, 1995, Ypsilanti, MI: High/Scope Press. Used with permission.)

Curriculum Model	Principal Use[1]	Supplemental Use[2]	Don't Use But Have Heard of[3]	Never Heard of	No Response
Any model	32.6	45.5	20.6	0.7	0.6
Bank Street	0.7	10.9	47.1	37.0	4.3
Creative Curriculum	5.1	24.6	21.8	45.3	3.2
Direct Instruction	0.4	12.2	35.3	48.0	4.1
High/Scope	10.4	33.4	35.8	16.8	3.6
Kamii–DeVries	2.8	21.9	31.0	39.8	4.5
Montessori	2.7	24.7	67.1	1.3	4.2
Other model	10.4	11.8	—	—	77.8

Note. Developmentally appropriate practice was not included because it was regarded not as a model but rather as a set of criteria for models.

[1] "Principal use" combines the questionnaire alternatives of "primary" use and "exclusive" use.

[2] "Supplemental use" is the questionnaire alternative of using a curriculum model "as one of several."

[3] "Heard of" is the questionnaire alternative of "don't use it but heard of it."

recognizing Montessori, 80% recognizing High/Scope, 59% recognizing Bank Street, 56% recognizing Kamii–DeVries, 52% recognizing Creative Curriculum, and 48% recognizing Direct Instruction.

As educated early childhood leaders, 86% of the respondents have examined one or more curriculum models, by engaging in either training or study of the model. Montessori and High/Scope, the most widely known of these curriculum models (80%–95%), are also the most widely examined (60%–68%). The Creative Curriculum, Kamii–DeVries, and Direct Instruction are at the next level of both awareness (48%–56%) and examination (25%–34%). Compared with these three models, Bank Street is more widely known (59%) but less widely examined (23%). Of the respondents, 52% have received training in some curriculum model, 34% have studied some curriculum model but not received training in it, and 10% have never trained in or studied any curriculum model.

Use

As shown in Table 3.3, 78% of the respondents use one or more curriculum models *in some way* in their programs: 44% use the High/Scope educational approach, 30% use the Creative Curriculum, 27% use the Montessori method, 25% use the Kamii–DeVries constructivist approach, 13% use Direct Instruction, 12% use the Bank Street Developmental-Interaction approach, and 22% use another curriculum model. Of the respondents without bachelor's degrees, 65% use one or more curriculum models, as compared with 81% of those with a bachelor's degree or more. The following percentages of respondents in various settings use curriculum models:

100%, college child-care centers and laboratory schools
96%, Head Start agencies
82%, public school early childhood programs
76%, nonprofit child-care centers
74%, private school early childhood programs
72%, for-profit, child-care centers
67%, group child-care homes
63%, family child-care homes

Earlier, we distinguished between principal and supplemental use of a curriculum model. Teachers adopt and use a *principal* curriculum model as either the exclusive source or the guiding framework for their educational practices. Teachers use *supplemental* curriculum models as sources of educational practices, guided by either their principal curriculum model or their own eclectic choices. Of the respondents, 33% use a principal curriculum model; 67% do not and therefore may be considered partially or totally eclectic, either using various supplemental curriculum models without preference for one of them (46%) or using no curriculum model at all (26%). As shown in Table 3.3, up to 10% use a particular model as their *principal curriculum model*, and 11% to 33% use a particular model as a *supplemental curriculum model*.

A *principal* curriculum model is used by larger percentages of respondents who have bachelors' degrees or work in Head Start, college-based programs, or public schools. Of the respondents without bachelor's degrees, 29% use a principal curriculum model, compared with 34% of those with bachelor's degrees or more. The following percentages of respondents in various settings use a principal curriculum model:

55%, Head Start agencies
40%, college child-care centers and laboratory schools
37%, public school early childhood programs
33%, for-profit, child-care centers
31%, family child-care homes
29%, nonprofit child-care centers
27%, private school early childhood programs
14%, group child-care homes

This last set of findings speaks most directly to the extent of acceptance of curriculum models as guiding frameworks in various types of early childhood programs. Head Start agencies are the only type in which a majority uses principal curriculum models. While all college child-care centers and laboratory schools use curriculum models, as noted above, only 2 in 5 use a principal curriculum model. Only 3 in 8 public school early childhood programs espouse curriculum models — more than most types of early childhood programs, but still a minority. About one-third of other types of early childhood programs use a principal curriculum model, except for group child-care homes, where use is surprisingly lower than in family child-care homes and the other types of child-care agencies.

THE FUTURE

The general direction of early childhood programs today is toward expansion, institutionalization, and professionalization. Early childhood programs are expanding and institutionalizing because of the movement of mothers into the labor force and because of the growing recognition of the importance of early childhood education to children's development. As these trends continue, the public increasingly will see early childhood programs as educational rather than custodial.

As early childhood programs become seen as educational, there is the danger that some will think that these programs must provide teacher-centered education to groups of students rather than learner-centered education of students by creating settings and circumstances for learning. However, NAEYC, the Association for Childhood Education International, and other associations concerned with early childhood have taken clear positions in support of general principles of learner-centered education and developmentally appropriate practice. Further, five of the six most prevalent early childhood curriculum models are largely consistent with these general curriculum principles.

However, developmentally appropriate practice is more widely professed than practiced, and only one-third of early childhood leaders claim to use a principal curriculum model to guide their educational thinking and practice. Two-thirds of early childhood leaders are eclectic, claiming no principal curriculum model. Yet only when early childhood programs use a validated principal curriculum model can they claim evidence of effectiveness. Generalizable evidence of the effectiveness of eclectic programs does not, and cannot, exist and because every eclectic program is different from every other eclectic program.

These observations raise the question of how much autonomy teachers should have. We believe that teachers should have the same kind of autonomy as scientists and artists. In all three cases, the practitioner intelligently interprets principles to develop raw materials into refined products that stand the test of some type of evaluation. The teacher intelligently interprets principles of learning and child development to contribute to children's learning and development and then verifies this contribution by evaluation. Such intelligent interpretation of principles is what treatment replication is all about and thus is what permits program providers to generalize findings from validating research to their own programs.

From this perspective, curriculum and evaluation should be organized by general principles and various curriculum models of demonstrated effectiveness. The use of unbridled eclecticism in programs is responsible only if the programs are subjected to valid evaluations; and, even then, such evaluations cannot be generalized to other eclectic programs. Regrettably, the majority of early childhood programs operating in the United States today are eclectic and are not receiving valid evaluations.

Too often, national evaluations virtually ignore the curriculum models involved. Widespread use of the Early Childhood Environment Rating Scale (Harms & Clifford, 1980), for example, acknowledges the importance of learner-centered education, but does not further distinguish among curriculum models. Many assessments of child outcomes are not even learner centered, instead focusing on teacher-centered assessment tools such as the Peabody Picture Vocabulary Test (Dunn, 1965).

Early childhood educators need to adopt valid curriculum models as guiding frameworks for their programs. The curriculum model adopted should serve as the guiding framework not only for program practices, but also for staff development, program monitoring, and program evaluation. Thus, one-day workshops should focus not on the latest unrelated trends, but on topics needed to better implement the curriculum model. Program monitoring should be based not on the supervisor's whims, but on the curriculum model's goals and objectives. Program evaluation should use assessment tools that not only offer psychometric validity and reliability, but also assess program practices and child outcomes appropriately in terms of the curriculum model espoused in the program. When the nation has not only enough programs for all young children living in poverty, but also the infrastructure to support the widespread use of valid curriculum models as guiding frameworks, we finally will be able to take full advantage of the promise of early childhood education.

Acknowledgment. This chapter is based on *Models of Early Childhood Education* by A. S. Epstein, L. J. Schweinhart, and L. McAdoo (Ypsilanti, MI: High/Scope Press, 1995).

REFERENCES

Bereiter, C., & Engelmann, S. (1966). *Teaching disadvantaged children in the preschool.* Englewood Cliffs, NJ: Prentice-Hall.

Biber, B. (1984). *Early education and psychological development.* New Haven, CT: Yale University Press.

Boehnlein, M. (1988, Summer). Montessori research: Analysis in retrospect [Special issue]. *The NAMTA Quarterly, 13*(3).

Bowman, G. W., Mayer, R. S., Wolotsky, H., Gilkeson, E. C., Williams, J. H., & Pecheone, R. (1976). *The BRACE program for systematic observation.* New York: Bank Street Publications.

Bredekamp, S. (Ed.). (1987). *Developmentally appropriate practice in early childhood programs serving children from birth through age 8 (exp. ed.).* Washington, DC: National Association for the Education of Young Children.

Burts, D. C., Hart, C. H., Charlesworth, R., Fleege, P. O., Mosley, J., & Thomasson, R. H. (1992). Observed activities and stress behaviors of children in developmentally appropriate and inappropriate kindergarten classrooms. *Early Childhood Research Quarterly, 7*, 297–318.

DeVries, R., Haney, J. P., & Zan, B. (1991). Sociomoral atmosphere in direct-instruction, eclectic, and constructivist kindergartens: A study of teachers' enacted interpersonal understanding. *Early Childhood Research Quarterly, 6*, 449–471.

DeVries, R., & Kohlberg, L. (1987). *Constructivist early education: Overview and comparison with other programs.* Washington, DC: National Association for the Education of Young Children.

Dodge, D. T. (1988). *A guide for supervisors and trainers on implementing the Creative Curriculum for early childhood* (2nd ed.). Washington, DC: Teaching Strategies, Inc.

Dodge, D. T., & Colker, L.J. (1992). *The Creative Curriculum for early childhood* (3rd ed.). Washington, DC: Teaching Strategies, Inc.

Dunn, L. M. (1965). *Peabody Picture Vocabulary Test manual.* Minneapolis, MN: American Guidance Service.

Epstein, A. S. (1993). *Training for quality: Improving early childhood programs through systematic inservice training.* Ypsilanti, MI: High/Scope Press.

Epstein, A. S., Schweinhart, L. J., & McAdoo, L. (1996). *Models of early childhood education.* Ypsilanti, MI: High/Scope Press.

Evans, E. D. (1975). *Contemporary influences in early childhood education* (2nd ed.). New York: Holt, Rinehart & Winston.

Gersten, R., & Keating, T. (1987). Improving high school performance of "at-risk" students: A study of long-term benefits of direct instruction. *Educational Leadership, 44*(6), 28–31.

Gilkeson, E. C., Smithberg, L. M., Bowman, G. W., & Rhine, W. R. (1981). Bank Street Model: A Developmental-Interaction approach. In W. R. Rhine (Ed.), *Making schools more effective: New directions from Follow Through* (pp. 249-288). New York: Academic Press.

Goffin, S. G. (1993). *Curriculum models and early childhood education: Appraising the relationship.* New York: Merrill.

Golub, M., & Kolen, C. (1976). *Evaluation of a Piagetian kindergarten program.* Unpublished manuscript based on paper presented at the Sixth Annual Symposium of the Jean Piaget Society, Philadelphia.

Harms, T., & Clifford, R. M. (1980). *Early Childhood Environment Rating Scale.* New York: Teachers College Press.

Hendrick, J. (1988). *The whole child: Developmental education for the early years.* Columbus, OH: Merrill.

Hohmann, M., Banet, B., & Weikart, D. P. (1979). *Young children in action: A manual for preschool educators.* Ypsilanti, MI: High/Scope Press.

Hohmann, M., & Weikart, D. P. (1995). *Educating young children: Active learning practices for preschool and child care programs.* Ypsilanti, MI: High/Scope Press.

Hyson, M. C., Van Trieste, K. L., & Rauch, V. (1989, November). NAEYC's *developmentally appropriate practice guidelines: Current research.* Paper presented at the preconference sessions of the meeting of the National Association for the Education of Young Children, Atlanta.

Kamii, C., & DeVries, R. (1980). *Group games in early education: Implications of Piaget's theory.* Washington, DC: National Association for the Education of Young Children.

Kamii, C., & DeVries, R. (1993). *Physical knowledge in preschool education: Implications of Piaget's theory.* New York: Teachers College Press.

Karnes, M. B., Schwedel, A. M., & Williams, M. B. (1983). A comparison of five approaches for educating young children from low-income homes. In Consortium for Longitudinal Studies, *As the twig is bent — Lasting effects of preschool programs* (pp. 133–170). Hillsdale, NJ: Erlbaum.

Kohlberg, L., & Mayer, R. (1972). Development as the aim of education. *Harvard Educational Review, 42,* 449–496.

Lindauer, S. L. K. (1993). Montessori education for young children. In J. L.

Roopnarine & J. E. Johnson (Eds.), *Approaches to early childhood education* (2nd ed., pp. 243-259). New York: Macmillan.

Mallory, B. L., & New, R. S. (1994). *Diversity and developmentally appropriate practices: Challenges for early childhood education.* New York: Teachers College Press.

Miller, L. B., & Bizzell, R. P. (1983). The Louisville experiment: A comparison of four programs. In Consortium for Longitudinal Studies, *As the twig is bent — Lasting effects of preschool programs* (pp. 171–199). Hillsdale, NJ: Erlbaum.

Montessori, M. (1964). *The Montessori method.* New York: Schocken.

Roopnarine, J. L., & Johnson, J. E. (Eds.). (1993). *Approaches to early childhood education* (2nd ed.). New York: Macmillan.

Schweinhart, L. J. (1993, July). Observing young children in action: The key to early childhood assessment. *Young Children, 48*(5), 29–33.

Schweinhart, L. J., Barnes, H. V., & Weikart, D. P. with Barnett, W. S., & Epstein, A. S. (1993). *Significant benefits: The High/Scope Perry Preschool study through age 27.* Ypsilanti, MI: High/Scope Press.

Schweinhart, L. J., McNair, S., Barnes, H., & Larner, M. (1991). Observing young children in action to assess their development: The High/Scope Child Observation Record study. *Educational and Psychological Measurement, 53,* 445–455.

Schweinhart, L. J., & Weikart, D. P. (1988). Education for young children living in poverty: Child-initiated learning or teacher-directed instruction? *Elementary School Journal, 89,* 213–225.

Schweinhart, L. J., Weikart, D. P., & Larner, M. B. (1986). Consequences of three preschool curriculum models through age 15. *Early Childhood Research Quarterly, 1,* 15–45.

Smithberg, L. M. (1977). *Checklist of model implementation.* New York: Bank Street College.

Weikart, D. P. (1972). Relationship of curriculum, teaching, and learning in preschool education. In J. C. Stanley (Ed.), *Preschool programs for the disadvantaged.* Baltimore, MD: Johns Hopkins University Press.

Zimiles, H. (1993). The Bank Street Approach. In J. L. Roopnarine & J. E. Johnson (Eds.), *Approaches to early childhood education* (2nd ed., pp. 261–273). New York: Macmillan.

CHAPTER 4

Evaluating Early Childhood Programs: The British Experience

Tony Bertram and Christine Pascal

This chapter explores the context of early childhood programs in the United Kingdom and identifies the need to evaluate their quality. We describe the principles for making these judgments and how they operate. We outline what we have learned about the evaluation process thus far and indicate the issues that have emerged. We make particular reference to our ongoing research, a major United Kingdom initiative called the Effective Early Learning Research Project.

EARLY CHILDHOOD PROGRAMS IN THE UNITED KINGDOM

National statistics for education and care in the United Kingdom conceal wide local variations in what is available. Compared with countries in continental Europe, there has been little coordinated government policy in this area. As a result, education, health, and social service agencies; voluntary bodies; and private businesses have all developed separate approaches and separate advisory and inspection systems to evaluate, assess, and develop their settings. In addition, a great variety of *ad hoc* arrangements begun by desperate parents has led to fragmentation and a lack of coherent policy.

It is symptomatic of the muddle that has resulted from years of governmental neglect and prevarication that reliable statistical evidence of even the extent and nature of existing provision is difficult to obtain (Department for Education, 1992; Government Statistical Service, 1993; Moss, 1994). Yet despite this lack of governmental commitment, the United Kingdom has some of the best programs for young children in the world coexisting with some of the poorest.

The Characteristics of UK Provision

There are a number of distinguishing features that make early childhood programs in the United Kingdom markedly different than those in other countries.

• *Early childhood teachers are college graduates.* Early childhood teachers have the same pay and conditions as high school teachers and the same length and status of training; that is, they are graduates of 4-year, postsecondary university programs. Because there is no employment disparity between teachers of children of differing ages, it is not uncommon to find trained high school teachers, who may have returned to teaching after having their own families, choosing to teach young children. In a survey of "reception" classes (the first class of the primary schools) in a large English city, Pascal (1990) found that more teachers who had been trained for high school teaching were working with 4-year-olds than were teachers who had been trained for that age range.

• *Children start school sooner than in most other countries.* The legal age for admission to school is 5 years, but in England and Wales schools increasingly are admitting children at the age of 4 years. In Northern Ireland the legal age for compulsory attendance is 4 years, although mostly this is part-time, half-day attendance. In Scotland, however, it is unusual for 4-year-olds to be in formal school. Most of the 84% of UK 4-year-olds who receive some form of publicly funded educational provision are in reception classes. Children aged 4–5 years attend school full time for about 6 hours a day and are likely to be in classes of 25–35 pupils.

• *Many school-based programs may be inappropriate.* Many early childhood educators are worried that much of this school-based provision focuses too narrowly, too formally, and too soon on inappropriate attempts to deliver a nationally prescribed curriculum that, they feel, is in danger of excluding the children's real needs and interests and is not matched to their level of development (Early Years Curriculum Group, 1989).

• *Nursery education has different characteristics.* Those 3- and 4-

year-old children (26%) who live in areas where there is publicly funded nursery provision benefit from staff ratios of between 1 to 10 and 1 to 15. Nurseries usually have buildings designed specifically for young children and employ nursery trained college graduate staff members supported by appropriately trained aides. Most children attend nursery education part time for 4 hours a day, either morning or afternoon. There is an active and exploratory curriculum with opportunities for movement, choice, and play. Nursery teachers are trained in observation techniques and use them as the basis for tailoring their curriculum to meet the children's needs. There is no requirement to deliver a formally prescribed curriculum in most nurseries.

• *There is little publicly funded, extended day care.* Publicly funded child care outside of school hours and during holidays is minimal (less than 1%) for young children.

• *Programs for preschool children are spotty, diverse, underfunded, and uncoordinated.* Most 3- and 4-year-olds outside the school system attend play centers (40% in 1986) run mainly by parents and volunteers. Only 1 in 4 of these centers or "playgroups" is supported by public funds, and where they are assisted, grants on average cover less than half the costs. The average attendance for each child is about 6 hours a week. These programs usually are housed in buildings that are likely to have other predominant functions, such as village and church halls. Training courses for their staff vary from 10 to 120 hours.

Currently, only 3% of nursery and preschool programs for 3- to 5-year-olds are privately funded, although this is a form of provision that is likely to expand following new government initiatives, which will be described later. Hours of operation tend to be longer than in publicly funded programs and more suited to the demands of working parents.

• *There is little publicly funded provision for children under the age of 3.* Center-based, public programs for children under the age of 3 are funded mainly by health and social service agencies. These often are targeted at children who have special needs or whose families are seen as "at risk." Only 2% of children aged 0–2 years have access to these publicly funded programs. Most of the children whose parents do not have access to relatives or friends willing to help, will be cared for outside the home by family-based caregivers called "child minders," who are required to register with local authorities, although few do.

Government Policy

Current government policy in relation to preschool education continues to be one of choice and diversity at a time when demand for places has increased substantially due to changing social and economic conditions. Policy continues to emphasize the shared responsibility of parents, businesses, and local communities and to argue for continued diversity. This lack of central direction and national standards serves to perpetuate the inequalities and inadequacy that families with young children face in the United Kingdom today. In this context, programs for children under the age of 5 remain patchy, diverse, and, compared with other European countries, at a low level. This has been called "a national scandal" (Ball, 1994).

Recently the government has made a "cast iron" commitment to provide access to center-based education for all 4-year-olds whose parents want it. It is doing this through the mechanism of a voucher system, an idea adopted from the United States, which will allow parents to choose where to spend £1,100 — an inadequate amount to fully pay for service — for preschool for each 4-year-old child. The vouchers will not be means tested but will be available to all. There is a stipulation that vouchers can be spent only in approved settings that have an educational commitment and a mechanism for validation. Inspection also is currently being considered.

Social Changes

Educational programs for young children in the United Kingdom cannot be considered without reference to the social context in which they live. The position of children in society continues to worsen. Recent studies by Wilkinson (1994) and Holtermann (1995) and the Rowntree Foundation Report (1995) have documented the effects of increasing inequality on children. These reports highlight the social and psychological effects of poverty on family life and the development of the young. It is in this broad context of increasing social inequality, with in some areas of the country as many as 46% of young children growing up in households with no earners, that we must set any further development of education and care for young children. Any move toward establishing universal preschool education must be placed in a context of the need for wider care and services for young children.

The reality of current programs for children under the age of 5 falls far short of meeting these urgent needs. The availability of high-quality education and care for the young is a lottery, dependent on such factors as place of residence, age, and family income. Where programs are available, young children are learning in a vast array of different educational and care settings — public, private, and voluntary sectors of education, social services, and health. These include local authority nurseries and primary schools, day-care centers, family centers, playgroups, private kindergartens, workplace child-care centers, and nurseries.

Each of these settings operate with different aims, funding, resources, staffing, and quality control procedures. This diversity means that the quality and effectiveness of the early learning experiences they offer are variable and difficult to judge.

We have never been better informed about the need for quality in providing for young children. The lack of appropriate provision in the United Kingdom must be set alongside the increasing volume of valid evidence from across the world that demonstrates that high-quality pre-school education can have a significant and long-term effect on children's learning and can lead to better social behavior and more productive citizenship. Research has shown clearly that investments in high-quality, early learning experiences at this stage pay dividends as children grow through the schooling system to adulthood (Sylva & Wiltshire, 1993).

NATIONAL REPORTS AND POLITICAL INITIATIVES

In view of this emphasis on quality, concern has been expressed in many quarters, and in many recent reports (Ball, 1994; Department of Education and Science, 1990; House of Commons, 1994; Moss, 1994; National Commission on Education, 1993; Pascal, 1990), as evidence has accumulated of the poor quality of early education experienced in some settings at this critical time in children's development. The poor quality is due to many factors: poor physical facilities, lack of equipment, unsuitable expectations and objectives, inappropriate curriculum, poor staffing ratios, inadequate monitoring, and — perhaps most important — lack of appropriate and ongoing training.

The pursuit of quality in education and, in particular, in early childhood education, is currently high on the political and social agenda in the United Kingdom. A series of major national reports (Ball, 1994; Department of Education and Science, 1990; House of Commons, 1994; National Commission on Education, 1993) have argued strongly that educational programs for 3- and 4-year-olds should be expanded. Each report has stressed the importance of high quality in this expansion and has specified in some detail, at both a policy and practical level, what this should entail. The reports highlight the need for a national system of quality review and assurance and for a coordinated strategy of evaluation and improvement in early childhood settings.

There are a number of initiatives at present that indicate that action is being planned. Following Prime Minister John Major's "cast iron" commitment to universal nursery education at the Conservative Party conference in November 1994, a task force was set up at the Department for

Education to put this policy in place. We await the details of how the voucher scheme will operate in practice, but already the government has indicated that it will be funded by taking money presently given to local education authority providers. The trial scheme, which invited authorities to participate, has been taken up by only four of more than 100 authorities. The Labour Party, currently out of office, also has established an Inquiry Team that aims to develop a policy of integrated, coherent and comprehensive provision of early years services that will ensure that all 3- and 4-year-olds whose parents wish it have access to quality preschool education. These initiatives should be welcomed but will take time to implement. There is agreement that long-term and carefully planned development is required at a national level. However, given the financial constraints, it also is clear that these long-term targets will come too late for many children who need more effective early learning experiences immediately, as they will not get another chance at their childhood.

This factor has meant that demand for expansion has been accompanied by pressure for the development of procedures to facilitate quality evaluation and improvement in all preschool settings. Recent reports have pointed to the urgent need for the introduction of strategies to improve the quality of existing provision, but as the Royal Society of Arts Report (Ball, 1994) points out,

> The diverse pattern of provision in the UK . . . makes it difficult to ascertain and monitor the quality of learning experiences offered to young children. There is a lack of thorough and systematic quality review, and a need for appropriate and rigorous procedures for quality development and assurance for all center based early learning. One of the purposes of a national evaluation of the diversity of provision would be to enable parents to make informed choices. At present, there are no incentives to encourage the evaluation of quality and the pursuit of strategies of improvement. (para. 6.12)

The Effective Early Learning (EEL) Research Project, substantially funded by charitable foundations and local authority providers, addresses these issues directly and is taking action to influence this situation so that more children in the United Kingdom have opportunities for high-quality and effective early learning.

THE EFFECTIVE EARLY LEARNING RESEARCH PROJECT

Given the context described above, British experience in evaluating early childhood programs is not extensive. As noted, there is no coordinated and coherent system of education for young children, and this has led to the development of a diverse and complex plethora of early childhood programs, many of which rarely are monitored and evaluated. Added to this is the paucity of funding available for the development of evaluation strategies and for evaluation studies in the early childhood field. However, with the recent political focus on developing programs for young children, and the emphasis on value for money and accountability that permeates all policy initiatives, there has been an increase in evaluative activity. Some of the evaluative initiatives have a clear focus on measuring or assessing quality as part of a policy for quality inspection or assurance. Examples of these include the British Standards Institute (BSI) BS 5750 or BSEN/ISO 9000 Scheme (1991), the Office for Standards in Education (OFSTED) Inspection Framework (1993), and the PLA (Pre-school Learning Alliance) Accreditation Procedures (Pre-school Playgroups Association, 1993). Other evaluative initiatives are more geared toward quality improvement or total quality management, developed as part of providers' commitment to raising standards. Examples of the latter include the Thomas Coram Self Evaluation Materials (Munton, Mooney, & Rowland, 1995), the Strathclyde "Evaluating Ourselves" Project (Wilkinson & Stephen, 1992), and the Effective Early Learning Research Project (Pascal & Bertram, 1994; Pascal, Bertram, & Ramsden, 1994; Pascal, Bertram, Ramsden, & Georgeson et al., 1995). Of all of these schemes, the Effective Early Learning Research Project provides the most comprehensive, extensive, and well-tested evaluation study in early childhood ever undertaken within the United Kingdom (Williams, 1995).

The EEL Research Project began in May 1993 and is completing its second, developmental phase of operation. The next phase will involve an extensive dissemination program for the EEL evaluation and improvement process and a comparative analysis of quality in different types of early childhood settings.

Aims and Approach

The EEL Project grew out of the urgent need for procedures to facilitate quality evaluation and improvement in the diverse range of settings in which children under the age of 5 are being educated in the United Kingdom. It also responded to the lack of a substantial empirical database on the quality and effectiveness of early learning offered in these settings. It focuses particularly on programs for 3- and 4-year-olds, as these children currently are in a wider range of programs than any other age group, but has applicability throughout the early childhood years (and beyond). The project is operating throughout the United Kingdom and is being carried out by a team of practitioner researchers, directed by Professor Christine Pascal and based at Worcester College of Higher Education.

The key aims of the project are

1. To develop a cost-effective strategy to evaluate and improve the quality and effectiveness of early learning available to 3- and 4-year-old children in a wide range of educational and care settings across Scotland, Northern Ireland, England, and Wales.
2. To rigorously and systematically evaluate and compare the quality of early learning provided in a diverse range of early childhood educational and care settings across the United Kingdom.

The project provides a clear and targeted strategy for change and improvement that builds on the existing range of programs for young children and attempts to extend the skills and expertise of all those who work with young children. It brings together those in education and child care in the voluntary, public, and private sectors. It centers around the development and application of an innovative and cost-effective set of evaluation and improvement procedures that may be used for training, institutional development, monitoring, and review in all early childhood settings. The development of quantitative and qualitative instruments to evaluate the quality of provision in different settings is also a key feature of the project.

The project has two interlinked and complementary elements: *research* and *development*. A main thrust of the project's work is to *develop* and improve the quality and effectiveness of young children's learning. However, the process of evaluation also provides a wealth of detailed qualitative and quantitative data from early childhood settings across the United Kingdom. Data are collected on such things as training, staff ratios, curriculum, facilities, teaching styles, interactions, daily programs, planning and assessment procedures, equal opportunities, home/school partnership, and quality control procedures. These data will allow a comparative evaluation to be made of different kinds of provision and also will validate a set of *research instruments* for quality monitoring and review of early childhood services.

The links between the research process and practice are clear in this project, which is grounded in practice; the research is informed by and informs practitioners. The roles of researcher and practitioner have become blurred in the process. All the members of the research team are practitioners by training and were able to take on this role within the settings where they worked. This gives them credibility within the settings and helps to break down some of the distancing and mystique that sometimes surround research. It also ensures that the knowledge generated by the project has a powerful and direct application to the realities of life in these early childhood settings.

How Quality Is Defined

"Quality" is a much overused word that is in danger of losing its meaning. Attempts to identify key elements in any definition of quality, whether related to early learning or any other aspect of life, have proved to be problematic and contentious. The difficulty lies in the concept of quality itself. As early philosophers pointed out, quality is a subjective and personal notion. Pirsig (1974) points out, "Quality is neither mind nor matter, but a third entity independent of the two. . . . Even though quality cannot be defined, you know what it is" (p. 14).

The EEL Project is based on the belief that quality is a value laden, subjective, and dynamic concept that varies with time, perspective, and place (Pascal & Bertram, 1994). This belief has grown out of our experience that has shown that to lay down precise, fixed, static definitions of quality is inappropriate. Rather, we have found that evaluation is more powerful, accurate, and valid if quality is viewed as a dynamic, developmental concept whose definition grows out of the shared and agreed-upon perspectives of those who are closest to the experiences being assessed.

The notion of quality as being centered in experience and enlightened awareness is not a romantic notion. Business gurus such as Handy (1994) and Peters (1992) support it. Japanese car manufacturers recognize that quality comes not from manuals and targets sent down from on high, but by empowering individuals to take pride in producing work of the highest quality. Employees make judgments about that, with support and help from external moderators and with continual training. The "intuitive feel good" approach, as Williams (1995, p. 15) calls it, has a very hard-nosed and rigorous edge, and has been tested by some of the most demanding managers in the world of industry and commerce. Other factors in defining quality that we feel need to be taken into account are those of time and place. Quality is not a fixed point on a scale; it changes over time. What may be high quality at one time, in one set of circumstances, may not be viewed as high quality at a later time, or in a different place, or in different circumstances. A definition of quality therefore has to allow for its dynamic nature.

We were also mindful that there are aspects of practice that provide a core set of conditions that favor high-quality early learning experiences. There is wide consensus about the essentials of quality in early childhood programs. These are discussed amply in much of the literature in the field and are outlined in several UK national reports (House of Commons, 1989, 1994; Ball, 1994; Department of Education and Science, 1990). The consensus also extends worldwide. In the United States, the Carnegie Task Force report (1994) and the guidelines on developmentally appropriate practice of the National Association for the Education of Young Children (Bredekamp, 1987) affirm these same core elements of quality. New Zealand and Australian early childhood experts concur (Early Childhood Care and Education Working Group, 1988). The EXE (Experiential Education) Project in Belgium (Laevers, 1994a) and the worldwide High/Scope program (Hohmann et al., 1979) also can be viewed as fitting these core values. There is thus a strong, historical, comparative, diverse grouping of early childhood expertise that shares this view of high quality and agrees on the areas that must be evaluated for it to be achieved.

Developing an Evaluative Framework for Quality

Although quality is dynamic and developmental and allows for differing value bases, it was also clear to us that to be successful, any evaluation project needs to employ a clear and systematic framework for its activity. The EEL Project, therefore, developed a framework for evaluating quality that builds on the consensus about what constitutes quality in early childhood and also the knowledge base we have about effective early learning. It is flexible and allows for individual interpretation, but is framed around a number of clear "domains" or "dimensions" of quality practice that allow for comparability and cohesiveness within the project as a whole. The framework employed in the EEL Project (Pascal & Bertram, 1994; Pascal et al., 1995) may be taken as typical of most other evaluative frameworks for early childhood within the United Kingdom and demonstrates the breadth of issues that any evaluation of quality must embrace.

Working closely with practitioners and policy makers and synthesizing the evaluative literature, we have identified a framework including the following 10 dimensions. These are the areas that need to be evaluated.

1. *Aims and objectives* — the written and spoken statements of policy in which the aims and objectives of the provision for learning are made explicit. This dimension also focuses on issues such as how the policy statements are formed, who is involved in their formation, and how they are communicated to involved parties. The extent to which these aims are initiated, shared, communicated, and understood by all involved parties also needs to be considered.

2. *Learning experiences/curriculum* — the range and balance of

learning activities provided and the learning opportunities they present for young children. The curriculum is interpreted very broadly to embrace children's all-around cognitive and social development. This dimension considers the extent to which the activities and experiences offered provide learning opportunities in language and literacy, mathematics, science, technology, physical, human and social, moral and spiritual, aesthetic, and creative areas of experience. It also may include reference to the UK National Curriculum (or its equivalent) where appropriate. When considering issues of continuity and progression, the extent of differentiation within learning experiences to cater for individual needs also is addressed.

3. *Learning and teaching strategies* — how the experiences and activities are organized and structured to encourage learning and discovery. The extent of children's independence and autonomy and the rules that govern behavior and participation are considered. Who is participating in the activities and what roles are being adopted by adults and children are key issues. The competencies being displayed by children in their actions also are highlighted.

4. *Planning, assessment, and record keeping* — how learning is planned, who is involved in planning, and how far planning builds on previous assessment of children's activity. The assessment of children is considered, and the efficacy of the methods of recording their activity and experience is noted also. Access to and sharing of records and the use to which they are put fall within the considerations of this dimension.

5. *Staffing* — the opportunities for involvement of staff in children's learning. Issues of staff deployment, ratios, management policy, and attitude toward learning are relevant. Opportunities for staff development and training are noted. Attention also is given to the way staff interact with children and the way they support children's learning.

6. *Physical environment* — the context in which learning occurs. The use of space, both inside and out, to create an environment for learning is considered. The availability, condition, and appropriateness of learning resources are documented.

7. *Relationships and interactions* — how children and adults interact. How far and in what ways relationships are expressed and developed in the activities are considered. The social rules and codes of conduct that operate are seen as significant. The opportunities for self-initiated learning and the degree of staff intervention would fall within this dimension. The involvement of children and their interactions in the activities are highlighted as a means of reflecting on the quality of the educational experience the activities provide.

8. *Equal opportunities* — the way in which the setting and the learn-

ing experiences within it reflect and celebrate cultural and physical diversity and challenge stereotypes and the extent to which children with special educational needs are included. The equipment and the activities are scrutinized with regard to issues of race, gender, disability, and social class.

9. *Parental partnership, home and community liaison* — the nature of the partnership with parents and the ways in which they and other members of the local community are involved in the learning process. The extent to which the learning builds on and reflects the children's home and community environment is explored. Links between the setting and other early childhood settings also are noted.

10. *Monitoring and evaluation* — the procedures by which the quality and effectiveness of the learning processes and provision are monitored and evaluated. Who is involved in these processes and how the results of this process are acted upon, are considered.

Approaching Evaluation Democratically

Another underlying conception of the EEL Project is a "democratic approach" to quality evaluation (Pfeffer & Coote, 1991). As quality evaluation is a value-laden enterprise, we believe it is best achieved through the active involvement of participants in the process. Thus, the evaluation process is viewed as being "done with" participants and not "done to" them. The subjectivity of the definition is thus acknowledged and the shared perceptions of quality are celebrated as central to the debate about quality in each particular setting. Quality is defined by the shared reflections and agreement of experienced practitioners, parents, and children. It is validated and scrutinized for accuracy by those closest to the learning experiences being evaluated. The EEL Project is founded firmly on democratic principles, and the team has worked hard to establish a feeling of partnership and shared ownership of the whole research process. Our philosophical commitment to this approach was reinforced with the hope that it also would help the evaluation and improvement process become a major vehicle for the professional development of practitioners. We also hoped that it would ensure that the individual settings would become more responsive, more fit for their purpose, and that those within them would be empowered by the process (Pfeffer & Coote, 1991).

Developing the Evaluation and Improvement Process

Although little work has been done to develop evaluation strategies for early childhood programs, we in early childhood education should not feel we have to start from scratch in our search for them. There is much experience we can draw upon, and a growing wealth of literature on educational evaluation, school improvement, and the wider field of total quality management. There is also much in this literature to reassure us that quality evaluation need not be a threatening process but can be achieved in a positive, empowering way.

Common Strategies in Quality Evaluation. Looking across the literature, we have found substantial agreement as to the strategies that appear to facilitate effective quality evaluation and improvement and those that do not (Fullan & Hargreaves, 1992; Goddard & Leask, 1992; Handy, 1994; Hopkins, 1986, 1992; Louis & Miles, 1991; Murgatroyd & Morgan, 1993; Sallis, 1993; Scheerens, 1992; West-Burnham, 1992). These common strategies reveal that

- Judgments about quality need to be made.
- An outside perspective is required, but the assessed and the assessor should know and trust each other.
- Evaluation should emerge from an open, honest, and collaborative dialogue using a shared vocabulary.
- This dialogue should be generated over an extended period of time.
- The dialogue should have a clear, systematic, and agreed-upon framework and format.
- The evidence for evaluation should be gathered together and shared together.
- The evaluation process should lead to action plans.
- The action should be followed through, supported, and monitored.
- The settings should take ownership of the process and its outcomes.
- All participants in the process should be encouraged to make a contribution that is acknowledged and valued.
- Compulsion and hierarchies do not work. Collaboration and participation do work.

These common characteristics of effective quality evaluation provide a sound basis from which to plan further action in the field of early childhood.

Six Principles of Evaluative and Improvement Action. This consensus and the experience of 4 years of development work on the EEL Project have convinced us that any quality evaluation and improvement process for early childhood should adhere to the following six principles of action:

1. Adopt a dynamic, developmental approach that views the processes of evaluation and improvement as inseparable.
2. Utilize procedures that are shared, democratic, and collaborative.
3. Implement a bottom-up process that is opted into and not imposed.
4. Create a rigorous, systematic, and agreed-upon evaluative framework that is implemented over an extended period of time.
5. Ensure that action is supported and has outcomes that are monitored.
6. Aim to develop a process that empowers and develops practitioners, parents, and children.

The Four-Stage Evaluation and Improvement. Building on the above principles of action, quality is evaluated using the EEL framework by taking the participants through a systematic and rigorous four-stage process of evaluation and improvement.

1. *Evaluation* during which researchers and participants work together to document and evaluate the quality of early learning within the setting.
2. *Action planning* during which participants meet to identify priorities for action and to generate an action plan to implement them.
3. *Improvement* during which the action plan to improve the quality of provision is implemented.
4. *Reflection* during which participants are encouraged to reflect upon the evaluation and improvement process and to review the impact of the action taken in the light of experience.

During the evaluation stage, the quality of practice in relation to each of the 10 dimensions of quality is documented carefully and evaluated using a number of research methods in which the project participants are trained. These include detailed observations of children and adults; interviews of parents, colleagues, and children; documentary analysis; and the administration of a number of questionnaires. One of the key and innovative features of this project is that it allows a detailed, rigorous quantitative and qualitative assessment to be made of the quality of educational provision across a wide range of different early childhood settings.

Key Research Measures

The process of quality assessment has been enhanced by the utilization of two key observation techniques that measure the effectiveness of the learning and teaching processes. These are the *Child Involvement Scale*, which measures the level of involvement of children in the activities offered, and the *Adult Engagement Scale*, which measures the qualities of effective teaching demonstrated by adults. The social-psychological underpinning of these techniques and their methodology are detailed by Laevers (1994a). As these two techniques are so central to the project's action, a short summary of their content and the way we have used them is outlined below.

The *Child Involvement Scale* is an observation instrument that aims to measure the level of a child's "involvement" in an activity. We were attracted to it because it is child focused and it attempts to measure the processes of learning, rather than to concentrate on outcomes. We also have found it to be grounded in a commonsense (and theoretically underpinned) view of effective early learning that all the practitioners in the project have found accessible and easy to use. It is based on the notion that when children are learning at a "deep level" (Laevers, 1993), they display certain characteristics, which Laevers summarizes in the concept of "involvement." This concept is linked directly to the child's exploratory drive and also captures the level of concentration and motivation of the child. Laevers argues that the level of involvement a child displays is a key indicator of the quality and effectiveness of the learning experience. Involvement levels are deduced from the presence or absence of a number of "involvement signals," including concentration, energy, creativity, facial expression and posture, persistence, precision, reaction time, language, and satisfaction (Laevers, 1994b).

Children's involvement thus can be graded on a scale of 1 to 5; Level 1 is when a child displays *no involvement*, and Level 5 is when a child displays *intense involvement*. Working in conjunction with Laevers, the Worcester team have utilized an English translation of the instrument (Laevers, 1994b) that has been used successfully within the project and that we believe has the potential for much wider application.

The *Adult Engagement Scale* (Bertram, 1995) provides the second part of the quality assessment process. This instrument also is based on a method developed by Laevers's EXE Project but has been modified substantially for use in the EEL Project. This evaluative instrument provides an assessment measure of the quality of an adult's interactions with a child. The instrument is based on the notion that the style of interactions between the educator and the child is a critical factor in the effectiveness of the learning experience. The EEL Project identifies three core elements in a teacher's style that shape the quality of such interactions.

1. *Sensitivity* — the sensitivity of the adult to the feelings and emotional well-being of the child, including elements of sincerity, empathy, responsiveness, and affection.

2. *Stimulation* — the way in which the adult intervenes in a learning process and the content of such interventions.

3. *Autonomy* — the degree of freedom that the adult gives the child to experiment, make judgments, choose activities, and express ideas; also, how the adult handles conflict, rules, and behavioral issues.

These two quantitative research methods provide hard data of the effect of action on the learning in each setting, as scores obtained in the evaluation stage can be compared with scores following the improvement stage. These scales are both attempts to measure qualitative aspects of the teaching and learning process.

All the qualitative and quantitative data collected are collated into a detailed and carefully structured evaluation report of the quality of early learning within each setting. The report is then fed back to the practitioners in the study setting for validation by the contributors. When agreed upon, the report is used to develop and implement an *action plan* for the improvement of practice within the setting. At the end of the improvement stage the two assessment instruments (*Involvement* and *Engagement*) are administered again and compared with the previous results to capture any changes in the quality of learning engendered by the improvement process.

LESSONS LEARNED ABOUT
EVALUATION IN EARLY CHILDHOOD

Experience with evaluation projects in the United Kingdom, and in particular the EEL Project, has taught us a lot about evaluative processes and their potential for improving the quality of programs for young children. More than anything else, it has deepened our respect for the professionalism and commitment of those who work with young children. It also has provided us with some clear indications of how high-quality and effective early learning may be achieved in the United Kingdom. Although we are still at an early stage of reflecting on the process of evaluation, some clear and tangible issues have emerged.

• *Evaluation and improvement are possible and desired in all settings.* We have been impressed by the commitment the practitioners involved in the EEL Project have displayed to evaluating and improving their practice and the quality of early learning they offer. All sectors and providers expressed a great desire to develop their knowledge and expertise and were very open to evaluative strategies that would facilitate this. Participants came from all sectors of the early childhood world and all were excited, energetic, and positive at the prospect of working together to evaluate and improve their programs. There was much goodwill and desire to work across the sectors in a multiprofessional way that has resulted in different providers in a local area networking and supporting each other.

In all the settings where we have worked, we have documented clear and identifiable changes in practice through the use of the EEL evaluation strategies. These changes cover many different aspects of practice, from the physical environment, the curriculum, relationships with parents, and organizational matters, to developing the role of play in learning. Improvements in the quality of the early learning experiences offered can be claimed in all settings that have completed the evaluation and improvement cycle. This is very strong evidence of the power of the evaluative process as a vehicle for change.

• *A democratic approach is effective but requires some external support.* In the EEL Project we have tried to ensure that quality is defined by the shared reflections and agreement of experienced managers, practitioners, parents, and children. The definition is validated and scrutinized for accuracy by those closest to the experience that is being evaluated. The project is founded firmly in democratic principles and we have worked hard at putting in place a process that depends on partnership, collaboration, and teamwork. Other UK quality evaluation initiatives have adopted a similar inclusive, collaborative approach (e.g., Pre-school Playgroups Association, 1993; Wilkinson & Stephen, 1992). Others have tended to view the process as being carried out more effectively by an external team of "experts" who come into an early childhood setting and implement the quality evaluation process (e.g., BSI, 1991; OFSTED, 1993). We believe that if ongoing quality evaluation is viewed as part of a complex set of continuously evolving relationships among providers, children, and their families, then it is crucial that approaches adopt a participative, collaborative mode of operation. This is a key issue to be addressed by those concerned with developing quality. We have found that parents, children, and practitioners need to be encouraged to work in an open, honest, and supportive partnership that is directed toward ensuring the highest-quality early learning experiences possible.

• *Evaluation and improvement should go hand in hand.* We are convinced that quality evaluation, inspection, or accreditation should not be separated from the improvement process. It appears helpful if those who evaluate quality also are involved in the improvement process. Continuity is needed and must be facilitated, along with the extended dialogue that accompanies and follows from the evaluation process. Those who evaluate quality need to feed into the development process.

It also has become clear that self-evaluation and development are less effective than self-evaluation and development, which is then externally validated. Settings needed the support, advice, and encouragement of an outside perspective to move on. The settings found the democratic approach — in which all practitioners were involved — attractive, as it gave them a feeling of self-worth and professional responsibility. They all indicated that the outside support was critical at key points in the evaluation process. The level of this support varied according to the setting and the issues it chose to tackle. We felt this was appropriate as some settings were more developed than others and more used to handling the kind of process we were taking them through. There was consensus that regardless of whether the setting provided high quality, all needed to continue to develop and an external source of new knowledge and opinion was invaluable.

• *The evaluative framework used must be rigorous but flexible.* There are three issues that need careful consideration in developing evaluative frameworks. First, to be effective any evaluative framework must be rigorous, systematic, and based on the best knowledge we have about effective teaching and learning in the early years. This will involve the development and utilization of accessible and practicable techniques for gathering and analyzing evidence on which to base the evaluation process, and the training of practitioners in employing them. At the heart of these techniques should be focused observations of adults and children within a setting, but they also will include a range of other qualitative and quantitative methods of gathering information. The model of practitioner as researcher should be viewed as central to the quality evaluation and improvement process.

Second, while the framework itself has to be robust and transferable, it also has to be flexible so that each element within it can be interpreted to meet the particular context in which it is being applied. The diverse range of early childhood settings within the United Kingdom, and the need for these to be responsive to the families and local community they serve, has demanded that there be room within any quality framework for it to be applied in a range of different ways. This flexibility should allow individual settings to offer parents real choice, while reassuring them that the core elements of quality are being addressed.

Third, all those participating in the evaluative process must be aware of this quality framework and agree on its validity and applicability to their particular context. Where dispute arises as to the relevance or appropriateness of any aspect of the framework, the effectiveness of the whole process is threatened. The evaluative framework being used must have credibility and acceptance among all members of the organization that is being evaluated. This requires good communication, time for everyone to familiarize themselves with the framework, and opportunities for an open dialogue about it.

• *The need for time.* Experience also has taught us that a "dip stick" approach to quality evaluation and improvement severely limits its effectiveness. In order to obtain a comprehensive, truly representative, and valid picture of a program's quality that can be used as the basis for fundamental improvement, a long-term time frame has to be used. The Effective Early Learning Project's evaluation and development process takes between 6 and 9 months to complete just one cycle of focused development. Other schemes also have extended time periods for their implementation. The Strathclyde Project took over 12 months, and the PLA Scheme has no time limits. We have found it is important that the process of quality evaluation and improvement not be viewed as a short, sharp blast of activity to be done periodically and then put aside. Rather, we would promote a model of ongoing, professional activity directed at a constant cycle of evaluation and improvement. In this way short-, medium-, and long-term goals can be planned for and worked at systematically, and at a pace that individual settings can manage within the normal ebbs and flows of their activity. We have found this to be not only practical and realistic, but also motivating for those involved because they feel in control.

• *The need for evaluative instruments that assess process as well as outcomes.* Evaluating the quality of the processes that go on within any early childhood setting is a very tricky task. It is not easy to identify the constituent elements within a quality experience and to gather hard evidence about changes in them. We are just beginning to understand the subtle qualitative nuances, interpersonal relationships, and factors that constitute effective teaching and learning at this stage, but it is clear that these are the critical factors in determining a quality education. As a result of the lack of well-developed techniques, process measures do not seem to carry the same attraction to those who currently are evaluating quality in early childhood. Outcome measures that can provide tangible and often quantifiable evidence often are seen, mistakenly in our view, as preferable. This is despite the fact that the outcomes of educational inputs in these early stages may not be evident until children reach maturity.

Yet, we would be wrong to polarize the debate. It is important that we focus our attention on the development of evaluative instruments that can assess the quality of any early childhood program. Some of these instruments may focus on educational outcomes, and these would include, among others, a child's social competence, emotional well-being, behavioral characteristics, linguistic skills, and mathematical competencies. However, given the emphasis placed on learning processes at this stage (Department of Education and Science, 1990), we urgently need to develop evaluative instruments that provide reliable and accessible evidence of the quality of these processes. These measures are beginning to emerge and to be utilized within quality evaluation schemes. More work clearly needs to be done in this important area of developing assessment techniques, as well as in convincing decision makers of the validity and reliability of such process measures. Among the quality schemes currently available to early childhood providers in the United Kingdom few are addressing at all the issue of monitoring the impact of improvements on the quality of teaching and learning.

• *The process can result in professional development of practitioners.* One of the primary aims of the EEL Project was to use the evaluation and improvement process as a cost-effective and targeted process of professional development for the participating practitioners. All participants were trained in the observation and data-gathering process, and shown how to interpret the data and use them for developing an action plan for improvement. The aim was to generate in each study setting a "research community" and to encourage the practitioners to use their new skills to investigate and evaluate their practice more systematically and rigorously.

Practitioners have reported changes in their thinking and understanding of their practice. In particular, they report that they are observing the learning process more critically and more regularly and using this information to inform their planning.

• *The process empowers the practitioners.* Part of professional development should be about becoming more confident, having an awareness of practice, having a rationale, and being able to articulate it. Evidence is emerging that practitioners who are working with the EEL methodology are empowered by the process. Taking responsibility for evaluating their practice, being given the tools to undertake this and the means to move their practice on, has given the practitioners a sense of self-worth and control over their professional lives. They report higher self-esteem and a growing belief in the importance and complexity of their work. They also are able to communicate this to those to whom they are accountable.

We believe that strong and confident practitioners working in an open and self-critical context provide the right conditions for long-term development and change. It is exactly these conditions that the EEL process aims to encourage so that working together for improvement becomes part of the ethos of every early childhood setting.

CONCLUSION

Putting in place high-quality early learning experiences that are available for all children will not be achieved overnight, nor will it come cheap. Substantial investment in quality programs for young children in the United Kingdom is urgently needed and long overdue. Yet, as limited resources are made available to us, we need to determine how these might be used most effectively and what kind of quality provision we are aiming to put in place. The development of rigorous, systematic, manageable, and appropriate evaluation strategies for early childhood education will be critical in the evolution of policy. The question of quality in early childhood is a crucial one, and one that we in the United Kingdom cannot afford to get wrong.

REFERENCES

Ball, C. (1994). *Start right: The importance of early learning* (Royal Society of Arts Report). London: RSA.

Bertram, A. D. (1995, September). *Adult engagement styles and their use in staff development.* Paper presented at the Fifth European Early Childhood Education Research Association Conference, Paris.

Bredekamp, S. (Ed.). (1987). *Developmentally appropriate practice in early childhood programs serving children through age 8.* Washington, DC: National Association for the Education of Young Children.

British Standards Institute. (1991). *Quality systems: Part 8. Guide to quality management and quality systems elements for services.* London: Author.

Carnegie Task Force. (1994). *Starting points: Meeting the needs of our young children.* New York: Carnegie Corporation of New York.

Department for Education. (1992). *Pupils under five years of age in schools in England — January 1991* (Statistical Bulletin 11/92). London: Author.

Department of Education and Science. (1990). *Starting with quality: The Rumbold report.* London: Her Majesty's Stationer's Office.

Early Childhood Care and Education Working Group. (1988). *Education to be more.* Aukland: New Zealand Ministry of Education.

Early Years Curriculum Group. (1989). *Early childhood education and the National Curriculum.* Stoke on Trent: Trentham Books.

Fullan, M., & Hargreaves, A. (1992). *What's worth fighting for in your school?* Milton Keynes: Open University Press.

Goddard, D., & Leask, M. (1992). *The search for quality*. London: Paul Chapman.

Government Statistical Service. (1993). *Education statistics for the UK: 1992 Edition*. London: Her Majesty's Stationer's Office.

Handy, C. (1994). *The empty raincoat: Making sense of the future*. London: Hutchinson.

Hohmann, M., Banet, B., & Weikert, D. P. (1979). *Young children in action: A manual for pre-school educators*. Michigan: High/Scope Press.

Holtermann, S. (1995). *The effects of tax and spending programs on children*. London: Barnardo's Children's Society.

Hopkins, D. (1986). *Improving the quality of schooling*. London: Falmer Press.

Hopkins, D. (1992). *Evaluation for school development*. Milton Keynes: Open University Press.

House of Commons. (1989). *Educational provision for the under fives* (Vols. 1 & 2; Report of the House of Commons Education Committee). London: Her Majesty's Stationer's Office.

House of Commons. (1994). *Educational provision for the under fives* (Report of the House of Commons Education Committee). London: Her Majesty's Stationer's Office.

Laevers, F. (1993). Deep level learning — An exemplary application on the area of physical knowledge. *European Early Childhood Education Research Journal, 1*(1), 53–68.

Laevers, F. (Ed.). (1994a). *The Innovative Project experiential education and the definition of quality in education*. Leuven, Belgium: Katholieke Universiteit.

Laevers, F. (1994b). *The Leuven Involvement Scale for Young Children LIS-YC* (Manual and videotape; Experiential Education Series No. 1). Leuven, Belgium: Center for Experiential Education.

Louis, F., & Miles, M. B. (1991). *The empowered school*. London: Cassell.

Moss, P. (1994). The early childhood league in Europe: Problems and possibilities in cross-national comparisons of levels of provision. *European Early Childhood Education Research Journal, 2*(2), 5–17.

Murgatroyd, S., & Morgan, C. (1993). *Total quality management and the school*. Milton Keynes: Open University Press.

Munton, A. G., Mooney, A., & Rowland, L. (1995). Deconstructing quality: A conceptual framework for the new paradigm in day care provision for the under eights. *Early Childhood Development and Care, 114*, 11–23.

National Commission on Education. (1993). *Learning to succeed* (Report of the Paul Hamlyn Foundation National Commission on Education). London: Heinemann.

Office for Standards in Education. (1993). *Handbook for the inspection of schools*. London: Her Majesty's Stationer's Office.

Pascal, C. (1990). *Under fives in infant classrooms*. Stoke on Trent: Trentham Books.

Pascal, C., & Bertram, A. D. (1994). Defining and assessing quality in the education of children from four to seven years. In F. Laevers (Ed.), *Defining and assessing quality in early childhood education* (Studia Paedagogica). Leuven, Belgium: Leuven University Press.

Pascal, C., Bertram, A. D., & Ramsden, F. (1994). *Effective early learning: The quality evaluation and development process.* Worcester: Amber Publications.

Pascal, C., Bertram, A. D., Ramsden, F., Georgeson, J., Saunders, M., & Mould, C. (1995). *Effective early learning: Evaluating and developing quality in early childhood settings.* Worcester: Amber Publications.

Peters, T. (1992). *Liberation management.* London: Pan MacMillan.

Pirsig, R. (1974). *Zen and the art of motorcycle maintenance.* London: The Bodley Head.

Pfeffer, N., & Coote, A. (1991). *Is quality good for you?* London: Institute for Public Policy Research.

Pre-school Playgroups Association. (1993). *Aiming for quality.* London: PLA.

Rowntree Foundation. (1995). *Inquiry into income and wealth* (Vols. 1 & 2). York: Joseph Rowntree Foundation.

Sallis, E. (1993). *Total quality management in education.* London: Kogan Page.

Scheerens, J. (1992). *Effective schooling: Research, theory and practice.* London: Cassell.

Sylva, K., & Wiltshire, J. (1993). The impact of early learning on children's later development. *European Early Childhood Education Research Journal, 1*(1), 17–40.

West-Burnham, J. (1992). *Managing quality in schools.* London: Longman.

Wilkinson, R. (1994). *Unequal shares.* London: Barnardo's Children's Society.

Wilkinson, E., & Stephen, C. (1992). *Evaluating ourselves.* Glasgow: University of Glasgow.

Williams, P. (1995). *Making sense of quality: A review of approaches to quality in early childhood services.* London: National Children's Bureau.

CHAPTER 5

Using Standardized Measures
for Evaluating
Young Children's Learning

William L. Goodwin and Laura D. Goodwin

In this chapter, we first define "standardized" measures and set boundaries for this category of instruments. Some recent concerns involving the use of standardized measures in general, and with young children in particular, are then reviewed. Next, attention is given to the realities that surround many evaluation endeavors and that concern young children and measurement. Some principles for the use of standardized measures in early childhood education evaluations are presented. The chapter concludes with some examples of the use of measures in early childhood evaluations, as well as a list of some contemporary compendia of measures.

STANDARDIZED MEASURES

Most measures used in education are intended to provide a systematic procedure for describing performance or behaviors. *Standardized* measures are ones that typically include fixed administration and scoring procedures, empirical tryout of items, set apparatus or format, and tables of norms. Using established procedures sets a common task for children and allows interpretation of their performance relative to that of the children in the norming sample. The representativeness and relevance of the norms are critical for sound norm-referenced interpretations of individual children's scores (see Hopkins, Stanley, & Hopkins, 1990). While not discounting the importance of the norms, the scope of this chapter precludes a full discussion of norming procedures and interpretations of norm-referenced scores.

Most standardized measures are published commercially and are produced for general use. Therefore, they usually are based on common educational objectives that are held widely by practitioners and institutions in diverse settings. Rarely do these common objectives coincide exactly with the specific objectives of an individual classroom teacher or a given early childhood project. At the same time, the norms allow the comparative evaluation of scores — across settings, time, institutions, and so on.

Common types of standardized measure include intelligence and aptitude tests, achievement tests, readiness tests, screening measures, diagnostic tests, psychomotor measures, and personality and attitude measures. A great deal has been written about these different kinds of measure (e.g., Bailey & Wolery, 1989; Bracken, 1991; Cohen & Spenciner, 1994; Goodwin & Driscoll, 1980; Goodwin & Goodwin, 1993; Wortham, 1990). Here, we refer to certain of these types of measure, but only in specific contexts. We also should indicate that other types of standardized measure could be valuable in some evaluations, even though they do not directly assess children's learning and may not be normed. For example, there are a number of instruments available for assessing the quality of early education settings; an excellent compilation and succinct review was provided by Harms and Clifford (1993). Similarly, measures exist for the evaluation of educational environments, including child-care settings, kindergarten classrooms, and the like (Fraser & Walberg, 1991).

CONCERNS ABOUT STANDARDIZED MEASURES

Mention the word *test* in most early childhood educational environments, and the reaction is typically instantaneous and negative. Why is this the case? This section reviews several of the concerns that have been expressed about standardized measures, especially when thought of in terms of *testing* young children. While not exhaustive, the areas of concern include the weak linkage between tests and "real life," the fairness of the tests for certain groups, the negative impact of standardized tests on young children's curriculum, and the misuse of high-stakes tests, even with young children.

Numerous organizations and authors have challenged our country's allegiance to standardized tests and instead have promoted alternative assessment procedures. Most prominent, perhaps, is an approach termed "authentic assessment" using, of course, "authentic tests" (Wiggins, 1989a, 1989b). Discouraged by secondary school testing and grading practices that he felt were due to standardized tests, Wiggins proposed instead a dramatic shift to assessment methods that would gauge the depth of students' intellectual processing. In his view, authentic tests are ones that measure those capacities and habits considered essential — and do so in context. Emphasis would shift from student passivity, reception, and recognition to student construction, production, and performance. Examples he gave included an oral history project for first-year high school students and an end-of-course simulation "exam" in economics. We see counterparts to these ideas for young children, many of which have existed for some time. They include work samples, as well as ratings scales, checklists, and informal observation (Goodwin & Goodwin, 1993).

Another prevalent concern involves the extent of possible bias in measuring instruments. This is essentially a question of fairness that should be addressed as part of the estimation of the validity of any measure. Test bias has been defined as "differential validity of a given interpretation of a test score for any definable, relevant subgroup of test takers" (Cole & Moss, 1989, p. 205). Concerns have centered on ethnic, cultural, language, and gender bias and, secondarily, on bias related to the variables of age and socioeconomic status. Since many early childhood programs serve children from school-disadvantaged backgrounds; from ethnic, linguistic, and minority groups; and from low socioeconomic status homes, bias is an important consideration in test selection, use, and interpretation. Compounding the concern is the lack of agreed-upon methods for detecting test bias, although a number of models have been developed and operationalized (Cole & Moss, 1989).

Numerous sources have reported deleterious effects of standardized measures, especially achievement tests, on programs and curricula for young children. Some considered achievement tests for the primary grades as inappropriate or even counterproductive (Kamii & Kamii, 1990a, 1990b; Perrone, 1990). Kamii and Kamii (1990b) criticized achievement tests for not measuring true learning (because children's construction of knowledge, thinking, and development of autonomy were ignored) and for pushing the curriculum and accompanying expectations for children into lower and lower grades. Similarly, the National Association for the Education of Young Children (NAEYC) (1988) and Shepard and Smith (1988) lamented the increased academic emphasis in kindergarten and even earlier as educators scrambled to prepare their students for standardized tests. The curriculum became what was needed for children to perform creditably on the tests. A good review of the issue as it affects young children and early childhood educators was provided by Shepard (1991). Overall, these and other authors wished to derail the practice of measurement-driven instruction whereby achievement tests dictate curriculum (Airasian, 1988; Haertel, 1989). In a similar vein, Sigel (1987) defined "hothousing" as "the process of inducing infants to acquire knowledge that is typically acquired at a later developmental level" (p. 212). Societal conditions leading to hothousing have been deplored (e.g., Elkind, 1987; Hills, 1987).

Another troubling issue is the misuse of test results to make high-stakes decisions about individual children (e.g., Meisels, 1989; Shepard & Graue, 1993). For example, Shepard and Graue reviewed many extant "readiness" tests (including some intelligence tests, developmental screening measures, certain academic readiness tests, and the Gesell School Readiness Test). They concluded that, too often, such tests were not used for their original, validated purposes or, possibly worse, were used interchangeably. Especially problematic was the use of readiness tests to make high-stakes decisions such as denying school entrance and placing children in at-risk or 2-year kindergartens.

In the eyes of many, these concerns are compounded by two additional matters, one factual and the other more intuitive. First, the use of standardized measures in society continues to increase (e.g., Neill & Medina, 1989), with estimates of annual increases of 10–20% since 1950 (Haney & Madaus, 1989). Such increased usage is especially noteworthy given the many calls for reform in this regard (e.g., Cannell, 1988; Haney, 1989) and litigations involving test fairness (Chachkin, 1989). Second, many perceive a developmental mismatch when very young children are required to take paper-and-pencil "tests"—some struggling, some innocently nonchalant as they have yet not learned what "serious business" test taking is, and others possibly devastated when they learn that their personal performance was in some sense found wanting.

REALITIES SURROUNDING THE USE OF STANDARDIZED MEASURES

One might surmise from the prior section that it would be good to avoid standardized measures altogether in evaluating young children's learning. In our view, however, the issue is complex. Meisels, Steele, and Quinn-Leering (1993) stated well the dilemma facing educators in terms of test use.

> Most educators are extremely ambivalent about standardized tests. They
> love them, and they hate them; they adopt them, and they reject them;
> they need them, and they do not understand them. However, whenever
> a new trend in education emerges, a national commission reports its
> recommendations, or a novel idea is introduced, standardized tests are
> usually mentioned as the preferred means of measurement, implementa-
> tion, or evaluation. (p. 279)

While educators typically may be ambivalent and early childhood
educators even negative, one tends to find greater support for standardized
measures in the general public. When polled in 1994, for example, 73% of
the respondents in a countrywide survey thought it very or quite important
that students pass a national standardized achievement exam based on a
national curriculum for grade promotion and high school graduation
(Elam, Rose, & Gallup, 1994).

Thus, one reality bearing on this issue is the fact that a very large
constituency believes in standardized measures. One reason for this allegiance is that test results represent "truth" for a large segment of the
population. The societal support for testing was linked by Resnick (1981)
to values such as equal opportunity, efficiency, and clear national standards. Anyone who knows measurement well and watches talk shows on
television is frequently struck by the general public's "blind" attachment
to — or even reverence for — standardized tests.

Another reality is that many programs for young children are dependent for their funding on various governing boards and legislative bodies.
For policy makers, test scores serve as an attractive outcome measure,
relatively inexpensive to obtain, easy to understand, and connoting that
they "mean business" (Baker, 1989). In like manner, Kamii (1990) observed the vote-getting game, whereby school board members and legislators could demonstrate accountability by requiring the administration of
standardized tests in public schools. Recently, Goodwin (1994) noted that
early childhood program leaders should have solid evaluative data "at the
ready" to support their programs, because legislators and other funding
agencies could request such verification at almost any time, akin to a
high-stakes pop quiz. Relatedly, a condition of receiving funds in many
grant competitions is the utilization of quantitative, established procedures to measure outcomes — which often dictates the use of standardized
measures.

Yet a third reality is that standardized tests must be given to young
children in some cases. The NAEYC position statement (1988), referred to
earlier, recognized this as it endorsed the *Standards for Educational and
Psychological Testing* (American Psychological Association [APA], Ameri-

can Educational Research Association [AERA], & National Council on Measurement in Education [NCME], 1985) and added a "utility" criterion. This called for using standardized tests only if it was clear that benefits to children would result. Also apparent is the fact that early childhood special educators are required to assess children in the process of determining their eligibility for special services; such assessment very often includes the administration of standardized measures (Bailey & Wolery, 1989; Bracken, 1991; Cohen & Spenciner, 1994; Culbertson & Willis, 1993; Salvia & Ysseldyke, 1991).

An additional reality pertains to the way in which standardized measures are administered. If established administration procedures are not followed, the reliability and validity of the outcomes are weakened. Some of the shortcomings alleged as integral to standardized measures may, in fact, be due to careless administration. For example, Wodtke, Harper, Schommer, and Brunelli (1989) observed standardized group testing in 10 kindergartens. Their study revealed numerous departures from prescribed testing conditions and environments (e.g., differences in group size, providing no or insufficient breaks between subtests, poorly lit spaces or rooms for testing, and allowing interruptions during testing) and many variations in teacher behaviors (e.g., repeating items, rewarding high performance, modifying instructions, and cueing correct answers). Also, they observed inappropriate child behaviors during testing—such as calling out answers, copying, "mutual aid societies," and disruptive and inattentive actions. The authors questioned the worth of scores generated under such conditions and wondered, as we do, how often classroom testing departs from the assumed methodological ideal.

Another reality concerns the nature of development in very young children and how this process compounds the difficulty of constructing reliable and, therefore, valid standardized measures for them. More specifically, developmental processes in young children often are characterized by unevenness—starts, stops, spurts of great activity, and periods of little change. This unevenness translates to lower stability reliability in their performance on standardized measures. Accentuating this reality is the observation made elsewhere that many young children simply are poor at taking tests; this results in additional error in the measuring process. Thus, anyone planning to use standardized measures with youngsters as part of the process of evaluating programs for them indeed has taken on a formidable challenge.

Finally, we point out a reality associated with political conditions, as well as the bias concern mentioned in the previous section. Developing valid, unbiased measures is extremely expensive, frustrating, and time-consuming. Such an effort was underway in the late 1970s and early

1980s, constructing a new battery of measures for use in Head Start centers (Taub, Love, Wilkerson, Washington, & Wolf, 1980). Determined to avoid bias to the extent possible, this project assembled representative groups of Head Start parents to indicate outcome behaviors desired for their children. These behaviors were categorized and reviewed by teams of measurement experts from diverse ethnic backgrounds. Test specifications were drafted and measure development commenced. However, for multiple reasons, only parts of the original test battery — primarily the cognitive components not notably different from pre-existing tests — were completed. One reason for this redirection was a change in the administration in Washington, DC, which considered measures of social competence, applied strategies, and physical development and health to be of little value and therefore cut the project's budget dramatically. Other reasons were fuzzy and difficult to pinpoint (Raver & Zigler, 1991). This experience illustrates well that a firm and continuing commitment must be made if standardized measures of merit are to be developed.

PRINCIPLES FOR USING STANDARDIZED MEASURES

Given extant realities, it appears likely that standardized measures will continue to play a prominent role in many early childhood education evaluations. That being the case, it is crucial that those commissioning and conducting such evaluations follow sound principles of selection and use. The following list of principles, while not exhaustive, is offered in that spirit.

1. *Standardized measures used in evaluations must match important evaluation questions.* Too often, one gets the sense that many measures used in evaluations were selected simply because they were available. It is important for the evaluator of an early childhood program to examine the goals and objectives of the program and to discern the central evaluation questions. This process often will necessarily focus on the program's stated mission, particularly in terms of desired experiences and outcomes for children. Standardized instruments might be appropriate for the measurement of the desired child outcomes, and available measures should be examined in that light. The skilled evaluator will select for use only those standardized measures that match well the questions posed for the evaluation. If the match is poor, it is unreasonable to expect the measure to gauge the program's effects.

2. *Standardized measures used in evaluations must have purpose fidelity.* This principle emphasizes the requirement that measures be used

for the purpose(s) for which they were developed. We call this "purpose fidelity," and it applies to the use of measures in evaluations as well as in other contexts. It is not very difficult to find examples of the use of measures for purposes other than those intended by the developers. For instance, many early childhood "compensatory" programs in the late 1960s often used the scores from standardized IQ tests as one of their primary outcome variables. The mismatch is apparent when one considers that the real interest of the programs was in preparing children to perform better, academically and socially, when they reached school age. In defense of those programs, it should be noted that the available supply of standardized measures for very young children was limited at that time (and still is, although considerable measure development has occurred in the past quarter century). Evaluators seeking suitable measures might identify one or more that *appear* to have "purpose fidelity"; however, they need to examine thoroughly the technical information in accompanying manuals in regard to the measures' stated purposes.

3. *Standardized measures used in evaluations must have psychometric respectability.* It is critical that there be adequate evidence of the *validity* and *reliability* of the measures used in an evaluation, and that these psychometric data match the intended uses of the measures. The meaning of measurement validity has changed and evolved over the past 50 years; as defined in the most recent edition of the *Standards for Educational and Psychological Testing* (APA, AERA, & NCME, 1985), validity "refers to the appropriateness, meaningfulness, and usefulness of the specific inferences made from test scores. Validation is the process of accumulating evidence to support such inferences" (p. 9). Reliability refers to the consistency of scores produced by a measure. There are a number of specific types of both validity and reliability that might be estimated for any one measure (Hopkins, Stanley, & Hopkins, 1990). The evaluator needs to determine the degree of validity and reliability for any measures contemplated for use. Other things being equal, those measures with stronger psychometric respectability should be chosen. The field is well aware that, in general, the younger the child, the more difficult it is to develop measures with adequate validity and reliability (Goodwin & Driscoll, 1980).

4. *Standardized measures used in evaluations must be administered under set procedures.* The work of Wodtke and his colleagues (1989), mentioned above, described how difficult it can be to administer standardized tests to kindergartners following pre-established conditions. Our own experiences contain similar encounters in attempting to use standardized instruments with young children. Nevertheless, it is critical that the measures be administered under standard conditions — the conditions prescribed by the developers — or the interpretations of the results will be

clouded. Some standardized measures for young children have been developed in ways that take these difficulties into account; for example, they allow frequent breaks for the children, permit the examiner to choose the amount of the test to be covered in a single session, or are explicit about the degree of "prompting" or item-repeating that is permissible. Also in evidence frequently are short practice exercises that are done prior to the actual measure. These allow the children to become familiar with the format, pacing, and demands of the measure.

5. *Standardized measures used in evaluations must be interpreted and applied appropriately.* Some of the criticisms of standardized measures may be due to human error; that is, the user/interpreter of the measure's results may do foolish or uninformed things with the information. Elsewhere, we have wished for "psychometric literacy" in those persons who administer, interpret, and make decisions based on scores from such measures.

> Little direct attention has been paid to the psychometric literacy of those thousands of professionals who use and interpret the results of measures and assessments in early childhood education. How qualified are they to be skilled and wise in such matters? To what extent have their preparation programs addressed psychometric literacy? . . . We have heard of countless examples of misuse or misinterpretation of a child's performance on a measure. This should not happen. We also hear or read frequently about young children's interpretations of the "testing experience." Such views range from the comic to the tragic. . . . Psychometric literate professionals should help to reduce such tragedies, misuses, and misinterpretations. (Goodwin & Goodwin, 1993, p. 456)

Evaluators of early childhood programs certainly need to be psychometrically literate and, accordingly, would follow principles 2 through 4 above.

In closing this section, we feel compelled to state the obvious: In many cases, standardized measures that conform to the five principles are not commercially available, or they fall short in some regards. That being the case, evaluators of early childhood programs must be aware of other measuring procedures that might be more suitable in a given evaluation. Several of these — observation, performance assessments, children's products — are elaborated elsewhere in this *Yearbook* (Chapters 6, 7, and 8). Our first principle may say it best: Measures must be selected that match and will answer the crucial evaluation questions. At the same time, the task of measure selection is complex and issue ridden (see, for example, Fein, 1993; Walsh & King, 1993; Zimiles, 1993a, 1993b).

EXAMPLES OF THE USE OF STANDARDIZED MEASURES

In this section, we present summaries of several published studies in early childhood education that were evaluative in nature and utilized one or more standardized measures. We focus, of course, on the measures, and thus we will not provide extensive detail about the studies themselves.

Brody, Stoneman, and McCoy (1994) evaluated the apparent contributions of protective and risk factors to the competence of former Head Start children. Once the children were in kindergarten, their primary caregivers (80% were mothers) and teachers provided information for use in the study, as did the children themselves. Caregivers provided information concerning developmental goals, family processes, and their own psychological functioning. Teachers and children, on the other hand, provided data related to literacy, socioemotional status, and cognitive competence. Standardized measures used included subscales of the Temperament Assessment Battery (Martin, 1988), subscales of the Pictorial Scale of Perceived Competence and Social Acceptance for Young Children (Harter & Pike, 1983), and the Peabody Picture Vocabulary Test–Revised (Dunn & Dunn, 1981). Protective factors, especially endorsement of child independence, promotion of developmental goals, caregiver self-esteem, and responsive, cognitively challenging caregiver–child interactions were found to enhance literacy and socioemotional competence in the children. Conversely, conflict in family relationships and caregiver distress were related to negative outcomes for children.

In a somewhat similar study, Frede and Barnett (1992) evaluated both the implementation of the High/Scope approach in public preschools and its effects on at-risk children's performance in first grade. Considerable attention was given to developing and utilizing a measure of the fidelity of implementation of the High/Scope curriculum. Standardized measures were used for pretesting and posttesting: the DIAL-R (Mardell-Czudnowski & Goldenberg, 1983) was used as an indicator of prior ability, while the Cognitive Skills Assessment Battery (Boehm & Slater, 1981) served as the outcome (posttest) measure. Results indicated that better-implemented programs led to greater school success by children than programs with partial implementation of the High/Scope approach.

Phillips (1992) examined the effectiveness of a two-tiered kindergarten system for at-risk, 5-year-old children. Operationally the two-tiered system consisted of one year using a developmentally appropriate curriculum and a second year with a greater academic orientation. After their fourth year of school, this group of children was compared with at-risk children who had attended academic kindergarten and been retained, and with at-risk children who had not been retained. Standardized tests — the Cooperative Preschool Inventory (Caldwell, 1974) and the Primary Mental Ability Test (Thurstone, 1974) — were first used as part of the process to select children for the two-tiered approach. Among the outcome measures, many of which were teacher ratings and report-card, grade-point averages, were standardized measures such as subtests of the Iowa Test of Basic Skills (Hieronymus, Hoover, & Lindquist, 1986). Children who attended the two-tiered kindergarten program performed better on most social competence, academic, and self-perception measures, although some subgroup differences in these effects were noted.

The examples above are representative of many current evaluations in early childhood, as they utilize a mixture of standardized and nonstandardized measures. A more comprehensive illustration of the role of standardized measures in such evaluations was provided by Karweit (1993). She examined preschool and kindergarten programs for at-risk students. Her detailed tables list the measures used in numerous types of relevant evaluation. For example, in a summary table of the effects of full-day and half-day kindergarten programs, 18 studies were reviewed. All except one of these studies utilized one or more standardized tests; most of them included standardized achievement measures, while some used reading tests and child development inventories. In another table, Karweit summarized the early childhood programs validated by the national Joint Dissemination Review Panel that had used random assignment or matched control-group designs in their evaluative comparisons. Of the 20 programs named, 18 based their claims for effectiveness on data from one or more standardized instruments. Commonly used measures included achievement tests, school-related measures for younger children (such as readiness tests), and development-linked measures. Her chapter is a strong testimonial to one of our earlier points: that funders and endorsers/validators of programs typically require quantitative data generated by standardized instruments for evaluation purposes.

COMPENDIA OF STANDARDIZED MEASURES
FOR EARLY CHILDHOOD EDUCATION

While not specific to early childhood, likely the best-known and most frequently used source of information about published measures is the *Mental Measurements Yearbook* series. Now in their twelfth edition (Conoley & Impara, 1995), the yearbooks list and review many standardized tests covering a wide range of disciplines and specialty areas. Critiques by measurement and content-area experts help the user identify potential measures for evaluations and other research studies. A later entrant, with similar characteristics, is titled, *Test Critiques*; appearing annually, its most recent volume is the tenth (Keyser & Sweetland, 1994).

A number of other books and compendia list and describe early childhood measures. Cohen and Spenciner (1994) included descriptive summaries of measures in the areas of screening instruments, developmental batteries, adaptive behavior instruments, achievement tests, and measures for exceptional-child assessments. Aylward (1991) elaboratively described measures of intelligence and cognition appropriate for use with young children. She also reviewed tests of visual-spatial and visual-motor skills, as well as adaptive behavior inventories. Wortham (1990) presented illustrations of many standardized measures in use with young children, as well as an appendix of selected pertinent instruments. Culbertson and Willis (1993) described in depth the assessment processes and measures for exceptional children and their families. Three other books of note include Bailey and Wolery (1989), Bracken (1991), and Salvia and Ysseldyke (1991); the first two reviewed pertinent instruments in detail, while the latter discussed numerous measures and contained a chapter on assessment with infants, toddlers, and preschoolers. Three final sources contained shorter, more succinct descriptions of standardized early childhood measures. Boehm (1992) described assessment instruments for young children, while Axtman (1992) scanned infant assessment measures. Gullo (1994) provided a glossary of assessment instruments in early childhood education, categorized as developmental screening tests, readiness/achievement tests, and diagnostic tests.

SUMMARY

In this chapter, we defined standardized measures and then discussed the complex issues surrounding their use in early childhood education evaluations. Numerous legitimate concerns about their use exist; simultaneously, however, a series of realities dictate their use in many situations. The ambivalent reputation that such measures have, and the checkered reception that they often receive among early childhood educators, should not preclude their wise use in warranted situations. A set of principles for the use of standardized measures in early childhood evaluations was offered; these included the need for measures to match well the important evaluation questions, to have purpose fidelity, to exhibit psychometric respectability, to be administered under preset conditions, and to be interpreted with psychometric literacy. While not exhaustive, the five principles provide important guidelines for evaluators and others faced with the difficult problem of choosing and/or developing suitable measures for evaluation efforts.

REFERENCES

Airasian, P. W. (1988). Measurement-driven instruction: A closer look. *Educational Measurement: Issues and Practice, 7*(4), 6–11.

American Psychological Association, American Educational Research Association, & National Council on Measurement in Education [APA, AERA, & NCME]. (1985). *Standards for educational and psychological testing.* Washington, DC: American Psychological Association.

Axtman, A. (1992). Infant assessment: Issues and glossary. In L. R. Williams & D. P. Fromberg (Eds.), *Encyclopedia of early childhood education* (pp. 300–302). New York: Garland.

Aylward, E. H. (1991). *Understanding children's testing: Psychological testing.* Austin, TX: PRO-ED.

Bailey, D. B., & Wolery, M. (1989). *Assessing infants and preschoolers with handicaps.* New York: Merrill.

Baker, E. L. (1989). Mandated tests: Educational reform or quality indicator? In B. R. Gifford (Ed.), *Test policy and test performance: Education, language, and culture* (pp. 3–23). Boston: Kluwer.

Boehm, A. E. (1992). Glossary of assessment instruments. In L. R. Williams & D. P. Fromberg (Eds.), *Encyclopedia of early childhood education* (pp. 293–300). New York: Garland.

Boehm, A. E., & Slater, B. R. (1981). *Cognitive skills assessment battery.* New York: Teachers College Press.

Bracken, B. A. (Ed.). (1991). *The psychoeducational assessment of preschool children* (2nd ed.). Boston: Allyn & Bacon.

Brody, G. H., Stoneman, Z., & McCoy, J. K. (1994). Contributions of protective and risk factors to literacy and socioemotional competency in former Head Start children attending kindergarten. *Early Childhood Research Quarterly, 9*, 407–425.

Caldwell, B. M. (1974). *Cooperative preschool inventory.* Princeton, NJ: Educational Testing Service.

Cannell, J. J. (1988). Nationally normed elementary achievement testing in America's public schools: How all 50 states are above the national average. *Educational Measurement: Issues and Practice, 7*(2), 5–9.

Chachkin, N. J. (1989). Testing in elementary and secondary schools: Can misuses be avoided? In B. R. Gifford (Ed.), *Test policy and the politics of opportunity allocation: The workplace and the law* (pp. 163–187). Boston: Kluwer.

Cohen, L. G., & Spenciner, L. J. (1994). *Assessment of young children.* New York: Longman.

Cole, N. S., & Moss, P. A. (1989). Bias in test use. In R. L. Linn (Ed.), *Educational measurement* (3rd ed., pp. 201–219). New York: Macmillan.

Conoley, J. C., & Impara, J. C. (Eds.). (1995). *The twelfth mental measurements yearbook.* Lincoln: University of Nebraska Press.

Culbertson, J. L., & Willis, D. J. (1993). *Testing young children: A reference guide for developmental, psychoeducational, and psychosocial assessments.* Austin, TX: PRO-ED.

Dunn, L. R., & Dunn, C. (1981). *Peabody picture vocabulary test–revised.* Circle Pines, MN: American Guidance Systems.

Elam, S. M., Rose, L. C., & Gallup, A. M. (1994). The 26th annual Gallup poll of the public's attitudes toward the public schools. *Phi Delta Kappan, 76,* 41–56.

Elkind, D. (1987). *Miseducation: Preschoolers at risk.* New York: Knopf.

Fein, G. G. (1993). In defense of data adoration and even fetishism. *Early Childhood Research Quarterly, 8,* 387–395.

Fraser, B. J., & Walberg, H. J. (Eds.). (1991). *Educational environments: Evaluation, antecedents, and consequences.* New York: Pergamon.

Frede, E., & Barnett, W. S. (1992). Developmentally appropriate public school preschool: A study of implementation of the High/Scope curriculum and its effects on disadvantaged children's skills at first grade. *Early Childhood Research Quarterly, 7,* 483–499.

Goodwin, W. L. (1994, December). *Preparing leaders skilled in ECE program evaluation.* Paper presented at the annual meeting of the National Association for the Education of Young Children, Atlanta.

Goodwin, W. L., & Driscoll, L. A. (1980). *Handbook for measurement and evaluation in early childhood education: Issues, measures, and methods.* San Francisco: Jossey-Bass.

Goodwin, W. L., & Goodwin, L. D. (1993). Young children and measurement: Standardized and nonstandardized instruments in early childhood education. In B. Spodek (Ed.), *Handbook of research on the education of young children* (pp. 441–463). New York: Macmillan.

Gullo, D. F. (1994). *Understanding assessment and evaluation in early childhood education.* New York: Teachers College Press.

Haertel, E. (1989). Student achievement tests as tools of educational policy: Practices and consequences. In B. R. Gifford (Ed.), *Test policy and test performance: Education, language, and culture* (pp. 25–50). Boston: Kluwer.

Haney, W. M. (1989). Making sense of school testing. In B. R. Gifford (Ed.), *Test policy and test performance: Education, language, and culture* (pp. 51–62). Boston: Kluwer.

Haney, W., & Madaus, G. (1989). Searching for alternatives to standardized tests: Whys, whats, and whithers. *Phi Delta Kappan, 70,* 683–687.

Harms, T., & Clifford, R. M. (1993). Studying educational settings. In B. Spodek (Ed.), *Handbook of research on the education of young children* (pp. 477–492). New York: Macmillan.

Harter, S., & Pike, R. (1983). *Procedural manual to accompany: The pictorial scale of perceived competence and social acceptance for young children.* Denver, CO: University of Denver.

Hieronymus, A. N., Hoover, H. C., & Lindquist, E. F. (1986). *Iowa test of basic skills*. Chicago: Riverside.

Hills, T. W. (1987). Children in the fast lane: Implications for early childhood policy and practice. *Early Childhood Research Quarterly, 2*, 265–273.

Hopkins, K. D., Stanley, J. C., & Hopkins, B. R. (1990). *Educational and psychological measurement and evaluation* (7th ed.). Englewood Cliffs, NJ: Prentice Hall.

Kamii, C. (Ed.). (1990). *Achievement testing in the early grades: The games grown-ups play*. Washington, DC: National Association for the Education of Young Children.

Kamii, C., & Kamii, M. (1990a). Negative effects of achievement testing in mathematics. In C. Kamii (Ed.), *Achievement testing in the early grades: The games grown-ups play* (pp. 135–145). Washington, DC: National Association for the Education of Young Children.

Kamii, C., & Kamii, M. (1990b). Why achievement testing should stop. In C. Kamii (Ed.), *Achievement testing in the early grades: The games grown-ups play* (pp. 15–38). Washington, DC: National Association for the Education of Young Children.

Karweit, N. (1993). Effective preschool and kindergarten programs for students at risk. In B. Spodek (Ed.), *Handbook of research on the education of young children* (pp. 385–411). New York: Macmillan.

Keyser, D. J., & Sweetland, R. C. (Eds.). (1994). *Test critiques* (Vol. 10). Austin, TX: PRO-ED.

Mardell-Czudnowski, C. D., & Goldenberg, D. S. (1983). *Developmental Indicators for the Assessment of Learning–Revised*. Edison, NJ: Childcraft.

Martin, R. P. (1988). *The Temperament Assessment Battery for Children–Manual*. Brandon, VT: Clinical Psychology.

Meisels, S. J. (1989). High-stakes testing in kindergarten. *Educational Leadership, 46*(7), 16–22.

Meisels, S. J., Steele, D. M., & Quinn-Leering, K. (1993). Testing, tracking, and retaining young children: An analysis of research and social policy. In B. Spodek (Ed.), *Handbook of research on the education of young children* (pp. 279–292). New York: Macmillan.

National Association for the Education of Young Children. (1988). NAEYC position statement on standardized testing of young children 3 through 8 years of age. *Young Children, 43*(3), 42–47.

Neill, D. M., & Medina, N. J. (1989). Standardized testing: Harmful to educational health. *Phi Delta Kappan, 70*, 688–697.

Perrone, V. (1990). How did we get here? In C. Kamii (Ed.), *Achievement testing in the early grades: The games grown-ups play* (pp. 1–13). Washington, DC: National Association for the Education of Young Children.

Phillips, N. H. (1992). Two-tiered kindergartens: Effective for at-risk 5-year-olds? *Early Childhood Research Quarterly, 7*, 205–224.

Raver, C. C., & Zigler, E. F. (1991). Three steps forward, two steps back: Head Start and the measurement of social competence. *Young Children, 46*(4), 3–8.

Resnick, D. P. (1981). Testing in America: A supportive environment. *Phi Delta Kappan, 62*, 625–628.

Salvia, J., & Ysseldyke, J. E. (1991). *Assessment* (5th ed.). Boston: Houghton Mifflin.

Shepard, L. A. (1991). The influence of standardized tests on the early childhood curriculum, teachers, and children. In B. Spodek & O. N. Saracho (Eds.), *Yearbook in early childhood education: Vol. 2. Issues in early childhood curriculum* (pp. 166–189). New York: Teachers College Press.

Shepard, L. A., & Graue, M. E. (1993). The morass of school readiness screening: Research on test use and test validity. In B. Spodek (Ed.), *Handbook of research on the education of young children* (pp. 293–305). New York: Macmillan.

Shepard, L. A., & Smith, M. L. (1988). Escalating academic demand in kindergarten: Counterproductive policies. *The Elementary School Journal, 89*, 135–145.

Sigel, I. E. (1987). Does hothousing rob children of their childhood? *Early Childhood Research Quarterly, 2*, 211–225.

Taub, H. P., Love, J., Wilkerson, D. A., Washington, E. D., & Wolf, J. M. (1980). *Accept my profile: Perspectives for Head Start profiles of program effects on children*. Black Rock, CT: Mediax Interactive Technologies.

Thurstone, T. G. (1974). *PMS readiness level examiner's manual*. Chicago: Science Research Associates.

Walsh, D. J., & King, G. (1993). Good research and bad research: Extending Zimiles' criticism. *Early Childhood Research Quarterly, 8*, 397–400.

Wiggins, G. (1989a). A true test: Toward more authentic and equitable assessment. *Phi Delta Kappan, 70*, 703–713.

Wiggins, G. (1989b). Teaching to the (authentic) test. *Educational Leadership, 46*(7), 41–47.

Wodtke, K. H., Harper, F., Schommer, M., & Brunelli, P. (1989). How standardized is school testing? An exploratory observational study of standardized group testing in kindergarten. *Educational Evaluation and Policy Analysis, 11*, 223–235.

Wortham, S. C. (1990). *Tests and measurement in early childhood education*. Columbus, OH: Merrill.

Zimiles, H. (1993a). The adoration of "hard data": A case study of data fetishism in the evaluation of infant day care. *Early Childhood Research Quarterly, 8*, 369–385.

Zimiles, H. (1993b). In search of a realistic research perspective: A response to Fein, and Walsh and King. *Early Childhood Research Quarterly, 8*, 401–405.

CHAPTER 6

Using Observational Techniques for Evaluating Young Children's Learning

Doris Bergen

From the moment of birth, and even before birth, human beings are observers of their world. Research on infant perception suggests that neonates have been auditory observers while still in the womb because they can demonstrate recognition of their mother's voice. Young infants use all of their sensory modalities to observe and begin to organize their object and interpersonal worlds (Bornstein, 1988). Throughout their childhood years, human beings are astute observers of their experience and they use the information gained from observation to construct knowledge (Piaget, 1962).

Adults also use their observational skills constantly as they try to understand the behavior of other people, as well as the phenomena of the object world. Most adults are so familiar with obtaining information through observing the naturally occurring activities, the objects, and the persons around them that they rarely are aware that they are using observational skills to make sense of their experience. As the context for this discussion of observational techniques, however, it is important to note that everyone uses observational techniques for evaluation purposes. Indeed, from an ethological perspective, observing and evaluating are biologically based human behaviors necessary for survival. Thus, the basic abilities do not need to be taught. Although early childhood educators have used observational techniques to help them evaluate child behavior, judge effectiveness of curricular activities, and monitor child progress, their observations often have been intuitive, unsystematically collected, and globally categorized; thus, the inferences made from them may or may not have been valid.

Observational techniques using the naturally occurring child environments of home, school, and neighborhood were extremely popular during the "child study" era, and many of the techniques used today were described initially by early researchers and educators (e.g., Dawe, 1934; Gesell, 1925; Olson, 1929; Parten, 1932). Their observations formed the basis for standardized developmental milestone tests used now in early childhood (Bergen, 1994). Naturalistic observational data also formed the base from which Piagetian developmental theory was derived (e.g., Piaget, 1926, 1932, 1954). Indeed, data obtained from naturalistic observational techniques have provided the early childhood field with much of its current knowledge base on all domains of development (Bergen, 1988, 1994).

Although standardized, norm-referenced tests and rating scales have been the primary mode of evaluation for children of public school age, the commitment to naturalistic observation has remained strong among early childhood researchers and educators. Recently, the importance of ecologically based evaluation for all ages has been stressed and the use of qualitative methods to describe behaviors in context has been strongly recommended (e.g., Denzin & Lincoln, 1994; Guba, 1978; Wozniak & Fischer, 1993).

Pressures for testing young children also have increased, as has the variety of techniques for observing children in natural environments. Particularly in early childhood education, alternatives to evaluation by testing have been designed and promoted (e.g., Meisels, 1993). This chapter will provide the rationale for the use of naturalistic observation as an evaluation method, describe the features that are common to observational techniques, and suggest methodological cautions that apply to these procedures. It will describe time-honored observational techniques and some newly designed versions that incorporate aspects of earlier techniques. It also will give predictions for future directions in the use of naturalistic observation for evaluation of children's learning.

RATIONALE FOR USING NATURALISTIC OBSERVATION

In a now classic chapter on observational child study, Herbert Wright (1960) wrote that observational methods "leave nature and society to their own devices." He defined direct observation as "a scientific practice that includes observing and associated recording and analysis of naturally oc-curring things and events" (p. 71). According to Wright, there are four reasons for using these methods in child study: (1) ecological—studying relationships between behavior and environment; (2) normative—classify-ing what is typical behavior; (3) systematic—studying relationships among universal behavior variables; and (4) idiographic—evaluating par-ticular children as individuals.

One reason for using observational techniques is that certain charac-teristics of young children make unnatural testing situations less likely to show typical child performance (e.g., Linder, 1993). There are also cer-tain types of child behavior, such as play, that can be observed more comprehensively in natural environments (Bergen, 1988). In addition, some behaviors, such as peer social interactions, must be observed in con-text if they are to have validity (Schneider, Rubin, & Ledingham, 1985).

Characteristics of Young Children

A number of characteristics of young children that make naturalistic ob-servation appropriate have been identified (e.g., Bailey, 1989; Linder, 1993). One of these is that children are less likely to perform well in a standardized testing situation that requires attending to an examiner and performing requested tasks when those tasks are not of interest to them. Young children usually do not have a concept of "test," nor do they have in mind the "script" and "roles" that must be adhered to in a formal testing situation. Even if they do perform some of the tasks, they are often inconsistent in paying attention, and they do not realize that they cannot choose to do some and not others of the tasks. Second, children may have difficulty relating to an examiner who is not familiar to them or have problems in separating from their parents. Finally, because most tests rely on verbal directions, young children whose language skills are not fully developed may be unable to understand the task or to produce the verbal responses required. All of these problems are exacerbated if children come from cultural or language groups that stress different behaviors with unfa-miliar adults or in unfamiliar situations.

A special advantage of naturalistic observation is that it allows observ-ers to gain information about the ways young children perform various skills that they might not reveal in a formal testing environment, especially those that can be assessed well only when other people (peers and parents) are present. Another characteristic of young children that makes them good subjects for observation is that their behavior is less likely to change when they are being observed. They may show some initial interest or concern but usually return to their typical pursuits. Especially if they are being observed in their own classroom by familiar adults, they will be likely to show typical developmental behaviors during the naturalistic observation period.

Characteristics of Behaviors to Be Evaluated

Many child behaviors that can be observed quite easily in a naturally occurring environment are extremely difficult to observe in a testing situation. They include such behaviors as play, humor, aggression, empathy, social skills, and others that are ephemeral in expression, difficult to elicit, and/or context specific (Bergen, 1994). Often these behaviors are assessed by having parents or teachers use a checklist or rating method to indicate whether the behaviors have been observed. Unfortunately, this approach is an "observation once removed" method and relies on unsystematically collected observational data. In regard to analysis of data collected, Martin (1994) offers a sequence of types of behavior from which appropriate inferences about children's stage of development can best be made from observation. Those for which inferences from observation may be especially valid are physical skills, language/communication, social interaction, and emotions. Those that might be more difficult to infer from observational data include personality, moral understanding, cognition, and spirituality. Thus, to evaluate cognitive processes and academic skills through observation, the environment would have to be one in which opportunities to demonstrate those skills are afforded by the materials and activities available.

Characteristics of Contexts

Certain behaviors, especially those requiring evaluation of child interactions with peers, parents, or teachers, can be different when the settings of potential interaction vary. For example, child interactions with parents at home and at school, or child communication with familiar or unfamiliar peers, are likely to be quantitatively and qualitatively different. Therefore, another reason why observation in a range of typical settings is useful is that it makes it possible to evaluate the person/environment variables that may affect demonstration of learning (Bergen & Mosley-Howard, 1994; Wright, 1960). The kind of observation that has been planned systematically to be done in a range of settings has been called an "ecological assessment" (Bergen & Everington, 1994). However, even when the same setting is used to observe young children's behavior and learning, the observer may note that different situations occurring each day will influence the observational data collected. These context factors must be taken into account in the evaluation of young children's learning.

FEATURES COMMON TO OBSERVATIONAL TECHNIQUES

Although there are numerous ways to conduct observations in the naturally occurring environment, all of the methods have some common features. First, they are part of a systematic observation plan that is followed on a consistent basis. Second, the role of the observer is determined initially and, once prescribed, is maintained. Third, the objectivity, reliability, validity, and generalizability of the observations are addressed. Fourth, contextual factors that might influence child behavior are specified.

Systematic Nature of Observation Plan

A major difference between the everyday observations that human beings make and the type of naturalistic observation that teachers should use in evaluating young children's learning is that in the former information is neither collected nor recorded in a systematic manner. Thus, it risks being subjective and inconsistent, with salient behaviors likely to be noted more than less obvious ones, and prior mind-sets about the child subject to reflection in the behaviors that are noted. Also, because of the human tendency toward selective memory, the observer may recall episodes that are of special interest or that have higher emotional content rather than the entire range of behaviors that were observed. Teacher expectations about what behavior should be seen also may influence the recall or the evaluation of the behavior.

An interesting cross-cultural study that compared teacher reports with actual classroom observation may serve to illustrate how ongoing but unsystematic observations of teachers may be biased due to one or more of these factors (Weisz, Chaiyasit, Weiss, Eastman, & Jackson, 1995). These researchers investigated results of an earlier study that showed Thai children to have many more behavior problems, as reported by teachers, than did a comparable American sample. The subsequent observational study, in which independent observers collected data on the behaviors, found the opposite — that the American children showed more behavior problems. In this second study, both groups of teachers rated the children higher in behavior problems than the observational data indicated. However, the Thai teachers reported a higher rate of behavior problems than the American teachers, even though the independent observations showed the opposite! The researchers explain their findings as a cultural expectation effect, because the expectations for child politeness and compliance are higher in the Thai culture. This example points out the problems in using teacher report data that are not backed up by systematically (and independently, if possible) collected observations. It confirms the importance of teachers not only having clearly specified plans for collecting observational data and following these plans systematically, but also being aware of their own cultural biases in using these data to make inferences.

Open/Closed Nature of Plan. In planning observational techniques, it is useful to categorize the types of observations on a continuum of "open to closed" methods (Wright, 1960). Open techniques sample long or continuous segments of naturally occurring behavior over regular intervals, record with narrative and sequential methods, and describe by classifying and interpreting themes or constructs. There is usually a wealth of narrative information gained from open methods, which sometimes can be daunting in interpreting learning progress. Closed methods use shorter units of behavior, with a sampling plan that focuses on more narrowly prescribed behavioral events or units of time; recording codes usually are used, and data often are quantified in the analysis (e.g., counting how often a specific behavior occurred). These methods also may constrict the environment in some way, such as rearranging the classroom space. There are many variations of observational techniques that teachers can consider, some of which incorporate both open and closed dimensions.

Operational Definitions of Behavior. Another part of a systematic plan is to determine the operational definitions; that is, to decide what kinds of behaviors are going to be observed. Although this seems like a very straightforward decision, it is surprising how often naturalistic observation is conducted with a "just record anything" approach. Unfortunately, this may result in a confounded data set that includes behaviors (e.g., hitting peers); impressions (e.g., always in trouble); and judgments (e.g., a "mean" child). While it is true that ethologically oriented researchers often collect a wide range of data without specifying the exact behaviors they want to observe, they do this to generate hypotheses rather than to evaluate children. To evaluate with observational techniques, the teacher must state clearly the operational definitions for behaviors that are to be observed. For example, if children's social skills are to be evaluated, specific behaviors, such as sharing toys, helping other children, or asking to enter a group, must be identified for observation.

Roles of Observers

Traditionally the person doing naturalistic observation has played a non-participant role, trying to be as quiet, noninitiating, and "invisible" as possible while recording behavioral data. More recently, a model from anthropology has been followed, which has a participant observer who interacts with the subjects while observing their behaviors. Technology also has provided an alternative option; by recording activities on video-tape, the observer has the leisure to do the actual note taking or coding after the events have taken place. This method is now preferred by many researchers and it also is used in some team assessments of young children. It can be a useful addition to direct observation for teachers.

Nonparticipant Observer. Ideally this role works best if there are other teachers, teacher aides, or parent volunteers in the classroom. Then the teacher can become the nonobtrusive recorder of children's learning behavior. In actual practice, the role may be hard to maintain because the children are still likely to want to interact with the teacher. A number of suggestions are given by Martin (1994) for responding in a way that is warm but still conveys that the teacher is busy. For example, avoiding eye contact and attention-getting clothing, staying at a distance, and respond-ing briefly if asked what he or she is doing help the teacher to be nonobtru-sive. If observations are done on a regular basis, the children become accustomed to seeing the teacher in that role. Of course, adequate supervi-sion must be provided by other staff members. Other nonobtrusive options involve training an aide or volunteer to record the observational informa-tion, exchanging data-collecting duties with another teacher, or using a closed system that does not require long-term sustained attention.

Participant Observer. The participant observer role can work well for the teacher if the activity focus is one in which teacher participation can be low-key and noninitiating. For example, sitting at a table handing out materials for children and responding to their comments, as necessary, can still be a good forum for observing children's learning behavior. As a participant, teachers rarely can take notes or complete forms while the activity is ongoing. However, having a series of cards on which reminder ideas can be jotted quickly after the activity or at the end of the day, or using audiotape recording to assist in recall can make this process effective. One very important difference between nonparticipant and participant observation should be noted. In the first, the observer attempts to stay objective and to insert as little of his or her personal interaction into the setting as is possible. Conversely, in participant observation the observer does record his or her side of interactions with children, responses to the phenomena being observed, and feelings about the affect being experienced. This information on observer interactions that may have influenced child behaviors will form part of the context for the child evaluation.

Technologically Assisted Observation. The use of videotape technology to record observations can be a welcome addition or it can seem to be an intrusion in the classroom. In order for the observations to be valid, a period of time must be allocated for getting the children accustomed to seeing the camera in the room and to having the teacher or other staff member involved with it. There are some distinct advantages to videotaping for evaluation purposes. First, the videotape may record behaviors that in-class observational recording will miss. Second, it can be analyzed at the convenience of the teacher. Third, the records of behavior can illustrate to parents or other staff members the extent of the children's learning progress in a particular dimension. Fourth, it is especially useful for analyzing person/environment relationships. Fifth, if taped sequences are collected at different points in the year, they can give information on long-term progress. Because the size of cameras has decreased, this method is relatively unobtrusive. Often an aide or parent volunteer can be trained to collect the observations on focal children. Coding of the data can be assisted by use of a video playback that permits frame by frame review.

Audiotape recording also has been used extensively, especially to gather language samples. It has many of the same advantages as videotaping and, of course, is less obtrusive. However, the richness of data is not as great and, unless the observer describes the setting, the context cannot be considered in evaluating the children's learning. Some studies have had observers describe the setting and child behavior directly onto audiotape (e.g., White & Carew-Watts, 1973), and this method could be used by teachers observing children at school.

Laptop computers can be fitted with software to record and analyze data in the field. Some of the programs are capable of precise microanalyses of slight differences in behavior and physical responses, as well as analysis of molar observations, which focus on pattern categories of behavior such as turn taking or verbal exchanges. These techniques have been used in studies of parent–infant interactions, but they are also useful for recording classroom social interactions. An advantage to this technique is that once the data are recorded, the quantitative analysis can be accomplished easily, using the recorded data. Because most children are familiar with computers, this method can be relatively unobtrusive. It does, of course, require sophisticated hardware and software.

Reliability, Validity, Objectivity, and Generalizability

Although observational researchers have always had concerns about the extent of agreement between observers/coders (reliability), use of methods that measure what is intended to be measured (validity), unbiased collection and interpretation of data (objectivity), and factors that affect whether the findings can be applied to other settings (generalizability), teachers usually have not been concerned about these issues when observing the children in their class. However, these issues are important to consider if teachers want their observations to be maximally useful.

Gaining Reliability. When teachers use observational techniques, they rarely have another person to work with who can help them establish observer reliability—that is, to make sure they do not have "observer drift," in which the criterion changes with each observational attempt, or an "expectation bias" that results in a failure to record data that are incongruent with the bias, or a "fatigue effect" from having observed over a long period. If a teacher is fortunate enough to be team teaching, having another member of the team do some brief observational checks can establish reliability. An advantage of videotaped data is that a second observer can code some tapes to establish reliability. Just being aware of problems that can affect reliability also might help the teacher avoid them.

Establishing Validity. There are a number of ways that observations can be judged to be actually assessing the dimensions defined as important to observe. Content validity can be assessed by having another teacher review the operational definitions of the behaviors to be observed and give an opinion as to their validity. If there are other methods being used to assess the same behaviors or if other people on a team are looking at these from their professional perspectives, then the observational data can be compared with these other data sources to determine concurrent validity. One advantage of teaming for evaluation of learning is that the team usually can provide the validation. For example, the observational data on communication skills collected by the teacher within the classroom can be compared with data from the speech therapist's clinical observations or the parent's home observations.

Maintaining Objectivity. The goal of most observational techniques is to record observations without making judgments and to make inferences that are based on the factual data recorded, not on pre-existing opinions, emotions, or biases. However, postmodern thinkers assert that subjectivity is inevitable because there is no objective truth "out there" that can be perceived. They see objectivity as one of the fallacies of "modernity" (Giddens, 1990). From this perspective, the best that observers can do is to be aware of their subjective reality and to acknowledge it as part of their evaluation process. Particularly in the participant observation approach, "objective subjectivity" regarding the interactions that are occurring between the observer and the child is important to acknowledge.

Considering Generalizability. When teachers use observational techniques to evaluate young children's learning, they are not concerned about the typical issues of generalizability, which focus on applying findings to other groups and other settings. Rather, the generalizability question refers to whether the particular behaviors that have been observed during the repeated sampling of one child's behavior can be generalized as a consistent behavior pattern of that child. This question is very important for decision making based on the evaluation of the collected data. One observation of a child does not allow the teacher to make an assumption of generalizability about the observed behavior. A sampling plan that includes observation of the behavior at intervals across a number of days or weeks and across a range of settings would make an assumption of generalizability warranted. The question that teachers must answer is how small a sample of behavior over how short a time span and in how few settings can be used to decide if the behavior is one that characterizes the child. For example, is observing a high activity level in a child during story reading, free play, and snack time for 20 minutes on three different days a sufficient amount of observation to evaluate that child as hyperactive? These are the kinds of generalizability questions that teachers try to answer, using observational techniques.

Contextual Influences

In testing or experimental conditions, an attempt is made to minimize the influence of contexts, making them similar for all subjects and attempting to rid the setting of extraneous variables. In using observational techniques, however, the context variables are acknowledged and their influences are explored to provide a richness of interpretation to the evaluation. Contextual influences come from the settings in which observation takes place, from the situations that occur in those settings, and from the interactions among physical and social contexts.

Settings. Observational data analysis often has been criticized for its failure to take setting influences into account, especially when reporting presumed universals of child behavior. For educational evaluation, the influence of the classroom, playground, home, or other settings where the child is observed is always one of the crucial variables used. For example, if the child speaks in four-word sentences at home but not in school, the child's ability as a speaker may not be the problem; the teacher may decide to make changes in the school environment to encourage the child's verbal interaction. If one child's behavior with peers is socially competent on the playground but not in the classroom and another child shows little social interaction in either setting, the teacher's evaluation of these two children's social competence may be very different. If a child is unable to demonstrate academic readiness skills in a test situation but has no difficulty writing her name on her paper in class and matching pictures in the lotto game, then the teacher might request that the test examiner observe the child in the classroom. The influence of the setting on the behavior that is demonstrated was stressed initially by Lewin (1931), and many theorists and researchers have lent credence to its importance. Teachers are often aware of this intuitively, especially when parents talk about the child as a behavior problem at home, while the teacher does not notice those behaviors in school. If observational techniques are to be of greatest value, teachers must make the setting influences explicit when reporting their evaluations.

Situations. Even within the same setting, observational conditions are not always the same. On a particular day, there may be a visitor or a substitute staff member, a different arrangement of equipment, or a change in the time sequence of activities. Two situational changes that often affect child behavior are when the child's parent is in the classroom and when there is a change in the activity sequence due to a field trip or other special event. Teachers often expect children to show more dependent behavior when the parent is present and more "out of bounds" behavior when the routine activity sequence is disrupted. These types of situations will, of course, affect the substance of observational data. Before starting an observation, therefore, the situational conditions that exist before the observation starts (the antecedents) should be noted. For example, if a child's sociodramatic play is to be observed, but right before the observation starts the child and peers argue over who will have a particular doll and the child loses the argument, she may have a less active role in the play than would be usual for her. This type of antecedent condition should be recorded in the observational notes.

Interactions Among Child, Peers, and Adults. As the previous example shows, although observations may focus on particular children, in actual practice they usually include information on those children in interaction with other people. One of the most useful functions of observational techniques is to document social interactions, noting who initiates, responds, and seeks the social interactions and what the nature of those interactions is. For example, studies have described children's ability to enter into social play settings (Corsaro, 1985) and investigated cross-cultural differences in their cooperative and competitive behaviors (Madsen, 1971). When observing social interactions of dyads or groups, the observer makes all participants the focus of the observation, not just a focal child.

Attention to social interactive dimensions is of special helpfulness to teachers who wish to evaluate learning *potential* as well as learning achievements. Observation and analysis of adult–child interactions can assist teachers in determining children's "zone of proximal development," which is the level of difficulty that children can master with adult help (Vygotsky, 1962). For example, observing a child trying to do a puzzle alone and then trying to do it with the scaffolding help provided by an adult, could give teachers valuable information about the speed of learning and level of understanding reached with assistance, as well as the independent achievement level. Observations of peer interaction can help teachers determine the social skills children already possess and ones they are working on. Children's ability to use adult facilitation of social interaction with peers also can be observed systematically and progress can be noted over repeated observations.

USING A RANGE OF OBSERVATIONAL TECHNIQUES

There is a wide range of effective observational techniques for assessing educational environments and children's behavior in those environments. They include a number of time-tested methods as well as some newer approaches that incorporate aspects of traditional methods.

Traditional Techniques

Some traditional observational techniques, originally described by Wright (1960), are still useful for teachers today. They range from those on the "open" end of the continuum to those on the "closed" end.

Diary Descriptions. This method has been used by such notable scientists as Darwin (1877). It requires a systematic plan of recording a sequential account of behavior and learning changes; that is, each time a new behavior in the areas of interest (e.g., physical, language, cognitive) is noticed, a rich description of that behavior is added to the diary. Of necessity, it requires a close and continuous association with the child so that the new behaviors can be appropriately recorded in sequence. The style of narration, the timing of entries, and the description of results are all open to the observer's judgment. If done in an ongoing, systematic manner, however, diary descriptions can provide a very useful "case study" for evaluating children's learning. Teachers could use this approach in two ways. They could select a particular child (or a few children) whose learning in certain domains is of major interest and record at least weekly a rich description of the new behaviors that have occurred in that domain. Another way would be to give directions to parents and ask them to assist the teacher by recording new behaviors they notice each week. The parent probably would need to write in a diary provided by the teacher (with some "prompt" questions to aid in getting rich information). This approach is especially useful for learning more about children who have severe disabilities or special giftedness, whose parents usually are sufficiently motivated to continue the diary recording over a long period.

Specimen Descriptions/Running Accounts. Specimen descriptions have their origin in child development study in the work of Barker and Wright (1949). They consist of a continuous observation of a "behavior stream" for a particular time period, such as a full day, a week, or other specific period. The observer attempts to record "everything," including context information, in an objective rather than interpretive style. This is considered an open observational technique. Analysis of the content may use quantitative methods, such as counting the frequencies of various behaviors recorded, and qualitative methods, such as scanning the record for themes and describing rich examples of the themes.

While teachers are unlikely to use specimen descriptions (although videotapes of entire classroom days could be useful), they often use a truncated version of specimen descriptions called "running accounts." The intention of the observer is to record in the same manner as in a specimen description (all behaviors observed, plus context), but the time period is shorter (often an hour). This method was used by a number of early researchers of young children (e.g., Isaacs, 1930), and it is a method faculty often assign to students in child development classes. While these running accounts do not have all the advantages of a specimen description, they do provide a window on all the behaviors the child exhibits during a particular time period, and thus behaviors that otherwise would not be noted are included in the observation. If videotaped samples are collected routinely, a database on each child can be available for evaluating a variety of learning domains.

Anecdotal Records. This method has some characteristics in common with the methods already described; however, the choice of which behaviors to record and the timing of the recording may be either open (whatever is of interest) or more structured (specific times or developmental domains or types of events). Teachers often have used this technique to document particular child behaviors about which they had concerns. While anecdotal records can be useful in documenting these concerns, the method has been criticized because it is subject to bias if the operational definitions of the behaviors are not clearly specified and if the range of behaviors recorded does not include positive as well as negative incidences of these behaviors (Wright, 1960). For example, if a teacher is concerned about a child's social skills and chooses to record only anecdotes showing aggressive interactions, the evaluation of the child may be biased. The sampling plan for anecdotal recording should include an intent to record a range of child interactions so that a balanced picture can be obtained; the context influences should be clearly specified. Such a comprehensive sampling plan permits the records to be analyzed similarly to running accounts or specimen descriptions. These records can then be used as backup data when teachers do checklists or rating scales.

Event Sampling. Event sampling is a way to systematize the evaluation of a particular type of behavior by focusing on recording every instance of that class of behavior (e.g., every event in which that behavior occurs). Prior to the observation, the operational definition of the class of behavior and the types of behavior that are in that class are identified. The observer then focuses on describing these behaviors as they take place during the event. The recording method is structured to provide a certain set of consistent information, such as length of time of the event, foci of social interactions, or roles taken. Analysis is usually quantitative, with frequencies reported, but it also can be qualitative, with descriptions of themes, styles of interaction, or other relevant variables. For example, pretend play events often have been observed and categorized as to frequency and type of object use, roles taken, and scripts enacted (e.g., Roskos, 1990). The study of literacy-related play events, in which play interventions involving reading and writing materials are observed for child behavior changes, also has been of interest (e.g., Christie, 1994).

This method can be useful for teachers in evaluating particular learning domains, such as mathematical understanding or artistic skills. It is particularly useful for behaviors that occur on an infrequent or sporadic basis. Understanding of antecedents and consequences of the event can be enhanced by noting the conditions prevailing immediately before and after the event. Event sampling requires a constantly alert stance regarding the designated behavior events, however, and this might be hard for teachers to maintain. If a number of staff members can be observers and recorders of such events, the teacher is likely to get a more comprehensive picture.

Time Sampling. This closed technique is highly structured as to method of collecting observations. It specifies the time intervals at which information will be recorded and usually uses a checklist or other structured format for the recording of data. It is similar to snapping still photographs because it provides a picture of a moment in time when behavior is observed. The type of behavior observed can be relatively open, however, because while the class of behavior usually is specified (e.g., communication), all observed types of behavior in that class may be recorded (e.g., language, gestures, and nonlanguage verbal communication attempts). The time between "snapshots" (i.e., sampling intervals) is usually short, ranging from 5–10 seconds to 15–20 minutes, and typically about 1–5 minutes. Observations can be recorded directly onto a computer program and coded into preprogrammed categories. Analysis usually consists of quantifying the data (e.g., percentages, means) and making statistical comparisons.

While this method usually results in high reliability among observers, the range of information is more narrow than that from other approaches. Because of the time interval constraints, some relevant activity going on in the interim periods may be missed. However, a wealth of information can be obtained from time sampling. The method is most effective if the class of behavior to be observed is likely to occur rather frequently. It also can be useful as a check on teacher perceptions of frequency of behavior problem occurrence. For example, when teachers wish to change child behavior through behavior modification, they first use time or event sampling to determine the frequency of the behavior before the modifications start. They may be surprised to find that a behavior problem that seemed so salient really occurred infrequently! Time sampling, in particular, can offer a balanced look at the behaviors that children routinely show over a classroom day, can chart total classroom patterns of interaction and curricular use, and can map teachers' movement about the classroom.

Clinical Observation. This method is on the borderline between testing and observational techniques. Any of the strategies for observing and recording data used in running account, event sampling, and time sampling techniques can be used. However, the context of the observation is prescribed by controlling for setting, situation, or interaction influences. A typical example of this technique is Piaget's (1954) study of children's thinking, in which he asked children to solve structured problem situations. His data collection was very open; he recorded children's comments and described their reactions and solutions. Another example is that of DeVries (1970), who videotaped and described children's interactions and language during game play to study their sociomoral thinking level. Teachers rarely have used this method systematically, but they could evaluate young children's learning, especially on cognitive and sociomoral dimensions, using their classroom settings (e.g., dramatic play center, art center). A plan for observing behaviors of interest could be carried out in those settings. For example, if teachers wish to know whether children have mastered color concepts or letter symbols, a method of recording such behaviors in a center that required their use could give that information. When teachers rate children's achievements or needs, they usually rely on a set of data that they have obtained through ongoing but informal and unsystematic observation of classroom events. They could use "clinical observations" of learning domains that are difficult to document through informal observation to validate their ratings. Often teachers remark that the information they provide for early intervention team meetings is not considered as carefully as the information other professionals provide from test scores. Having clearly specified, clinically obtained data could make a difference in the effectiveness of their evaluation presentations.

New Approaches

Techniques that build on aspects of standard methods have been recommended recently as evaluation tools. They include reflective logs, anecdotal records with ratings, play-based assessment, arena assessment, and classroom environment manipulation.

Reflective Logs. This approach, in which teachers write a "diary," records not only newly emerging child behavior but also teachers' growth as they reflect on their interactions with children and discover what they have learned about themselves and the teaching process as they construct these "teacher stories" (Jalongo, 1992). It draws upon postmodern and critical theory concepts because it does not permit "objective" recordings to stand alone, provides rich interpretation of teacher–child interactions, and includes the teacher as participant observer. It acts as an evaluation of teachers' facilitation of children's learning, of scaffolding techniques effective with particular children, and of contextual influences that hinder or support learning. Data from reflective logs typically are reported as narratives, usually in case study format.

Anecdotal Records with Ratings. A method developed for use in Head Start programs combines a rating scale with anecdotal records

(*Child Observation Record,* 1992). The rating form identifies six competency areas and three to six behaviors in each area that give evidence of
competence. Teachers must base their ratings on the evidence gathered
from systematically collected anecdotal records. Because the competency
areas are wide ranging, the anecdotes also must cover the range of developmental domains. Ratings of behavioral indicators in each competency
area are combined to obtain an overall rating of competence in that area.
This approach improves upon both typical anecdotal record and rating
scale techniques because it includes a systematic plan of observation and
requires ratings to be backed up by evidence. Because this model has been
implemented only recently, it is not yet clear how effectively teachers will
use it. It does require teachers to do descriptive record keeping for every
child.

Play-based Assessment. Driven primarily by mandates to assess preschool children who are at risk for developmental delay, techniques that
draw upon observation of young children in play-oriented structured environments have been designed. The designers are primarily early childhood
special educators or psychologists who have concerns about standardized
testing of young children. They suggest play-based assessment, in which
children are observed by a team as they play in specially designed settings.
The data are used by the team to assess development in a range of domains, including that of play. For example, in the model designed by
Linder (1993) a team of professionals, with the child's parents, observe
and interact with the child in a sequence of play experiences (with peer,
with parent, alone, with staff) and then meet to discuss their observations
and to reach a team consensus on the child's developmental and learning
status. The sessions are usually videotaped and team members observe and
describe a range of child behaviors. Numerous other play-based assessment
procedures have been designed; many of these are described in Schaefer,
Gitlin, and Sangrund (1991). By studying play-based assessment methods,
teachers can gain ideas about developmental domains and processes to
observe, ways to describe the skills that are expressed in play, and how to
make inferences about children's learning progress from their observations.

Arena Assessment. This is a method derived from early childhood
special education. A team of observers is present and records information
while the parent or another team member interacts with the child. These
interactions may include play, informal testing, social interaction, or any
other procedures that the professionals think will enable them to get a
good picture of the child's abilities and needs. The team discusses and

comes to a group decision about the child's development and learning progress and formulates an intervention plan. While a full arena process will not be used routinely by regular early childhood teachers, if they have children with special needs in their classrooms, those children's evaluation may require teacher participation in arena assessment. With the present emphasis on inclusion, most teachers will need observational skills to participate in these team assessments. A number of systems are available that help the team integrate the information from various data sources and reach consensus judgments about children's status (e.g., Bagnato & Neisworth, 1990).

Classroom Environment Manipulation. Although this method, involving deliberate rearrangements of classroom space and equipment to observe what behavior changes might occur as a result, has been used most often by researchers, teachers can use it productively to evaluate contextual influences on particular child behaviors. Manipulations for research purposes have included rearranging the block and housekeeping center locations to encourage less gender-stereotypic play (Kinsman & Berk, 1979), adding specific literacy-related items to play centers (Christie & Enz, 1992), and putting a complex piece of climbing equipment in a prominent place to encourage social interaction (Witt & Gramza, 1969). If teachers are interested in encouraging certain kinds of behavior and discouraging others, they can observe child behavior before and after the change is made to evaluate the effects of their environmental manipulation. Given the strong influence of context on child behavior, this technique is of special interest when teachers want to discover the effects of their planned interventions.

THE FUTURE OF NATURALISTIC OBSERVATIONAL TECHNIQUES

In spite of the strong emphasis on testing in the American culture, naturalistic observational techniques have always been highly valued by early childhood researchers and educators because of the characteristics of young children and the domains of evaluation interest in early childhood education. The many excellent observational techniques used by researchers have not been used often by teachers, however, because of the complex nature of the teaching process, the many demands upon teachers' time, and the tendency to use informal and unsystematic observational methods.

Four factors may promote the use of systematically planned observational techniques in the future. First, teachers are being encouraged to be applied researchers who take the lead in answering questions about young children's learning and their own role in that learning. Second, observational techniques are compatible with the team approaches advocated in early intervention and the need to have clearly specified methods of documenting learning progress. Third, the availability of technological devices that make the recording of observational data less obtrusive and more comprehensive and assist in analysis of the information collected can make the use of observational techniques less onerous. Finally, and most important, early childhood educators are realizing that they must take the lead in finding alternatives to testing approaches because, without the ability to document their knowledge of the competencies the children in their programs possess, they will not be able to counter the testing bias of this society. Fortunately, there are some excellent time-tested and newly designed observational techniques to assist teachers in collecting relevant information on children's progress.

REFERENCES

Bagnato, S. J., & Neisworth, J. T. (1990). *System to plan early childhood services (SPECS)*. Circle Pines, MN: American Guidance Service.

Bailey, D. B. (1989). Using direct observation in assessment. In D. B. Bailey & M. Wolery, *Assessing infants and preschoolers with handicaps* (pp. 64–96). New York: Merrill.

Barker, R. G., & Wright, H. F. (1949). Psychological ecology and the problem of psychosocial development. *Child Development, 20,* 131–143.

Bergen, D. (Ed.). (1988). *Play as a medium for learning and development: A handbook of theory and practice*. Portsmouth, NH: Heinemann.

Bergen, D. (Ed.). (1994). *Assessment methods for infants and toddlers: Transdisciplinary team approaches*. New York: Teachers College Press.

Bergen, D., & Everington, D. (1994). Assessment perspectives for young children with disabilities. In D. Bergen (Ed.), *Assessment methods for infants and toddlers: Transdisciplinary team approaches* (pp. 216–233). New York: Teachers College Press.

Bergen, D., & Mosley-Howard, S. (1994). Assessment methods for culturally diverse young children. In D. Bergen (Ed.), *Assessment methods for infants and toddlers: Transdisciplinary team approaches* (pp. 190–206). New York: Teachers College Press.

Bornstein, M. H. (1988). Perceptual development across the life cycle. In M. H. Bornstein & M. E. Lamb (Eds.), *Developmental psychology: An advanced textbook* (pp. 151–204). Hillsdale, NJ: Erlbaum.

Child Observation Record. (1992). Ypsilanti, MI: High/Scope Educational Foundation.

Christie, J. F. (1994). Literacy play interventions: A review of empirical research.

In S. Reifel (Ed.), *Advances in early education and day care* (Vol. 6, pp. 3–24). Greenwich, CT: JAI Press.

Christie, J. F., & Enz, B. (1992). The effects of literacy play interventions on preschoolers' play patterns and literacy development. *Early Education and Development, 3*, 205–220.

Corsaro, W. A. (1985). *Friendship and peer culture in the early years.* Norwood, NJ: Ablex.

Darwin, C. (1877). A biographical sketch of an infant. *Mind, 2,* 267–294.

Dawe, H. C. (1934). An analysis of two hundred quarrels of preschool children. *Child Development, 5,* 139–157.

Denzin, N. K., & Lincoln, Y. S. (Eds.). (1994). *Handbook of qualitative research.* Thousand Oaks, CA: Sage.

DeVries, R. (1970). The development of role-taking as reflected by behavior of bright, average, and retarded children in a social guessing game. *Child Development, 41,* 759–770.

Gesell, A. (1925). *The mental growth of the preschool child: A psychological outline of normal development from birth to the sixth year.* New York: Macmillan.

Giddens, A. (1990). *The consequence of modernity.* Stanford: Stanford University Press.

Guba, E. G. (1978). *Toward a methodology of naturalistic inquiry in educational evaluation* (CSE Monograph Series in Education, No. 8). Los Angeles: University of California Press.

Isaacs, S. (1930). *Intellectual growth in young children.* London: Routledge.

Jalongo, M. R. (1992). Teachers' stories: Our ways of knowing. *Educational Leadership, 49*(7), 68–73.

Kinsman, C., & Berk, L. (1979). Joining the block and housekeeping areas: Changes in play and social behavior. *Young Children, 35*(7), 66–75.

Lewin, K. (1931). Environmental forces in child behavior and development. In C. Murchison (Ed.), *A handbook of child psychology* (pp. 94–127). Worcester, MA: Clark University Press.

Linder, T. (1993). *Transdisciplinary play-based assessment–Revised.* Baltimore, MD: Brookes.

Madsen, M. C. (1971). Developmental and cross-cultural differences in the cooperative and competitive behavior of young children. *Journal of Cross-Cultural Psychology, 2,* 366–371.

Martin, S. (1994). *Take a look: Observation and portfolio assessment in early childhood.* Don Mills, Ontario: Addison-Wesley.

Meisels, S. J. (1993). Remaking classroom assessment with the work sampling system. *Young Children, 48*(5), 34–40.

Olson, W. C. (1929). *The measurement of nervous habits in normal children.* Minneapolis: University of Minnesota Press.

Parten, M. (1932). Social participation among pre-school children. *Journal of Abnormal and Social Psychology, 27,* 243–269.

Piaget, J. (1926). *Language and thought of the child.* London: Routledge & Kegan Paul.

Piaget, J. (1932). *The moral judgment of the child.* New York: Free Press.

Piaget, J. (1954). *The construction of reality in the child.* New York: Basic Books.

Piaget, J. (1962). *Play, dreams and imitation in childhood.* New York: Norton.

Roskos, K. (1990). A taxonomic view of pretend play activity among 4- and 5-year-old children. *Early Childhood Research Quarterly, 5,* 495–512.

Schneider, B. H., Rubin, K. H., & Ledingham, J. E. (Eds.). (1985). *Children's peer relations and social skills: Issues and assessment.* New York: Springer-Verlag.

Schaefer, C. E., Gitlin, K., & Sangrund, A. (1991). *Play diagnosis and assessment.* New York: Wiley.

Vygotsky, L. (1962). *Thought and language.* Cambridge, MA: MIT Press.

Weisz, J. R., Chaiyasit, W., Weiss, B, Eastman, K. L., & Jackson, E. W. (1995). Multimethod study of problem behavior among Thai and American children in school: Teacher reports versus direct observations. *Child Development, 66,* 402–415.

White, B. L., & Carew-Watts, J. (1973). *Experience and environment: Major influences on the development of the young child* (Vol. 1). Englewood Cliffs, NJ: Prentice-Hall.

Witt, P., & Gramza, A. (1969). *Position effects in play equipment preferences of nursery school children.* Urbana, IL: Children's Research Center.

Wozniak, R. H., & Fischer, K. W. (Eds.). (1993). *Development in context.* Hillsdale, NJ: Erlbaum.

Wright, H. F. (1960). Observational child study. In P. H. Mussen (Ed.), *Handbook of research methods in child development* (pp. 71–139). New York: Wiley.

CHAPTER 7

Assessing Student Learning Through the Analysis of Pupil Products

Dominic F. Gullo

"By the year 2000, all children will come to school ready to learn" (U.S. Department of Education, 1991). This quotation, which represents the first education goal set forth by the National Governors' Association at their meeting in Charlottesville, Virginia, is a source of much controversy. One erroneous assumption that emanates from the "readiness goal" is that, for whatever reason, some children start school "not ready" to learn. Validation for this assumption may stem from the interpretation of assessment information used in determining a child's readiness status as well as the definition of readiness that one espouses. In reality, one's definition of readiness cannot be separated from measurement practice. That is, the practice of how one uses the information gleaned from measurement procedures, along with the assumptions one has related to what measurement tells us about children's readiness status, often leads to the determination of whether or not a child is said to be "ready."

According to the National Association for the Education of Young Children (Bredekamp, 1987), ongoing assessment in early childhood education should occur primarily to determine children's curricular needs. Based on information gleaned from assessment data, the early childhood curriculum should be modified to match the strengths and needs of individual children. What follows from this is a view of assessment as a means of determining the kinds of experiences for which children are ready

(Gullo, 1994). While readiness often is associated with the start of formal schooling, it also is used to describe "preparedness" for reading and math, as well as schooling itself. In addition, the concept is associated with the skills and knowledge necessary to participate successfully in kindergarten or prekindergarten. However, it should be evident from the above-noted relationship between assessment and readiness, that "readiness" issues occur throughout schooling.

There are others, however, who advocate a somewhat different relationship between assessment and readiness. Uphoff and Gilmore (1986), for example, view assessment as a means for determining whether children are ready for certain educational experiences. A central assumption of this position is that children should be assessed and be permitted to begin "formal" schooling based on their being similar in developmental status or level of academic performance with the rest of the children with whom they start school. In this manner, assessment may be used to restrict the experiences of some children or to delay their entry.

While assessment is not, in and of itself, a readiness issue, readiness as defined by schools and the society at large is an assessment issue. The issue revolves around how readiness is defined and how it is measured. Controversies about early childhood assessment abound (see, for example, Bredekamp & Rosegrant, 1992; Gullo, 1992, 1994; Meisels, 1987). The controversies surround two major issues — the mismatch between assessment and the child, and the mismatch between assessment and the curriculum.

The primary manner by which the early childhood education profession has addressed these controversies has been through advocating alternative assessment or authentic assessment practices. Alternative assessment and authentic assessment are the terms used to describe the kinds of procedures used in lieu of or in addition to the more "standard" paper-and-pencil type assessments. Authentic assessment procedures encompass many different types of gathering procedures as well as many different types of information used as evidence for developmental change and academic progress. Some of these are discussed in other chapters of this volume.

In this chapter, one specific type of evidence resulting from the assessment process will be discussed — pupil-produced products. The use of pupil-produced products responds to many of the problematic concerns addressed earlier. For purposes of this discussion, pupil-produced products are defined as those materials that are generated by the child through active engagement in the curriculum activities. Thus, they can be either tangibles, such as a picture or a writing sample, or intangibles, such as the processes evident in the observation of children engaged in curriculum activities, including block construction, manipulation of objects, or dramatic play. In this manner, using pupil-produced products to assess children's developmental or academic status can be thought of as a contextualized form of assessment.

The chapter is divided into four sections. In the first section, problems associated with early childhood assessment will be identified. Assessment of pupil-produced products will be discussed in light of these problems. In the second section, general principles guiding the assessment process, vis-a-vis the use of pupil-produced products, will be described. The basis for making decisions, about which types of products to use and how to use the information obtained, will be discussed. Two types of strategies for using pupil-produced products will be presented in the remainder of the chapter. In the third section, portfolio assessment will be described. Questions such as, "How do I use a portfolio?" "What do I include in the portfolio?" and "What criteria do I use for selecting material to be included in the portfolio?" will be answered. Finally, in the fourth section of the chapter, assessment of processes will be discussed. While the third section of the chapter is primarily concerned with the assessment of the "what" (what products do pupils produce?), the fourth section is concerned with the assessment of the "how" (how do pupils produce these products?). Finally, at the conclusion of the chapter, some issues will be raised relative to the efficacy of using pupil-produced products for assessment in early childhood education.

PROBLEMS WITH EARLY CHILDHOOD ASSESSMENT

When teachers think of assessment, they often think of the paper-and-pencil tests that were pervasive in their own schooling — the tried and true multiple-choice or true-or-false tests that children have suffered through for decades. While the more "objective" method of assessment may provide valid information regarding older children, children in the early childhood years pose a challenge for teachers attempting to assess their current performance status or progress. The challenge stems from mismatch. One mismatch exists between the child's developmental capabilities and the performance expected in various assessment formats. A second mismatch exists between the content and strategies assessed and the content and strategies emphasized in the curriculum.

Assessment and Child Development

In its policy statement on assessment, the National Association for the Education of Young Children (1988) states that early childhood assessment practices should reflect and take into account children's level of developmental capabilities and performance. Early childhood professionals should be cognizant of the fact that the developmental characteristics of children may affect children's behavior in response to assessment procedures, as well as the assessment outcomes. It should be recognized that the developmental characteristics of individual children, or of a group of children, within the same developmental stage, may affect how they will respond in and to various assessment situations (Cryan, 1986; Gullo, 1994; Meisels, 1987). This is true for both formal as well as informal assessment procedures. There are a number of developmental characteristics that should be considered that may affect assessment practices in early childhood education. In this chapter, early childhood education is defined as prekindergarten (age 3 or 4) through third grade (age 8). Assessment issues related to prelinguistic infants and toddlers pose their own challenges and are beyond the scope of this chapter.

Developmental Limitations. Early childhood professionals should recognize that young children often operate under developmental limitations, which may influence the responses of children to certain assessment situations. When children in early childhood settings are assessed in order to determine whether they have acquired specific knowledge or skills during or following a particular curriculum activity, it should not be assumed that an inappropriate response or no response during the assessment process indicates that children do not have the knowledge or skills that are sought. One of the things that should be considered is whether the method used to assess the child is consistent with the child's individual and general age-related developmental capabilities to respond.

If, for example, the assessment method requires that the child use controlled fine motor movements, the inability to exhibit such movements may inhibit the child's ability to demonstrate that he or she has acquired the knowledge or skills being assessed. Likewise, the language used by the teacher to assess a child's performance may not be consistent with the child's own level of language development. The teacher's language may not reflect content that is familiar to the child because he or she comes from a different experiential or social background. If a question is not meaningfully stated for the child, the child will not respond in the anticipated manner, even if the information or skill being assessed is known or has been acquired.

Another developmental characteristic of children during the early childhood years is that they often demonstrate impulsive behaviors more than do children who are at more advanced levels of development. Impulsivity means that children will respond with the first thing that comes to their mind without reflecting on or considering alternative, and perhaps more appropriate, responses. An example of this might be the instance where a child is asked to circle a correct answer in response to a stimulus picture or question on an activity sheet or test form. Often children at this age will circle the first picture on the sheet or the first one that "seems" right, without looking to see if a subsequent picture is "more right" than the picture they circled. Again, the outcome is that the teacher is not getting an accurate picture of what the children really know, because the children's development supersedes their need to make sure that they are responding correctly or appropriately.

Motivational Differences. The next developmental consideration is that the motivation to do well in assessment situations differs depending on children's level of developmental accomplishments and experiential backgrounds. From experience with children, it is known that they often do not understand the importance or significance of their performance in assessment situations. For children, the reinforcement or incentive to perform may be simply to complete the task so that they can go on to a more comfortable or enjoyable circumstance. Professionals in early childhood education should be aware of young children's "lack of motivation" to perform according to external standards. It should be noted that "lack of motivation" is not meant in the pejorative sense. Rather, it is due to children's lack of understanding or appreciation for the significance of the task.

There are some groups of children who have more experience with "assessment-like" situations and therefore may be more motivated at earlier ages than others to perform. Children who come from middle socioeconomic status backgrounds are more likely to have engaged in these types of situations than children who come from homes of economic poverty. Because they are more likely to have had these types of experiences in their homes prior to commencing a formal education process, these children may be more comfortable answering questions or being assessed in other ways. Familiarity alone could account for middle socioeconomic children being more at ease, and therefore more motivated to do well, in assessment situations.

Children's Perception of Their Performance. Another developmental consideration is that there are differences in how children perceive themselves as compared with how others perceive them relative to their performance on various tasks. An important element affecting the assessment of children's performance is the degree to which they incorporate feedback into the internalized assessment of their own competence. Younger children's perception of their own competence is not consistent with teachers' ratings of their competence (Gullo & Ambrose, 1987; Stipek, 1981). Teachers often expect that the feedback given to children will be used by them to gauge their performance. Young children uniformly have an exaggerated perception of their own abilities and usually do not perceive teacher feedback as criticism that can be used to modify or determine their future behaviors. It is not until about 8 years of age that children's perceptions of their own competence match that of the teacher.

In addition, the feedback that teachers give young children with regard to their classroom performance is not consistent with the kinds of behaviors that teachers assess to determine academic competence. Teachers tend to focus on and give children feedback regarding their classroom behavior and social adjustment. Conversely, teachers tend to *assess* children's cognitive and academic performance (Apple & King, 1978). Thus, young children may get little direct and meaningful feedback regarding their academic performance.

Generalizing Knowledge. A final developmental consideration is that there are differences in how children generalize their performance or knowledge from situation to situation and context to context. It is not appropriate for teachers to assume that because a child is able to demonstrate that he or she has a specific skill or bit of knowledge within a particular academic context, the child will be able to generalize this knowledge or skill and demonstrate proficiency in all contexts (Hills, 1993; Meisels, 1993).

For example, if children are provided with experiences using literacy concepts and skills only in contexts where they manipulate objects, but never have opportunities for using representational symbols, these children may not be able to demonstrate what they know when assessed in a representational manner, with paper-and-pencil tasks. It is imperative that children be given opportunities to have experiences in many contexts, both those that are concrete and those that are representational in nature. In addition, children should be assessed in multiple contexts.

In summary, it has been shown that early childhood professionals should consider the child's developmental characteristics when assessing him or her. One should ask two questions before undertaking the assessment of an individual child: *What are the developmental characteristics of the child that will be assessed?* and *How do these developmental characteristics relate to, or affect, what is being assessed?*

The developmental status of some children may preclude the use of some assessment techniques. It is imperative that teachers take into account children's development when both selecting assessment procedures and interpreting assessment results. Using pupil-produced products as the primary assessment tool is one way to take these developmental considerations into account. In addition, it is imperative that early childhood assessment procedures occur within the context of the classroom while the curriculum is being implemented.

Assessment and the Early Childhood Curriculum

During the early school years, it is difficult to determine through assessment whether children have acquired specific, small bits of knowledge or skills. This is especially true if these bits of knowledge and skills are isolated from other types of knowledge and skills. Further, young children are not reliable "test takers" due to the many confounding personal, developmental, and environmental factors that affect their performance during these early years. Just as children do not develop each domain in an isolated manner, or in a uniform manner, they do not acquire knowledge or learn specific bits of information or skills without learning other things within the contextual framework of the curriculum. As a result, measuring whether children have acquired specific information may be a somewhat difficult, invalid, and unreliable task. The process of assessment must be consistent with the manner in which curriculum is viewed in early childhood education (Meisels, 1992; National Commission on Testing and Public Policy, 1990). Two implications related to the relationship between the assessment process and the early childhood curriculum emerge.

First, children should be assessed within the context of the classroom, while engaged in meaningful curriculum activities. Young children learn within a meaningful context and should be assessed within a meaningful context as well. During the early schooling years, it is often difficult for children to separate skills from knowledge, or process from product, and therefore a more holistic approach to assessment must be taken. Attention should be paid to *how* children are learning, as well as to *what* they are learning.

Second, assessment should *inform* curriculum practice. Teachers should not use assessment to determine which children are doing better or worse than which children, or which children are ready to go on to the next level and which children should stay where they are or go back. Rather, teachers should use the information that they get from assessment practices to help them understand *how* the curriculum is working for individual children. That is, teachers should use assessment information to help them understand where children are, so that modifications in the curriculum can be made to meet children's individual needs.

As should be evident, the assessment process should be an inherent part of the curriculum process. Assessment should not focus solely on outcome measures that are directed toward identified success markers. Rather, assessment should be viewed as a dynamic process, integral to and subject to curriculum development and implementation. Assessment should be a *continuous process* — one that occurs time and time again, over a long period. Assessment should be a *comprehensive process* — one that acknowledges the multidimensional aspects of learning and development. Assessment should be an *integrative process* — one that is not separate from the process of curriculum development and implementation.

To address the challenges of assessment as described above — as a process that fits into a developmentally appropriate early childhood curriculum — early childhood professionals have had to look beyond the paper-and-pencil test. The response has been overwhelming — why not use curriculum content and process as assessment tools? The processes and products that are inherent to curriculum implementation have formed the basis for assessment in early childhood today.

PRINCIPLES GUIDING EARLY CHILDHOOD ASSESSMENT PRACTICES USING PUPIL-PRODUCED PRODUCTS

A number of guiding principles are inherent in all of the information and practices presented in this chapter. These principles, or themes, are woven throughout and appear in different ways and different forms. It is important to note them. While it seems easy to list these principles as separate entities, it is important to understand that at times they are interrelated. Each of the four guiding principles discussed below should be kept in mind at all times when making decisions about assessment using pupil-produced products.

1. *Assessment practices that are developmentally appropriate should capitalize on the actual work of the classroom.* As has been discussed earlier, and will be discussed again, it is difficult to assess young children reliably if they are asked to perform tasks that seem unnatural or irrelevant. Context and relevance are important characteristics to consider both in developing curriculum (Bredekamp, 1987; Gullo, 1992) as well as in assessing how children are progressing (Gullo, 1994, 1995; Hills, 1993). Simply using concrete materials that children can manipulate for the pur-

pose of assessment is not sufficient to make the practice developmentally appropriate. A necessary condition is that the materials are relevant to the curriculum experiences of the children.

2. *Assessment practices that are developmentally appropriate should enhance both the teacher's and the child's involvement in the assessment process.* Assessment should not be something that teachers do to children. Rather, just as the curriculum should reflect a child-centered approach, so too should assessment practices reflect this approach. Both teachers and children should be active participants in the assessment process.

3. *Assessment practices that are developmentally appropriate should be informative to others.* In order for assessment practices and outcomes to be useful, they must serve as a source of information to more than just the classroom teacher. The information obtained from the assessment process should provide the basis for presenting to parents a clear picture of how their child is progressing (Hills, 1993). The child's future teachers also should be able to make curriculum decisions for the child based on assessment data. In addition, assessment should provide information to the district regarding the effectiveness of the curriculum for individual children.

4. *Assessment practices that are developmentally appropriate should provide a close match between assessment and the curriculum goals.* When schools engage in the practice of making decisions about assessment materials and practices without regard to the curriculum, they run the risk of collecting information that will be of little use in curriculum planning (Bergan & Feld, 1993). A greater risk is run when curriculum decisions are based on assessment information that has little bearing on curriculum content or implementation strategies (Meisels, 1989). It is important to ask the following questions when making decisions regarding assessment materials and procedures:

- What will the assessment materials and procedures reveal about children's level of development or academic progress?
- How will the information obtained from the assessment materials and procedures help in making curriculum decisions and/or modifications?
- How will the assessment process help children better understand their own accomplishments?

The answers to these questions should help one understand the level at which the assessment materials and procedures match the curriculum. In the remainder of this chapter, pupil-produced materials will be discussed as one means of addressing the issues related to developmentally appropriate assessment practices.

PORTFOLIO ASSESSMENT

The National Association for the Education of Young Children (Bredekamp & Rosegrant, 1992) defines assessment as "the process of observing, recording, and otherwise documenting the work that children do and how they do it, as a basis for a variety of educational decisions that affect the child" (p. 10).

As has been stated previously, one way in which early childhood professionals have responded to the need for an assessment process that fits within the paradigm of developmentally appropriate practice, and for a view of assessment data as useful information for educational decision making, has been to use pupil-produced products as the basis for assessing children. Out of this movement grew the need for a device that would enable teachers to systematically collect and organize materials that were deemed useful in describing the progress that children were making, both developmentally and academically. Portfolios became the answer.

According to Vavrus (1990), portfolios are a systematic and organized collection of the work that children do as they are engaged in classroom activities that reflect curriculum goals, content, and strategies. It should be noted that portfolios are not, in and of themselves, an assessment tool. Rather, they provide a convenient way to organize and store the information that is gathered about children (Gullo, 1994).

Purposes of a Portfolio

Portfolios provide a way for early childhood professionals to look at children's strengths in their developmental and learning processes. Portfolios also provide a means for targeting those areas of development and achievement where there is a need for support. According to Shanklin and Conrad (1991), portfolios are the means by which educational professionals become empowered as decision makers who then are able to determine what information is important to collect, what type of analysis protocol is appropriate, how the information resulting from the analyses will be used for decision making and curriculum modification, and how the information will be shared with others.

The information about children's developmental status and educational achievement found in portfolios has many uses for the early childhood educator (Nall, 1994; Shepard, 1989). In addition, many benefits for teachers, children, and families result from this method of assessment. It is difficult to differentiate the uses from the benefits, in that often the way in which teachers use the information contained in portfolios *is* the benefit. A number of these uses/benefits are discussed below.

Focus on Change. The information gathered for the portfolio, mainly in the form of pupil-produced products, allows one to focus on the changes in development and achievement that occur in children over time. By examining these products, teachers are able to chart children's progress in the curriculum. The information gathered as part of the portfolio permits teachers to focus both on children's developmental and educational processes as well as on products. For example, the art that children produce provides an effective medium for noting and documenting change in children. Like no other academic activity, art can be viewed as a reflection of the child's development and immediate environment. As such, creative art experiences that are focused on the child's interests and developmental capabilities provide teachers with valuable assessment information. Changes in children's conceptualization of the world often are represented through their art. Their use of form, perspective taking, and color is mirrored in their art as well. Less obviously, children's representational thinking ability and understanding of part–whole relationships also are reflected. From a maturational change perspective, one can tell much about children's fine motor ability from their artwork. Maturational changes can be assessed and documented in their ability to grasp; to make steady, controlled marks; and to make coordinated figures.

Focus on Individualization. The information contained in portfolios, when used properly, permits teachers to compare children's progress against themselves. As such, it focuses on the individual child, rather than on groups of children. Children's progress is measured against their own rate of acquisition and development of knowledge and skills. This information can be used to make appropriate modifications in the curriculum in response to children's strengths and needs. Because the focus is on the individual child, collecting pupil-produced products as a means of documenting developmental and academic progress does not rely on the "one chance" opportunity for children to demonstrate competence. Rather, information is collected on a regular basis, and often. Teachers thus have many opportunities to observe and record children's behaviors in multiple contexts. This improves both the reliability and validity of the observations and better ensures that what is observed reflects accurately the child's capabilities.

Focus on Curriculum. As was stated previously, it is important that assessment closely reflect curriculum content and strategies. Using pupil-produced products as assessment tools provides such a match. The resulting information is, therefore, relevant for further curriculum development and modification. When used appropriately, the materials contained in the portfolio provide a concrete and systematic means for modification of the curriculum. This serves two purposes. It not only supports the individual needs of the child, but helps teachers recognize more generally "what works" and "what doesn't work" in the curriculum itself. In addition, when pupil-produced products are collected for assessment purposes, the process of curriculum implementation is not interrupted. According to Maness (1992), teachers spend approximately 14 hours each year in preparing their students to take standardized tests, 26 hours in reading tests, and 18 hours in preparing teacher-made assessment measures.

Focus on Reflection. By participating in the process of collecting information to include in portfolios, teachers and children increase the opportunity to reflect on those things that they contribute to the teaching–learning process. To the extent that teachers encourage children to select their "best" work to include in the portfolio, children become aware of their own accomplishments. As this process is achieved, teachers gain the needed insights into how children view their own competencies. In observing and discussing with individual children, teachers can reflect on ways in which the curriculum serves the needs of the children in individual ways. When they become full participants in the process of collecting materials for inclusion in portfolios, both teachers and children have increased opportunities for learning about themselves.

Focus on Information Sharing. When pupil-produced materials are used to form the basis of evidence contained in portfolios, they provide concrete and meaningful information to present to parents, other teachers, administrators, and members of the public. This type of material allows the teacher to focus on what progress children have made, by presenting actual examples of children's work. It helps those with whom teachers are trying to communicate understand better the developmental progression of where children started, where they have reached, and where they will go next in the curricular process. It also educates others and gives them a better understanding of what the curriculum is like, how it is implemented, and what it is hoped will be accomplished through the curriculum.

Types of Portfolios

There are three types of portfolios that often are used in the field of early childhood education (Mills, 1989; Vermont Department of Education, 1988, 1989). The first type of portfolio is called the "works in progress" portfolio. It contains stories, artwork, problem-solving examples, and the like, that children are working on currently. Depending on the types of work collected and the frequency with which it is collected, this type of portfolio can become unmanageable within a short time. This type of portfolio potentially can contain all of the work that the child is doing and because of its "richness" soon can lose its potential for assessment.

The second type of portfolio is called the "current year" portfolio. This portfolio contains those particular selections of work that the teacher and the child have mutually agreed upon and that meet certain criteria. These are the pupil products that are analyzed by teachers in order to elucidate children's levels of accomplishments. Doing this gives teachers a better understanding of how to structure or restructure the curriculum for the child's next step.

The third type of portfolio is called the "permanent portfolio." The examples of pupil products contained herein are highly selective. This portfolio will accompany the child to his or her next class. While the number of examples of children's work contained in the "permanent portfolio" needs to be limited, the products should, at the same time, provide the receiving teacher with a clear understanding of the child's developmental and academic accomplishments.

Contents of a Portfolio

While there are many types of items that can be selected to be included in a child's portfolio, the items should reflect work that the child does naturally as part of the curriculum. As will be seen, at times it is not possible to include the "actual" product, as in the case of a block construction. In these cases other appropriate means should be used that represent the child's work.

Samples of Children's Work. According to Meisels and Steele (1991), actual examples of children's work should constitute the major contents of a portfolio. These examples may take different forms and include such things as writing samples, artwork, mathematical calculations, and photographs of children's projects. It is important that the work samples be dated so that progress can be documented. Attempts should be made to include samples from the beginning, middle, and end of the year. Teachers also should take great care to ensure that the samples are representative of the many types of opportunities that are available to the child in the classroom. In addition, every effort should be made to include samples that represent efforts that take place in multiple contexts. Work representing all areas of the curriculum should be included in the portfolio. It is easy to overrepresent those areas that are paper-and-pencil type tasks. Some of the work that is included in the portfolio should be chosen by the teacher, and some of the work should be selected by the child.

There are both advantages and disadvantages in using examples of children's actual work. According to Cryan (1986), children's actual work provides the early childhood professional with real and direct, rather than contrived or extrapolated, evidence of children's progress. In addition, if the samples are collected and dated, as suggested above, they can be interpreted and used later by individuals other than the teacher who collected the work.

According to Decker and Decker (1990), there are also some potential disadvantages in using children's actual work for assessment purposes. Storage is one potential disadvantage, as was addressed earlier. Given the number of children in a classroom, multiplied by the number of samples of work collected as representative, the amount of material to be stored could become staggering. One potential solution to this dilemma would be to use advanced, but existing, technology, such as computer scanners (Gullo, 1994). In this manner, pictures, writing samples, and examples of problems can be scanned and kept on a disk until a printed copy is needed.

Another potential disadvantage to using children's actual work is that it is difficult to know how many samples, or which samples, are truly representative of the child and his or her capabilities and potential. The potential disadvantages notwithstanding, the advantages of using children's work outweigh them.

Anecdotal Records. As was mentioned above, at times it is not appropriate to include the child's "actual" work. At these times it may be necessary to include a description of the work, especially if the work is deemed significant in documenting developmental or academic progress. One approach would be to use an anecdotal record to document this information. An anecdotal record is a brief, narrative description of an event. Anecdotal records should be used especially if no other means are available to document and understand an event (Boehm & Weinberg, 1987). Events such as a problem-solving process or a social interaction that takes place during an activity would be appropriately documented using an anecdotal record. Chapter 6 of this volume provides more in-depth discussion of observational techniques used for evaluation and assessment. As with other examples of children's work, anecdotal records should be dated so that a progression of development or academic accomplishments can be noted.

Curriculum Checklists. Checklists can be used to document a sequenced series of behaviors or skills that often are linked directly to educational or developmental goals (Gullo, 1994). According to Cryan (1986), a variety of descriptive characteristics can be included on checklists. A checklist might include behavioral categories such as social-emotional behaviors, interest, specific academic skills, specific knowledge, or specific concepts. Checklists can either describe behaviors of a general nature, such as problem-solving skills, social skills, critical thinking skills, or attitudinal characteristics, or describe specific skills such as word attack skills, steps in performing a science experiment, or concepts required to perform mathematical operations. If designed and used appropriately, checklists can serve as a guide for understanding children's development and academic progress, as well as for developing curriculum.

Other Items. Portfolios also may include other items that represent the actual work that children do. These include audiotapes, videotapes, reading logs, conference records, and test results. These items will add to the richness of the information that can be obtained from the examples of children's work described previously.

Criteria for Inclusion

When deciding which examples of children's work should be included in the portfolio, teachers should consider a number of criteria (Shanklin & Conrad, 1991). Teachers should ask themselves the following three questions:

1. What will the samples of children's work tell me about their level of development and/or academic progress?
2. How will the information obtained from the samples of children's work help me make decisions about curriculum development, individualization, and modification?
3. How does the actual process of collecting the samples of children's work assist children in understanding their own developmental and/or academic accomplishments?

Lastly, much has been written about quality standards for portfolios. Paulson, Paulson, and Meyer (1991) suggest a number of principles to consider when developing a portfolio system that includes the systematic collecting of children's work.

First, the process of selection of work examples should provide both the children and the teachers with the opportunity to learn something about the learning process. Through the process of selection, both are required to reflect about how the work demonstrates what has been learned, developed, or achieved.

Second, children should be encouraged to be active participants in the process of their own learning. As such, portfolios should be done with children, rather than done for children. Through the participation process, children are taught to value their work and themselves.

Third, portfolios should reflect the manner in which children's development and academic accomplishments progress over time. Rather than simply a listing or collection of work and tests, the portfolio should contain a wide array of work samples that reflect the progress that is being made by the child.

Fourth, to be effective and useful for instruction and curriculum development, portfolios should have some type of structure. A rationale, goals, standards, and a systematized procedure for selecting and collecting work samples should be considered an integral part of that structure.

Finally, the portfolio's function may change from the beginning to the end of the academic experience. The work collected over that time span to measure developmental change and academic progress may differ from the work that is passed on to the next teacher as the best evidence of change over time.

ASSESSMENT OF CHILDREN'S ACTIVE ENGAGEMENT IN THE CURRICULUM

While the focus of this chapter has been primarily on the tangible products that children produce as they are actively engaged in curricular activities, one cannot dismiss the activity itself as being both a pupil-produced product as well as a useful tool in the assessment process. Krechevsky (1991) describes one such model of assessment in Project Spectrum. Gardner's (1983) theory of multiple intelligences is the theory upon which Project Spectrum is built. The strategy used is the recognition that there is potential variation in all children and in all activities. Project Spectrum's goal is to identify children's domain-specific strengths in areas not necessarily addressed in traditional modes of assessment.

There are a number of features of Project Spectrum that are consistent with the characteristics of developmentally appropriate practice in curriculum and assessment development that have been described earlier in this chapter. In Project Spectrum the curriculum and assessment procedures become integrated. As was stated earlier, developmentally appropriate early childhood practices view the relationship between curriculum and assessment as transactional. That is, each simultaneously affects the other. By using activities embedded within the curriculum as a means to assess, and using the outcome of the assessment as a method to modify the curriculum, this relationship becomes actualized.

Procedures used in Project Spectrum embed assessment into real-world activities that are meaningful and relevant to children. By putting the problem-solving activity into a context for which children have a referent in reality, one is more likely to maintain the interest and motivation necessary to obtain valid and reliable assessment information.

The procedures used in Project Spectrum are thought to be intelligence fair. That is, they do not rely solely or primarily on logical thinking and language. The curriculum, and thus the assessment procedures, is sensitive to the multiple modes that children use to acquire and construct knowledge.

Finally, the procedures used in Project Spectrum identify and emphasize children's strengths. Rather than focus on what children do not know and cannot do, they focus on what children can do and do know. This process allows one to approach assessment and subsequent curriculum development from a positive vantage point. The modus operandi for Project Spectrum, as it should be in all early education settings, is that all children can learn.

ASSESSMENT ISSUES RELATED TO
USING PUPIL-PRODUCED PRODUCTS

While using pupil-produced products is not a panacea that will end all of the problems associated with assessment in early childhood education, it is a means for diminishing them. There are a number of issues that can be identified related to using pupil-produced products, or a contextualized form of assessment, that merit consideration.

First, because there is a lack of consistency in curriculum content and implementation from classroom to classroom and school to school, it is often difficult to determine benchmarks for academic success using a contextualized approach to assessment. This is especially true if assessment criteria are subjective and not uniformly applied from child to child or situation to situation.

Second, if a child is assessed using a contextualized approach, how generalizable is the information gathered for determining the extent to which the child has mastered, or not mastered, the skills, concepts, or processes being assessed?

Third, age and developmental factors also must be taken into consideration when using a pupil-product approach to assessment, since much of the assessment findings are subject to interpretation. While it seems as though a contextualized assessment approach is appropriate for children at the prekindergarten level and above, it is often difficult to determine or interpret the behavioral intentionality of younger children, especially those who are prelinguistic.

Finally, the proverbial, "don't throw the baby out with the bath water," applies here. One should not think of contextualized assessment approaches as doing away with the necessity for more formal, structured, or standardized assessment. In the hands of skilled clinicians, these tools are reliable, are valid, and add to the information gathered using other assessment approaches.

As has been stated repeatedly, the purpose of any assessment is to help teachers gain a better understanding of children's developmental and academic accomplishments so that curriculum experiences can be modified to meet their needs. While using pupil-produced products will not do away with the necessity for other forms of assessment, it does provide teachers with an assessment tool that is child centered and highly personalized—a tool that is often overlooked.

REFERENCES

Apple, M., & King, N. (1978). What do schools teach? In G. Willis (Ed.), *Qualitative education: Concepts and cases in curriculum criticism*. Berkeley: McCutchan.

Bergan, J., & Feld, J. K. (1993). Developmental assessment: New directions. *Young Children, 48*(5), 41–47.

Boehm, A. E., & Weinberg, R. A. (1987). *The classroom observer: Developing observation skills in early childhood settings*. New York: Teachers College Press.

Bredekamp, S. (1987). *Developmentally appropriate practice in early childhood programs serving children from birth through age 8*. Washington, DC: National Association for the Education of Young Children.

Bredekamp, S., & Rosegrant, T. (1992). *Reaching potentials: Appropriate curriculum and assessment for young children* (Vol. 1). Washington, DC: National Association for the Education of Young Children.

Cryan, J. R. (1986). Evaluation: Plague or promise? *Childhood Education, 62*, 344–350.

Decker, C. A., & Decker, J. R. (1990). *Planning and administering early childhood programs.* Columbus, OH: Merrill.

Gardner, H. (1983). *Frames of mind: The theory of multiple intelligences.* New York: Basic Books.

Gullo, D. F. (1992). *Developmentally appropriate teaching in early childhood education: Curriculum, implementation, evaluation.* Washington, DC: National Education Association.

Gullo, D. F. (1994). *Understanding assessment and evaluation in early childhood education.* New York: Teachers College Press.

Gullo, D. F. (1995). Art in the curriculum: Opportunities for child-centered assessment. *Teaching PreK–8, 25*(6), 14.

Gullo, D. F., & Ambrose, R. P. (1987). Perceived competence and social acceptance in kindergarten: Its relationship to academic performance. *Journal of Educational Research, 8*(1), 28–32.

Hills, T. W. (1993). Assessment in context: Teachers and children at work. *Young Children, 48*(5), 20–28.

Krechevsky, M. (1991). Project spectrum: An innovative assessment alternative. *Educational Leadership, 49*(6), 43–48.

Maness, B. J. (1992). Assessment in early childhood education. *Kappa Delta Pi Record, 28*(3), 77–79.

Meisels, S. J. (1987). Uses and abuses of developmental screening and school readiness testing. *Young Children, 42*(4–6), 68–73.

Meisels, S. J. (1989). High stakes testing in kindergarten. *Educational Leadership, 46*(7), 16–22.

Meisels, S. J. (1992). *The Work Sampling System: An overview.* Ann Arbor: University of Michigan.

Meisels, S. J. (1993). Remaking classroom assessment with the work sampling system. *Young Children, 48*(5), 34–40.

Meisels, S. J., & Steele, D. M. (1991). *The early childhood portfolio collection process.* Ann Arbor: University of Michigan, Center for Human Growth and Development.

Mills, R. (1989). Portfolios capture rich array of student performance. *The School Administrator, 47*(10), 8–11.

Nall, S. W. (1994). Assessment through portfolios in the all-day kindergarten. *National All-Day Kindergarten Network Newsletter, 4*(1), 1,3.

National Association for the Education of Young Children. (1988). NAEYC position statement on standardized testing of young children 3 through 8 years of age. *Young Children, 43*(3), 42–47.

National Commission on Testing and Public Policy. (1990). *From gatekeeper to gateway: Transforming testing in America.* Chestnut Hill, MA: Author.

Paulson, F. L., Paulson, P., & Meyer, C. (1991). What makes a portfolio? *Educational Leadership, 49*, 60–63.

Shanklin, N., & Conrad, L. (1991). *Portfolios: A new way to assess student growth.* Denver: Colorado Council of the International Reading Association.

Shepard, L. (1989). Why we need better assessment. *Educational Leadership, 46*(7), 4–9.

Stipek, D. J. (1981). Children's perceptions of their own and their classmates' ability. *Journal of Educational Psychology, 73,* 404–410.

U.S. Department of Education. (1991). *America 2000: An educational strategy source book.* Washington, DC: Author.

Uphoff, J., & Gilmore, J. E. (1986). *Summer children: Ready or not for school.* Middletown, OH: J & J Publishing.

Vavrus, L. (1990, August). Putting portfolios to the test. *Instructor,* pp. 48–51.

Vermont Department of Education. (1988). *Working together to show results: An approach to school accountability for Vermont.* Montpelier: Author.

Vermont Department of Education. (1989). *Vermont writing assessment: The portfolio.* Montpelier: Author.

CHAPTER 8

Assessing Social Competence in Early Childhood

Sally Atkins-Burnett, Julie Nicholson, and Samuel J. Meisels

Social competence is a major factor in children's ability to enjoy and benefit from school experiences. The importance of social competence for children's achievement and success in school renders it a critical construct for both teachers and researchers to understand. The objective of this chapter is to construct a working definition of social competence, briefly describe its importance for young children, and summarize the various instruments used to measure this construct throughout the early childhood years.

DEFINING SOCIAL COMPETENCE

According to Rubin and Rose-Krasnor (1992), definitions of social competence are as plentiful as researchers examining this aspect of personal and social development. Typically, these definitions incorporate social skills, attainment of social goals, maintenance of interpersonal relationships, and ability to make appropriate social judgments and act accordingly (also known as social problem solving). For example, Siperstein (1992) refers to social competence as the "marriage of social knowledge and social action" (p. iv). Schaefer and Edgerton (1983) propose a conceptual model of academic competence, social adjustment, and psychosocial development that integrates social and emotional behavior, motivation, approaches to learning, and cognition. Reschly and Gresham (1981) propose that social competence comprises both adaptive behavior (independent functioning skills, physical development, academic competencies, and language development) and social skills (interpersonal behaviors, self-related behaviors, and task-related behaviors). Social competence also has been examined in relation to outcomes (success in social roles), and to behavioral traits that are thought to be predictive of positive social behavior (Greenspan & Granfield, 1992).

In considering the issue of assessing social competencies, Chandler and Chapman (1991) question whether one should consider competencies as "private" and "intrapsychic" or as residing somewhere in the space between individuals, tasks, and contexts. Social competence, by its very nature, involves other individuals. Assessment of social competence must take into account the judgments of significant individuals in the child's social milieu. This is commonly referred to as social validity (Gresham, 1983, 1986). The most significant individuals in a child's life are peers, parents, and teachers, and many assessments of social competence include information from one or more of these sources.

For the purposes of this chapter, social competence is defined as *those skills and behaviors of a child that lead to positive social outcomes with the individuals residing in a given setting and that avoid socially unacceptable responses*. Following Strayhorn and Strain (1986), three "broad-band competencies" are described as paramount for achieving social competence.

1. Kindness, cooperation, and appropriate compliance (rather than hostile and defiant behavior)
2. Appropriate extroversion, that is, interest expressed in people and things, and active socialization rather than interactions that are withdrawn and timid
3. Pragmatic language abilities, that is, the social aspects of communication such as interpreting nonverbal cues, understanding and using humor, initiating and responding appropriately to overtures, and referential communication.

Assessment of social competence requires that attention be devoted to such intraindividual attributes as those listed above, as well as to contextual factors that support or influence individual competencies. It is essential to focus not only on the child's actions and behaviors, but also on his or her interactions with others and the judgments of those in the child's setting who are familiar with the child and the norms of the situation.

RESEARCH DESCRIBING THE
IMPORTANCE OF SOCIAL COMPETENCE

Social competence and the skills that contribute to that competence have been widely researched. Social skills distinguish between students in kindergarten through grade 3 whom teachers rate globally as high or low on adjustment (McConnell, Strain, Kerr, Stagg, Lenkner, & Lambert, 1984). They are significant predictors of academic achievement, kindergarten through grade 6 (Clark, Gresham, & Elliott, 1985; Reschly, Gresham, & Graham-Clay, 1985; Swartz & Walker, 1984). One study of fifth graders found teacher ratings of social skills to be the best predictor of future academic achievement, school adjustment, and delinquency in the next 3-year period (Walker, Stieber, & Eisert, 1991).

Skills that are positively correlated with popular sociometric ratings are considered important for social competence (Guralnick, 1986; Hartup, 1983). Among these are

- Ability to initiate and respond to social overtures, use peers as resources, and display appropriate affection, friendliness, sociability, leadership capabilities
- Possession of moderately high self-esteem, intellectual ability, academic performance
- Achievement of success experiences.

Overall, cooperation, communication, social participation, and validating/ supporting others are considered important predictors of peer acceptance (Oden & Asher, 1977).

In contrast, deficient social skills and behavior problems, particularly aggressive behaviors, correlate with children who are socially unpopular (Frentz, Gresham, & Elliott, 1991; Gottman, Gonso, & Rasmussen, 1975; LaGreca & Santogrossi, 1980; Oden & Asher, 1977). Specific social behaviors found to be negatively related to peer acceptance are

- Devious, aversive reactions (Hartup, 1983; Roff, Sells, & Golden, 1972)
- Depressed mood (Asher, 1990; Boivin, Poulin, & Vitaro, 1994)
- Withdrawal (Boivin, Poulin, & Vitaro, 1994; Rubin, LeMare, & Lollis, 1990)
- Aggression and disruptedness (Asher, 1990; Boivin, Poulin, & Vitaro, 1994; Dodge, 1980; Dodge & Frame, 1982; Volling, MacKinnon-Lewis, Rabiner, & Baradaran, 1993).

Although aggression is highly associated with peer rejection, it also is found with very popular children, but it is offset by the presence of socially competent behaviors (Volling et al., 1993). In combination with decreased prosocial and cooperative behaviors, aggression is predictive of peer rejection (Dodge, 1983; Parkhurst & Asher, 1992; Volling et al., 1993). Rejected children, whether aggressive or withdrawn, differ from nonrejected peers in terms of their inability to meet peer expectations of prosocial behaviors, teacher expectations of classroom behaviors, and their frequency of reactive aggression.

Lack of social skills correlates with several negative outcomes, including

- Increased school dropout rates (Ullman, 1957)
- Adolescent and adult mental health problems (Cowen, Pederson, Babigian, Izzo, & Trost, 1973; Kupersmidt, Coie, & Dodge, 1990; Rubin & Ross, 1988)
- Juvenile delinquency (Hartup, 1983; Roff, Sells, & Golden, 1972)
- Dishonorable discharge from military service (Roff, Sells, & Golden, 1972).

Several studies demonstrated that conduct problems persist over time into adulthood (Strayhorn & Strain, 1986). Apathy/withdrawal scores in preschool predict scores in the fourth grade (r = .28) (Kohn, 1977). Moreover, in a 4-year longitudinal study, attention problems and social rejection in kindergarten predicted later learning disabilities (Vaughn, Zaragoza, Hogan, & Walker, 1993), while teacher ratings of problem behaviors in the second grade predicted negative outcomes in the fifth grade (Hymel, Rubin, Rowden, & LeMare, 1990). If a child is labeled negatively by peers, negative interactions on the part of peers are more likely, and peers tend to overlook the positive behaviors of the child (Dodge, 1980; Hymel, Wagner, & Butler, 1990).

Some correlates of peer acceptance/rejection are not directly related to behavior. For example, physical attractiveness has a positive relationship with acceptance (Hartup, 1983; McConnell & Odom, 1986; Roff et al., 1972), unusual names have a negative relationship (Hartup, 1983; McConnell & Odom, 1986; Roff et al., 1972), birth order has a positive relationship (youngest are more popular) (Roff et al., 1972), familiarity has positive relationship (Hartup, 1983; Guralnick, 1986; Howes, 1988; Ladd, Price, & Hart, 1990), and handicapping conditions have a negative relationship (Hartup, 1983). Information about these areas should be obtained in considering whether the social skills practiced by a child will be adequate for a judgment of positive social competence by peers.

Several studies of social competence among children with disabilities also have been completed. Swanson and Malone (1992) conducted a meta-analysis of 39 studies that dealt with social skills and learning disabilities. They concluded that learning disabled children clearly have "lower social acceptance than their peers without handicaps" (p. 440). High effect sizes were found for personality problems, immaturity/inadequacy, and task-related behaviors. Poor pragmatic language skills were identified as another possible factor, but only three studies examined this area. Problems in motor coordination and physical activity also were found to correlate with peer ratings and loneliness. These studies defined peer ratings in terms of quality as well as quantity of social relationships (Doan & Scherman, 1987; Hartup, 1983; Hops & Finch, 1985; Page, Frey, Talbert, & Falk, 1992).

MEASURING SOCIAL COMPETENCE

Depending on the conceptualization of social competence, assessment has been undertaken in various ways. As in so many other areas of inquiry, how the behavior is defined determines how the construct is measured (Dodge, Pettit, McClaskey, & Brown, 1986; Gresham & Reschly, 1987). The various methods designed to assess social competence can be organized into two categories, direct and indirect measures.

Direct Measures

Direct measures of social competence include instruments used to collect information through observations or interviews with children. The four main types of direct measures used to evaluate children's social competence include naturalistic and experimental observations, hypothetical problem sets, self-rating scales, and sociometric techniques.

OBSERVATIONS

Some observational measures are conducted in a natural context, while others are conducted within experimental situations (e.g., Stipek, Feiler, Daniels, & Milburn, 1995; Turnure & Zigler, 1964). Naturalistic observations of children's social behaviors have been used to develop an understanding of children's peer relationships, determine appropriate goals for improving social behavior, and assess the outcome of social skills interventions (Honig & McCarron, 1988; LaGreca & Stark, 1986; Strassberg, Dodge, Pettit, & Bates, 1994). Many researchers have utilized naturalistic observational measurements during free play times, particularly when examining prosocial behaviors (e.g., sharing, helping, and cooperation). Aggressive behaviors and levels of play also are used frequently as observational categories. Some examples of the use of structured naturalistic observations with young children are the Bronson Social and Task Skills Profile (Bronson, 1985), Howes' peer play scale for children 1–5 years (Howes & Matheson, 1992), and Howes' adult scale for children younger than 5 years old (Howes & Stewart, 1987).

The Bronson Social and Task Skill Profile (Bronson, 1985) is based on an information processing model that emphasizes the importance of goal orientation and organizational skills. The observation categories record a "child's use of effective strategies for choosing and reaching goals in three areas: use of time in the classroom setting, mastery task activities, and social activities with peers" (Hauser-Cram, Bronson, & Upshur, 1993, p. 485). It has been used with children who are developmentally disabled as well as those who are typically developing. Six 10-minute observations per child are completed by a trained observer. Frequency and duration of both social and mastery variables are recorded during each observation (Bronson, 1994; Hauser-Cram et al., 1993).

Various experimental tasks have been used in observational studies, including behavioral role plays and simulations, mother–child problem-solving situations, and art, puzzle, and block-building tasks. Behavioral role plays and simulations entail creating situations where children are asked to act out or respond to particular parameters, with the investigator observing. However, Gresham (1986) cites seven simulation studies that do not demonstrate validity. The behaviors observed in these simulations do not predict sociometric status nor do they correlate with naturalistic observations of the same behaviors.

In other experimental observations, researchers observe social interaction and emotion regulation during problem-solving tasks. For example, Pianta and his colleagues observed problem-solving situations between mothers and children where the dyads worked together to complete a fine motor and a verbal task (e.g., block building, naming objects in a category) during a 15-minute period (Pianta & Castaldi, 1989; Lothman, Pianta, & Clarson, 1990; Pianta & Caldwell, 1990; Pianta & Nimetz, 1991). Prior to beginning the tasks, the mother is instructed (when the child is not present) to teach the tasks to the child and help the child to perform them correctly. Immediately after the interaction, the researcher completes five-point global ratings on the mother's supportive presence and quality of instruction, the child's reliance on the adult for help, and the child's negativity/anger and affection.

Stipek and colleagues (1995) conducted observations of an experimental situation where individual children were involved in art, puzzle, and block-building tasks. Observers rated each child's level of dependency, preference for challenge, anxiety, and pride in accomplishment. To measure dependency, observers recorded the similarity of the child's art construction to that created by the adult, the child's requests for assistance or for the examiner's opinion or approval, the number of times the child looked at the adult's creation or puzzle, and whether the child waited for the adult to begin before starting the puzzle task. Preference for challenge was measured by showing children cards with increasing numbers of objects to be counted or added, and by allowing children a choice of completing a puzzle that they previously had been unable to complete (under a timed condition) or one that they had completed. A child's challenge was determined by whether he or she selected a card with a higher number of items to count or a puzzle that he or she previously had been unable to complete. Anxiety ratings were completed as each child engaged in the various tasks. Ratings for pride in accomplishment were based on whether the child smiled upon completing the puzzle or verbally drew the examiner's attention to his or her completed puzzle. However, cultural differences in displays of emotion may make this rating category somewhat problematic, particularly among children for whom it may be inappropriate to draw attention to personal accomplishments.

Strengths. Naturalistic observations can be repeated frequently, and when observations are performed by someone outside the social milieu, subjective bias is minimized. They are also sensitive to treatment effects (Gresham & Nagle, 1980; LaGreca & Stark, 1986). Observations of experimental tasks are less costly than naturalistic observations and may be completed in a single time period. They are also useful for observing behaviors that may occur with low frequency in natural settings.

Concerns. Two concerns that face observational studies are cost and interrater reliability. Even when adequate interrater reliability has been achieved at the outset, there is potential for observer drift (i.e., differences in how raters interpret behaviors over time). Training observers, completing multiple observations, and arranging the time for coding the data contribute to the high cost of this type of measure. In an experimental setting, validity is affected by the unfamiliar adult and unfamiliar situations. In addition, cultural differences among children render some measures inappropriate for certain populations.

In order to obtain valid assessments of behavior, multiple observations in multiple settings may be necessary. For example, Gibb and Jacobson (1988, cited in Foster, Inderbitzen, & Nangle, 1993) found that unpopular boys utilized different entry strategies for cooperative and competitive tasks and needed to be observed on different occasions. Extended time for observations is also necessary. When examining family interaction, Patterson (1982, cited in Foster et al., 1993) found that 60–100 minutes collected over three to five sessions was the absolute minimum needed to evaluate performance.

Observers generally code the frequency of behaviors when using these measures. However, it may be the quality of the behavior (e.g., the type of eye contact) rather than the frequency that is important for social competence. In addition, the presence of an observer (or video equipment) may alter the child's responses. Finally, some behaviors that influence peer relationships may occur only away from adult surveillance (Foster et al., 1993).

HYPOTHETICAL PROBLEM SETS

Social problem-solving or hypothetical problem sets have been used in studies of social cognition. The child is presented with hypothetical dilemmas and asked to interpret a peer's intentions (attribution measures) or to generate and evaluate solutions to social problems. These measures answer the question, "Does the child know what skill should be used and can the child make social judgments?" Social problem-solving sets do not tell how often (or whether) the child actually uses these skills. Among children with poor social ratings, Bandura (1977) makes the distinction between skill deficits, performance deficits, self-control skill deficits, and self-control performance deficits. Social problem-solving sets assess only skill deficits. Presentation of the hypothetical dilemmas may be verbal, videotaped, or by using enactments (e.g., with puppets).

Mize and colleagues used hypothetical problem sets in studies with preschoolers. With preschoolers from low socioeconomic status (SES) families, the friendliness of the children's initial responses during enactments with puppets was more predictive of their peer group acceptance and teachers' ratings of social competence than the children's verbal scores on the Preschool Interpersonal Problem-Solving Test (Mize & Ladd, 1988). For middle-income preschoolers, the friendliness of their initial verbal responses with the puppets and the number of responses given during the enactment situation were the strongest predictors of their observed behavior and teacher ratings of their aggression and friendliness (Mize & Cox, 1990).

In another study, Hubbard and Cillessen (1993) asked boys aged 5–7 years (n = 220) to generate responses to hypothetical situations presented in a story format. The problems included group entry, object loss or damage, object conflict, and activity conflict. Results were coded according to use of social strategies (25 codes) and compared with sociometric classifications. Popular boys generated more strategies in the compromise/negotiate and wait/hover categories and had fewer aggressive responses than average boys. Rejected boys also could be differentiated from average boys according to their strategy use.

Dodge and his colleagues have published a large body of work using hypothetical measures in examining his social-information processing model. Dodge's model outlines five steps involved in social problem solving: encoding social cues; interpreting the cues; generating potential responses; deciding on the response and evaluating consequences; and enacting the chosen response. Variation in these processing steps has shown predictable variation in behavior (and peer status) across several studies (Crick & Dodge, 1994; Dodge, 1993; Dodge & Crick, 1990; Dodge & Feldman, 1990; Lochman & Dodge, 1994).

Dodge (personal communication, 1995) recommends three important areas to investigate in hypothetical problem sets with young children: attribution issues, responses to interpersonal dilemmas, and evaluations of the effectiveness of proposed solutions to interpersonal problems. When selecting which type of hypothetical dilemmas to use, it is important to consider the different types of information each focus area provides.

- *Attribution issues* concern the child's understanding of social cues and whether the child makes hostile or benign attributions in ambiguous situations. Dodge and his colleagues have found no developmental trends in this area.
- *Responses generated to interpersonal dilemmas* are examined for the appropriateness of the responses generated (coded as aggressive, nonaggressive/inept, or competent) and the number of solutions a child is able to generate (up to 10). Children's competence in this area increases with age.
- *Evaluation of effectiveness of solutions to interpersonal problems* is investigated by presenting different solutions to children and having them tell the examiner whether they believe these are good or poor solutions to the problems and the reasons why. Dodge has found some developmental trends in this area, but they are unreliable until the third grade or higher.

In measuring these three areas, Dodge and colleagues used a combination of videotaped scenarios and hypothetical stories. The videotaped vignettes (n = 24) were used to assess children's ability to attend to and encode social cues, generate a single response to hypothetical problems, and evaluate the effectiveness of the responses proposed by the administrator. The hypothetical stories (n = 8) were used to assess hostile/benign attribution and solution generation. Children were asked why a certain situation occurred and then asked to generate as many behavioral solutions as possible (up to 10). The mean number of solutions per problem was computed.

Dodge and associates (Dodge, Pettit, & Bates, 1994; Weiss, Dodge, Bates, & Pettit, 1992) administered these social cognitive measures to young children from a variety of ethnic groups and from homes with a wide range in SES (Hollingshead four-factor index ranged from 14–66 out of the possible range of 8–66). In the first two cohorts (n = 309 and n = 275), children with one or more ratings of aggression (as measured by peer and teacher reports) showed after a 6-month period "less attention to relevant cues, greater hostile attributional biases, a tendency to generate aggressive responses to hypothetical problems, and positive evaluations of the likely outcomes of aggressing" (Weiss et al., 1992).

Strengths. Some hypothetical problem sets have shown sensitivity to children's development in their problem-solving abilities over time. Children's responses to hypothetical dilemmas also may provide helpful information for researchers interested in interpreting children's scores on more global behavior rating measures. Dodge's hypothetical measures show a significant ability to discriminate children with aggressive problem behaviors. Given the current concern with the level of violence in schools, this measure could add to an understanding of its prevalence in a given area.

Concerns. The time needed for administration and scoring of children's responses to the hypothetical problem sets is not described within the various studies using these measures. While great attention was paid to balancing gender and ethnicity in the Dodge videotaped segments, little attention was paid to either of these issues in the illustrations that accompanied the hypothetical stories. Because each child is asked to "imagine this is you," in the various hypothetical stories, it is important that all children can identify with the illustrations presented. Using multiple sets of illustrations is one way to address this concern.

Finally, receptive language abilities may confound the results of social cognitive measures. Reliance on verbal hypothetical situations may reduce the applicability of these procedures to some populations, for example, preschool children or individuals with poor listening comprehension or limited cognitive and language ability.

SELF-RATING SCALES

Self-rating scales enable children to respond to varied stimuli (typically paper-and-pencil questionnaires) with judgments concerning specific aspects of their development. The topics addressed within self-rating scales range; however, they often focus on children's perceptions of self-concept, problems in school, sense of well-being, or school achievement. Three commonly used self-rating scales are reviewed below.

The Pictorial Scale of Perceived Competence and Social Acceptance for Young Children (Harter & Pike, 1984) is a self-rating scale that taps children's perception of their cognitive competence, physical competence, peer acceptance, and maternal acceptance. Children respond by first pointing to pictures that they believe are most like them and then indicate degree of similarity. A teacher rating scale is available that parallels the child instrument by documenting the teacher's perception of the child in the same areas.

This instrument has been used in many studies (e.g., Howes & Matheson, 1992) and allows for comparison with other samples. It fills a gap in the assessment realm by rating children's judgments about themselves in specified domains. Harter (1990) reports that for children younger than age 8, cognitive and physical competence combine into one factor, and social acceptance and conduct items combine into a second factor. Young children have difficulty differentiating discrete areas of self-concept because of their limited understanding of specific concepts such as self-worth (Harter, 1990). Although this measure reports on children's judgments about self, it does not give a clear picture of how these areas may differentially influence children's self-esteem. In addition, some difficulty is reported with primary age children's understanding of the task when this instrument is used with children with learning problems (E. Forman, personal communication).

The Loneliness and Social Dissatisfaction Questionnaire (LSDQ) (Asher, Hymel, & Renshaw, 1984; Asher & Wheeler, 1985; Cassidy & Asher, 1992) is a self-rating scale consisting of 16 questions related to children's feelings of social adequacy (e.g., "Is it easy for you to make new friends at school?"), loneliness (e.g., "Do you feel alone at school?"), and subjective estimations of peer status (e.g., "Do the kids at school like you?"). In addition, there are eight "filler" items focusing on children's hobbies and preferred activities (e.g., "Do you like playing card games?"). Early versions of this instrument required children to respond to a five-point Likert scale. The current adaptation asks children to respond to each question with a "yes," "no," or "sometimes." Factor analysis reveals that the items load on a single factor with low to moderate correlations (.25 to .58).

The LSDQ has been used in conjunction with peer sociometrics with elementary age children (K–6). The self-report of loneliness discriminated the children with low peer acceptance (i.e., those who were rejected by their peers). A subscale of three items from this instrument ("Do you feel left out of things at school?"; "Do you feel alone at school?"; "Are you lonely at school?") obtained the same relationship with sociometric status as did the full scale. Therefore, these questions might be useful in combination with other measures. The LSDQ has been used only with small samples, and test–retest reliability has not been demonstrated. In comparison to other measures of social competence, it examines a rather narrow construct.

The Young Children's Feelings About School measure (FAS) (Stipek et al., 1995) is a 16-item, self-report questionnaire designed to measure the effects of different instructional approaches on children's sociomotivational development. This measure is intended to provide information from the child's perspective of his or her enjoyment of and anxiety about school. Children's affect regarding school, particularly anxiety about school, has been associated with attention to task (Stipek & Mason, 1987), intrinsic motivation (Gottfried, 1990), resilience (Werner, 1990), and achievement (Short, 1992). In addition, students' emotional response to school appears to affect teacher reactions and support of the student (Skinner & Belmont, 1993). Studies involving older elementary age children have found that students' perception of classroom climate is related to subsequent achievement (Haertel, Walberg, & Haertel, 1979). Studies using the FAS suggest it is sensitive to differences in observational measures of the quality of child care and the nature of instruction (i.e., didactic, skills-based approaches vs. child-centered methods) (C. Howes, personal communication, 1994; Stipek et al., 1995).

Children are asked to respond by pointing to one of five schematic drawings. The drawings include faces ranging from an extreme frown to an extreme smile, or five circles of increasing size. The average time for administration is 10 minutes. One concern relates to the stimulus items, which include a sketch of a teacher who is female and the faces of children who all appear to be Caucasian. Although Stipek and colleagues (1995) reported no difficulties in using the instrument with children of various ethnic groups, the lack of diversity represented in the faces on the instrument may be problematic. When asked to select the face that is most like them, young children should be able to identify easily with the pictures. In addition, the FAS is reported as sensitive to marked differences in teaching style (classrooms that could not be clearly categorized as didactic/skills based or child centered/constructivist were eliminated from the study), although there is no indication of its sensitivity to more subtle differences in instruction.

Strengths. Self-report measures provide an important perspective related to the assessment of a child's social competence—the child's own perception of his or her classroom context or social skills. Understanding children's perceptions related to their social skills may provide useful information for individuals interested in interpreting children's scores on behavior report measures and/or designing intervention programs targeting children's social skills.

Concerns. Young children have difficulty understanding and differentiating some of the concepts measured by self-report instruments. Therefore, young children provide ratings for global perceptions without making fine distinctions between concepts. In addition, children may project what they desire instead of reporting their actual perceptions.

SOCIOMETRIC TECHNIQUES

Sociometric techniques include peer nominations, peer ratings, peer rankings, and popularity ratings by teachers. These methods present "snapshots" of interactions. More information is necessary in order to obtain a functional assessment of behaviors. Peer nominations ask children to name a number of children (usually three) whom they like (positive nominations) and three whom they do not like (negative nominations). Parents and teachers often object to negative nominations because of concern about possible negative side effects, but research does not substantiate these fears. Children also may be asked to nominate peers with whom they would like to play (or take with them on a vacation, etc.) or who possess certain attributes or behaviors (e.g., "shares a lot," "is mean," "gets angry easily").

One peer nomination technique asks children to identify peers who fill a social role or exhibit a certain attribute. For example, a child might be asked to nominate three peers who could best be described as angry, shy, or helpful (Eisenberg, McCreath, & Ahn, 1988; Volling et al., 1993). Some standardized measures using this format for peer evaluation include the Class Play (Bower, 1960), the revised Class Play (Masten, Morison, & Pelligrini, 1985), and the Pupil Evaluation Inventory (Pekarik, Prinz, Liebert, Weintraub, & Neale, 1976). In the Class Play procedure, children are asked to nominate peers who would best fill certain roles in a hypothetical play. Half the roles are negative, and half are positive. This approach is useful for assessing the behavioral characteristics of some children, but is not useful with children under the age of 8 because of their undifferentiated social perceptions. The Class Play procedure has been used most often with children 9–12 years old.

In peer rating scales, students are given a class roster and asked to rate from 1–5 how much they like each peer. With younger children, photographs are used, and they choose between a sad face, neutral face, and happy face for each classmate ("don't like," "kinda like," and "like a lot"). Young children may have difficulty differentiating social roles and skills of peers, basing their decisions on very visible negative behaviors, such as aggression and frequent disruptions (Coie, Dodge, & Kupersmidt, 1990). Young children also give peers who do well in school higher ratings. As children grow older, their social perceptions become more differentiated and they are more sensitive to interpersonal subtleties. For example, they develop increasing ability to determine peer norms, adjust to the viewpoints and communications of others, interpret interpersonal contexts, and flexibly adapt their behavior to the demands and feedback of a given situation (Bierman & Montminy, 1993).

When sociometric measures are used with young children, each child is first asked to name the photographs of all classmates in order to ensure recognition. Researchers have used pictorial sociometric ratings and nominations with children as young as 3 years of age and have obtained acceptable reliabilities on the children's ratings (Howes, 1988). Howes presented children with pictures of their classmates one at a time and asked to place the pictures in one of three different size bowls (large, medium, or small) to indicate how much they wanted that child as a friend. Peer ratings were computed as the average score each child received using this procedure. Reliabilities for ratings ranged from .76 for 3-year-olds to .84 for 6-year-olds, increasing with age in a linear fashion. Reliabilities for nominations ranged from .54 for 3-year-olds to .77 for 6-year-olds. The high reliabilities in this study may have been due in part to the amount of time the children spent together each day and the stability of their peer groups. Each child had been with the peer group a minimum of 8 months (range 8–60 months).

Vitaro and colleagues (Vitaro, Gagnon, & Tremblay, 1990; Vitaro, Tremblay, Gagnon, & Boivin, 1992; Vitaro, Tremblay, Gagnon, & Pelletier, 1994) have used peer nomination and ratings in a group-administered situation with children as young as kindergarten, employing booklets with photographs of all of the children in the class. They reported "adequate temporal stability" for the children's ratings; however, actual reliabilities were not available. For peer nominations, children were asked to circle the pictures of the children nominated for each category. For the peer ratings, children were asked to place one of three stickers (happy, neutral, or sad face) beneath the photograph of every child in the class to indicate how much they liked each child. This measure had less predictive accuracy than teacher behavior ratings.

Fantuzzo, Manz, and McDermott (1995) administered the Social Skills Rating System–Teacher Form (SSRS) (Gresham & Elliott, 1990) and the Howes (1988) sociometric techniques to inner-city Head Start and kindergarten children who had been in class together for 6 months. It took approximately 10 minutes for each child to complete the peer ratings. Only a 6% overlap was detected between the two measures. This suggests that sociometric ratings may extend the information received on teacher reports of behavior and increase understanding of peer relationships.

Strengths. Sociometric nominations of children older than 8 years have the strongest predictive validity of any of the methods of assessing socioemotional development. Cowen and colleagues (1973) found that, although teacher ratings of children were highly correlated with observed behaviors and problems in children, the sociometric nominations of third graders were more predictive of children who later experienced mental health problems.

Sociometric ratings can be reliably obtained from children as young as 3 years when their peer group has been together for at least 8 months (Howes, 1988). It appears that sociometric techniques will provide information that supplements, rather than supplants, teacher reports of behavior. Peers seem to have access to more diverse social behavior and situations than can be assessed through behavior rating instruments. When children rate the entire class rather than simply the extremes (i.e., positive and negative nominations), gender does not emerge as a significant factor influencing their judgments. Peer evaluations also appear less influenced by socioeconomic status than are teacher ratings (Ramsey, 1988, cited in Foster et al., 1993).

Peer ratings offer a reliable measure of peer assessment of interpersonal skills. Gresham and Stuart (1992) contend that "information provided by peers cannot be obtained from other sources and therefore represents unique and potentially valuable data regarding the child's social competence" (p. 224). Peer ratings are the most time-efficient and reliable method of obtaining this information.

Concerns. Peer ratings with children younger than second grade require the use of photographs of every child in the class in addition to individual administration. In a longitudinal design, it may be difficult to obtain ratings on children who move to new schools.

Indirect Measures

In addition to using direct measures and techniques, social competence also can be assessed using indirect methods. Indirect methods involve behavior ratings made by significant individuals in the child's life (e.g., teachers, parents, caregivers, peers). Ostensibly these ratings are based on ongoing interaction and observation of the child over time. The discussion of indirect measures includes two main categories, instruments that focus mainly on psychopathology and problem behaviors, and instruments that include both positive and negative behaviors.

MEASURES OF PSYCHOPATHOLOGY AND PROBLEM BEHAVIORS

Instruments measuring problem behaviors abound in the literature. Discussion here will be limited to two widely used instruments, the Child Behavior Checklist (CBCL) (Achenbach & Edelbrock, 1983) and the Behavior Problems Index (BPI) (Zill & Peterson, 1986).

The CBCL, Teacher Report Form (TRF), and Youth Self-Report (Achenbach & Edelbrock, 1988) are parallel rating scales for parents, teachers, and children over the age of 11 years. Raters record problems and competencies of children and report the degree to which stated behaviors are true for the child in the previous 6 months. The majority of the items (n = 118) address problem behaviors. A short social competency component on the CBCL asks parents to list the activities of the child (e.g., jobs, sports, hobbies, clubs), organizations in which the child participates, and the number of the child's close friends, and to rate the child's school performance and his or her ability to get along with others. These well-designed instruments are used very widely in research. There is both a conceptual and an empirical basis for the items. Norms are available by age and gender and the manuals present studies that demonstrate the reliability and validity of these instruments (Christenson, 1992).

The congruence of items across the three forms provides standardized descriptions of the child's behavior (as perceived by significant individuals in the child's life). Items included on the checklist show a significant relationship with referrals for behavioral and socioemotional problems. Classification information on the TRF indicates misclassification of approximately 28% of the sample, with a balance of false negatives and false positives. The TRF contains several items that allow for individualization.

Although well explained in the manual, the hand scoring can be tedious and take about 20 minutes to complete (computerized scoring is available). Because these instruments are heavily weighted toward psychopathology, they are appropriate for detecting children in need of referral, but they do not provide a comprehensive picture of a child's strengths.

The BPI (Zill & Peterson, 1986) contains 28 items representing six scales: headstrong, antisocial, anxious/depressed, hyperactive, dependent, and peer conflict. The items are designed to document the more common behavior problems exhibited by children aged 4 to 17. The BPI has been used in the National Longitudinal Survey of Youth (more than 10,000 children) and the National Health Interview Survey of Child Health (n =

15,416), providing a large database for comparison. It has been used with diverse populations and successfully discriminated between referred and nonreferred children (Zill, 1990, cited in Love, 1994). The BPI is used so widely that "it can now essentially be considered a benchmark for other measures" (Love, 1994, p. 20).

Strengths. Estimates of the prevalence of problem behaviors in children range from 10 to 25% (Love, 1994). Problem behaviors not only identify children at risk for future problems but also serve as indicators of the social support system since presence of problem behaviors correlates with the number of social risk factors (e.g., low maternal self-esteem, poverty, large family, unstable marriage). Problem behavior measures have high reliability, show strong concurrent validity (with observations and peer evaluations), and are predictive of future problems. They are relatively inexpensive to administer and their wide use in research allows for comparison with other samples.

Concerns. The problem behavior instruments primarily assess psychopathology and do not adequately measure skills related to a child's social competence or provide a balanced portrayal of the child. For example, many of the items on these instruments are negatively worded—"can't get along with teachers," "feels worthless " (BPI); "cruel to animals," "overweight," "secretive, keeps things to self," "talks too much," "whining" (CBC). Since prosocial behaviors and positive social skills appear to have a mediating effect on the aggressive tendencies of children and their subsequent popularity (Dodge & Feldman, 1990; Ladd, Price, & Hart, 1990; Volling et al., 1993), it is important to assess social competence areas as well as the problem behaviors. Therefore, if problem behavior measures are used, additional instruments assessing children's competencies and skills should be used as well.

MEASURES INCLUDING PROBLEM BEHAVIORS AND SOCIAL SKILLS

Some instruments are designed to assess the presence of social skills and competencies, as well as children's problem behaviors. Two instruments representative of this category, the SSRS (Gresham & Elliott, 1990) and the California Q-Set (Block & Block, 1980; Caspi et al., 1993) will be reviewed below.

The SSRS is the most psychometrically sound of the instruments in this category. It is one of the few instruments of its type to be normed on a nationally representative sample. The SSRS uses teacher, parent, and student (≥ grade 3) questionnaires to measure social competence and is available in a preschool version as well as a version for grades K–6. The latter version contains 57 items on the teacher form and 55 items on the parent form. The SSRS is designed to sample three domains: social skills, problem behaviors, and academic competence.

Within the domain of social skills, all three rating scales (i.e., teacher, parent, and student) measure common core behaviors from the subdomains of cooperation, assertion, and self-control. Five subscales were developed to measure these subdomains. Forming the acronym CARES, the five subscales are: 1) cooperation (behaviors such as helping others, sharing materials, and complying with rules and directions), 2) assertion (initiating behaviors, such as asking others for information, introducing oneself, and responding to the actions of others, such as peer pressure or insults), 3) responsibility (behaviors that demonstrate ability to communicate with adults and regard for property or work), 4) empathy (behaviors that show concern and respect for others' feelings and viewpoints), and 5) self-control (behaviors that emerge in conflict situations, such as responding appropriately to teasing, and in nonconflict situations that require taking turns and compromising). Problem behaviors that might interfere with social skills performance are rated according to their perceived frequency. Examples include: "Fights with others," "Is easily distracted," "Gets angry easily," "Acts sad or depressed."

The SSRS uses multiple raters who are familiar with the child's social context in order to assess the cultural and ecological validity of its items. Because of the differences among students and families in cultural mores, social competence instruments should ascertain the importance of a given behavior in that environment. On the SSRS, teachers and parents rate the importance of each item, as well as their perception of the frequency with which the child exhibits that behavior or trait. Parents are told that the questionnaire is designed "to measure *how often* your child exhibits certain social skills and *how important* those skills are to your child's development. Ratings of problem behaviors are also requested." Teachers are given similar instructions, being told that the questionnaire is designed to measure how often a student exhibits certain social skills and how important those skills are for success in their classroom.

The California Q-Set uses Q-sort methodology and requires an observer to compare individual attributes designating which is most characteristic of a particular child. A descriptive item pool known as a Q-set is sorted by an individual familiar with the child into a nine-category distribution ranging from extremely uncharacteristic (1) to extremely characteristic (9). Q-sorts provide a descriptive profile of a child's personality and allow for intraindividual trait comparisons (rather than interindividual comparisons or frequency of behavior). This methodology distinguishes the significance of specific behaviors for a child rather than the frequency rating. Q-sorts can be completed with different raters and compared for overlap. The profiles of individuals provided through Q-Sort methods can be analyzed in a variety of ways, including cluster analysis of individuals in the sample, factor analysis of the items, item analysis, or comparison of the child's profile to a hypothetical profile.

Designed to capture the wide variation in children's personal and social characteristics, the California Q-Set (Block & Block, 1980) contains 100 statements describing personal and behavioral attributes. The original Q-Set was limited in application due to the complexity of language used. Recent modifications (Caspi et al., 1993) simplified the items to enable its use with lay observers (e.g., parents). This instrument has been used with parents from a wide range of socioeconomic status (Caspi et al., 1993). An examiner remains present throughout the sorting procedure to answer questions, offer explanations, and offer reading assistance as needed. The rater does not need to make reference to a common set of norms regarding children's behavior; instead he or she needs only to indicate the salience of a trait or behavior for a particular child compared with the child's other traits.

The California Q-Set discriminates children with childhood disruptive disorders, externalizing problems, and self-reported delinquency. Inter-rater reliability with the common language Q-Set is stronger for professionals than for parents, but is acceptable for both. Completing the Q-Set can be a time-consuming procedure. As with other measures, multiple perspectives of the child are warranted. With each Q-sort taking approximately 1 hour to complete, the time and expense involved in using this technique would prohibit its use with large samples.

Strengths. Instruments that assess both problem behaviors and children's social skills provide a more balanced portrayal of children than instruments measuring only psychopathology and problem behaviors. Providing this more complete representation of children's skills is very important in light of the fact that prosocial behaviors and positive social skills appear to mediate the effects of problem behaviors.

Rating scales are brief and relatively inexpensive to administer. They can be completed by mulitple individuals in the child's environment to increase understanding of the range of the child's skills.

Concerns. Q-sort methodology is time-consuming and more complex to administer. Relative importance of different social skills has not been established.

CONSIDERATIONS FOR SELECTING
A MEASURE OF SOCIAL COMPETENCE

Several criteria are important to address when selecting a measure of social competence. The most important considerations include highlighting the specific purpose(s) warranting a measure of social competence (e.g., research, referral, intervention) and the psychometric qualities associated with the various instruments appropriate for these goals.

Goals of Assessment

Research Purposes. The type of social competence measure selected for research purposes will depend on the specific research question being addressed. For example, is the aim of the study to identify children at risk of social and emotional disorders? Or is the question geared toward a more complete assessment of children's social competence, where both problem behaviors and children's social skills and competencies should be measured? Time and expense are considerations when making decisions about using direct or indirect measures. Some measures (e.g., observational measures and coding of videotapes) add time and expense, but may add ecological validity to the data. Psychometric qualities (reliability and validity) of the various instruments are important criteria to consider throughout the selection process. Collecting data longitudinally using multiple raters and multiple instruments is one way to address concerns about the reliability and validity of the data being collected.

Classroom Purposes. In addition to the measures listed earlier, several instruments have been developed that provide guidelines to teachers for observing children's behaviors in social competence over time. *The Work Sampling System* (wss) (Meisels et al., 1994) is an authentic performance assessment for children preschool through grade 5. Personal and social development is one of seven domains measured in this assessment system. Developmental guidelines and checklists are provided to help focus and guide teachers' ongoing observations and documentation of their students' growth and development across all seven domains. The personal and social development domain in the wss has a dual focus. Personal growth is defined as children's feelings about themselves (e.g., their views of themselves as learners) and their sense of responsibility to themselves and to others. Social development includes children's interactions with peers, adults and family members, and particularly their skills in making friends, solving conflicts, and functioning effectively in groups. Examples of performance indicators within this domain include "manages transitions," "seeks help when encountering a problem," and "interacts easily with peers." Because the WSS is used with ongoing observations over time, ecological validity of the assessment of children's skills/behaviors is enhanced.

When social competence measures are used for classroom purposes, it is very important that observations and/or ratings be completed over time instead of as one "snapshot" during the school year. Children's development is dynamic, and a single observation or rating will fail to reflect changes taking place in children's social skills over the course of the school year. In addition, the child's behavior and reactions often will vary with the situation. If possible, it is always helpful to include observations and ratings from additional people familiar with the child's social behaviors (i.e., parents, playground supervisors, peers). Finally, it is very important that teachers use instruments that are psychometrically sound if the results are to be used for referring children for special services.

Developmental Change in Children's Social Competence

Overall, the social skills literature shows little relationship between social skills and age within the elementary school period. Walker and McConnell (1988) found no correlation between grade level and each of the three subscales of their test of social competence. Findings with the SSRS are similar. Little or no consistent developmental change with age was found across the SSRS on teacher or parent forms for children in grades K–6. The mean scores fluctuate from kindergarten through sixth grade. Gresham and Elliott (1990) conclude that "there do not appear to be any strong, consistent developmental trends in the social skills as assessed by the SSRS" (p. 120). This is consistent with other research and theories (Cairns, 1986; Stuart, Gresham, & Elliott, 1991; Pettit, 1992). Cairns (1986) asserts that there is a "conservation of social pattern" that dictates increasing resistance to change once a social pattern has been established. In other words, once a child has established a pattern of interpersonal interaction, the child seeks to repeat the familiar pattern in new interactions.

The only research in social competence that demonstrates detectable change among elementary students according to age/grade level is in the area of social cognition (Feldman & Dodge, 1987). When students in first, third, and fifth grades were presented with three kinds of socially important situations (i.e., initiating entry into peer group, responding to teasing, and response to ambiguous provocation), the children's ability to interpret peers' intentions and to generate, evaluate, and enact competent responses increased with age. However, interactions were detected among gender, sociometric status, and age, indicating the complexity of social-information processing particularly among children with low sociometric status. In order to discuss growth in individual children in the area of social competence, one would need to examine the cognitive processes a child uses in determining appropriate behavior.

Social Validity

An important consideration for any use of social competence measures is social validity (Anderson & Messick, 1974; Greenspan & Granfield, 1992; Gresham & Reschly, 1987; Swick & Hassell, 1988). Social validity refers to the social significance, social importance, and social acceptability that individuals place on the various skills and/or behaviors measured (Gresham & Elliott, 1990). That is, social competence measures are socially, ecologically, and culturally valid only if both the evaluators and participants share a common understanding for the significance or appropriateness of the various social skills and behaviors being assessed. One way to address social validity is to collect information regarding the importance of each assessed skill/behavior from someone representative of the child's community and cultural background (e.g., parent or significant family member). Using multiple raters (including raters familiar with the child's cultural background) to establish inter-rater reliability and to assess the child's behavior over time increases the social validity of the data collected.

CONCLUSION

Attaining social competence in early childhood predicts later school achievement and success. Conversely, young children who fail to acquire social competence are at risk for developing problems across both academic and social domains. For these reasons, reliable and valid measures of children's social competence are of critical importance for teachers and researchers interested in understanding various social factors influencing young children's development.

Various methods have been designed to measure social competence. These methods can be organized into two categories, direct and indirect measures. Direct measures include observations (naturalistic and experimental situations), hypothetical problem sets, self-rating scales, and sociometric techniques, such as peer nominations, peer ratings, peer rankings, and popularity ratings by teachers. Indirect measures include problem behavior checklists, Q-Sorts, and questionnaires/behavior rating scales, including both social skills and competencies and problem behaviors. When selecting a measure of social competence it is important to consider the goals of the assessment (research or classroom purposes), the time period of the assessment (should instrument be sensitive to developmental changes?), and the psychometric qualities of the instruments selected. Reliability and construct validity are always important considerations when selecting any measure of social competence. Social validity, or the social significance and acceptability of the skills/behaviors measured by the instrument for diverse populations and cultural groups, also should be examined. Finally, as children's development is a dynamic process, assessments of children's social competence should be completed longitudinally, over several time periods, using a variety of measures and several raters, including some who are familiar with the child.

Acknowledgment. This chapter is a shortened version of a paper prepared for the Early Childhood Longitudinal Study (Meisels, Atkins-Burnett, Nicholson, 1995) conducted in conjunction with the National Opinion Research Center, University of Chicago, and funded by the National Center for Education Statistics, U.S. Department of Education. The opinions expressed are those of the authors and do not represent the positions or opinions of the Department of Education.

REFERENCES

Achenbach, T. M., & Edelbrock, C. (1983). Child Behavior Checklist and Revised Child Behavior Profile. Burlington: Department of Psychiatry, University of Vermont.

Achenbach, T. M., & Edelbrock, C. (1988). Child Behavior Checklist/4–18. Burlington, VT: Center for Children, Youth and Families.

Anderson, S., & Messick, S. (1974). Social competency in young children. *Developmental Psychology, 10*(2), 282–293.

Asher, S. (1990). Recent advances in the study of peer rejection. In S. R. Asher & J. D. Coie (Eds.), *Peer rejection in childhood* (pp. 3–4). New York: Cambridge University Press.

Asher, S. R., Hymel, S., & Renshaw, P. D. (1984). Loneliness in children. *Child Development, 55,* 1456–1464.

Asher, S. R., & Wheeler, V. A. (1985). Children's loneliness: A comparison of rejected and neglected peer status. *Journal of Consulting and Clinical Psychology, 53,* 500–595.

Bandura, A. (1977). *Social learning theory.* Englewood Cliffs, NJ: Prentice-Hall.

Bierman, K. L., & Montminy, H. P. (1993). Developmental issues in social skills assessment and intervention with children and adolescents. *Behavior Modification, 17*(3), 229–254.

Block, J., & Block, J. H. (1980). The California Child Q-Set. Palo Alto, CA: Consulting Psychologists Press.

Boivin, M., Poulin, F., & Vitaro, F. (1994). Depressed mood and peer rejection in childhood. *Development and Psychopathology, 6*, 483–498.

Bower, E. M. (1960). *Early identification of emotionally handicapped children in school.* Springfield, IL: Thomas.

Bronson, M. B. (1985). *Manual for the Bronson Social and Task Skill Profile.* Chestnut Hill, MA: Boston College.

Bronson, M. B. (1994). The usefulness of an observational measure of young children's social and mastery behaviors in early childhood classrooms. *Early Childhood Research Quarterly, 9*(1), 19–43.

Cairns, R. B. (1986). A contemporary perspective on social development. In P. S. Strain, M. J. Guralnick, & H. M. Walker (Eds.), *Children's social behavior: Development, assessment, and modification* (pp. 3–48). Orlando, FL: Academic Press.

Caspi, A., Block, J., Block, J. H., Klopp, B., Lynam, D., Moffit, T. E., & Stouthamer-Loeber, M. (1993). A "common-language" version of the California Child Q-Set for personality assessment. In M. E. Hertzig & E. A. Farber (Eds.), *Annual progress in child psychiatry and child development* (pp. 123–149). New York: Brunner/Mazel.

Cassidy, J., & Asher, S. R. (1992). Loneliness and peer relations in young children. *Child Development, 63*, 350–365.

Chandler, M., & Chapman, M. (1991). Introduction: Issues in the identification of competence. In M. Chandler & M. Chapman (Eds.), *Criteria for competence* (pp. viii–xii). Hillsdale, NJ: Erlbaum.

Christenson, S. L. (1992). Review of the Child Behavior Checklist. In J. J. Kramer & J. C. Conoley (Eds.), *The eleventh mental measurements yearbook* (pp. 164–166). Lincoln, NE: Buros Institute of Mental Measurements.

Clark, L., Gresham, F. M., & Elliott, S. N. (1985). Development and validation of a social skills assessment measure: The TROSS-C. *Journal of Psychoeducational Assessment, 4*, 347–356.

Coie, J. D., Dodge, K. A., & Kupersmidt, J. (1990). Peer group behavior and social status. In S. R. Asher & J. D. Coie (Eds.), *Peer rejection in childhood* (pp. 17–59). New York: Cambridge University Press.

Cowen, E. L., Pederson, A., Babigian, H., Izzo, L. D., & Trost, M. A. (1973). Long-term follow-up of early detected vulnerable children. *Journal of Consulting and Clinical Psychology, 41*, 438–446.

Crick, N. R., & Dodge, K. A. (1994). A review and reformulation of social information-processing mechanisms in children's social adjustment. *Psychological Bulletin, 115*(1), 74–101.

Doan, R. E., & Scherman, A. (1987). The therapeutic effect of physical fitness on measures of personality: A literature review. *Journal of Counseling and Development, 66*(1), 28–36.

Dodge, K. A. (1980). Social cognition and children's aggressive behavior. *Child Development, 51*, 162–179.

Dodge, K. A. (1983). Behavioral antecedents of peer social status. *Child Development, 54*(6), 1386–1399.

Dodge, K. A. (1993). Social-cognitive mechanisms in the development of conduct disorder and depression. *Annual Review of Psychology, 44*, 559–584.

Dodge, K. A., & Crick, N. R. (1990). Social information-processing bases of aggressive behavior in children: Illustrating the value of basic research [Special issue]. *Personality and Social Psychology Bulletin, 16*(1), 8–22.

Dodge, K. A., & Feldman, E. (1990). Issues in social cognition and sociometric status. In S. R. Asher & J. D. Coie (Eds.), *Peer rejection in childhood* (pp. 119–155). New York: Cambridge University Press.

Dodge, K. A., & Frame, C. L. (1982). Social cognitive biases and deficits in aggressive boys. *Child Development, 53*, 620–635.

Dodge, K. A., Pettit, G. S., & Bates, J. E. (1994). Socialization mediators of the relation between socioeconomic status and child conduct problems: Children and poverty [Special issue]. *Child Development, 65*(2), 649–665.

Dodge, K. A., Pettit, G. S., McClaskey, C. L., & Brown, M. M. (1986). Social competence in children. *Monographs of the Society for Research in Child Development, 51*(2, Serial No. 213).

Eisenberg, N., McCreath, H., & Ahn, R. (1988). Vicarious emotional responsiveness and prosocial behavior: Their interrelations in young children. *Personality and Social Psychology Bulletin, 14*(2), 298–311.

Fantuzzo, J., Manz, P., & McDermott, P. (1995). *Preschool version of the Social Skills Rating System: An empirical analysis of its use with low-income children.* Manuscript submitted for publication.

Feldman, E., & Dodge, K. A. (1987). Social information processing and sociometric status: Sex, age, and situational effects. *Journal of Abnormal Child Psychology, 15*(2), 211–227.

Foster, S. L., Inderbitzen, H. M., & Nangle, D. W. (1993). Assessing acceptance and social skills with peers in childhood. *Behavior Modification, 17*(3), 255–286.

Frentz, C., Gresham, F. M., & Elliott, S. N. (1991). Popular, controversial, neglected, and rejected adolescents: Contrasts of social competence and achievement differences. *Journal of School Psychology, 29*(2), 109–120.

Gottfried, A. E. (1990). Academic intrinsic motivation in young elementary school children. *Journal of Educational Psychology, 82*(3), 525–538.

Gottman, J., Gonso, J., & Rasmussen, B. (1975). Social interaction, social competence, and friendship in children. *Child Development, 46*, 709–718,

Greenspan, S., & Granfield, J. M. (1992). Reconsidering the construct of mental retardation: Implications of a model of social competence. *American Journal on Mental Retardation, 96*(4), 442–453.

Gresham, F. M. (1983). Social validity in the assessment of children's social skills: Establishing standards for social competency. *Journal of Psychoeducational Assessment, 1*, 297–307.

Gresham, F. M. (1986). Conceptual issues in the assessment of social competence in children. In P. S. Strain, M. J. Guralnick, & H. M. Walker (Eds.), *Children's social behavior: Development, assessment, and modification* (pp. 143–179). Orlando, FL: Academic Press.

Gresham, F. M., & Elliott, S. N. (1990). Social Skills Rating System manual. Circle Pines, MN: American Guidance Service.

Gresham, F. M., & Nagle, R. J. (1980). Social skills training with children: Responsiveness to modeling and coaching as a function of peer orientation. *Journal of Consulting and Clinical Psychology, 48,* 717–729.

Gresham, F., & Reschly, D. J. (1987). Dimensions of social competence: Method factors in the assessment of adaptive behavior, social skills and peer acceptance. *Journal of School Psychology, 25(4),* 367–381.

Gresham, F. M., & Stuart, D. (1992). Stability of sociometric assessment: Implications for uses as selection and outcome measures in social skills training. *Journal of School Psychology, 30,* 223–231.

Guralnick, M. J. (1986). The peer relations of young handicapped and nonhandicapped children. In P. S. Strain, M. J. Guralnick, & H. M. Walker (Eds.), *Children's social behavior: Development, assessment, and modification* (pp. 93–142). Orlando, FL: Academic Press.

Haertel, G., Walberg, J., & Haertel, E. (1979, April). *Socio-psychological environment and learning: A quantitative synthesis.* Paper presented at the annual meeting of the American Educational Research Association, San Francisco.

Harter, S. (1990). Causes, correlates, and the functional role of global self-worth: A lifespan perspective. In R. Sternberg & J. Kolligan (Eds.), *Competence considered* (pp. 67–97). New Haven, CT: Yale University Press.

Harter, S., & Pike, R. (1984). The Pictorial Scale of Perceived Competence and Social Acceptance for Young Children. *Child Development, 55,* 1969–1982.

Hartup, W. W. (1983). The peer system. In E. M. Hetherington (Ed.), *Handbook of child psychology: Vol. 4. Socialization, personality, and social development* (pp. 103–196). New York: Wiley.

Hauser-Cram, P., Bronson, M. B., & Upshur, C. C. (1993). The effects of the classroom environment on the social and mastery behavior of preschool children with disabilities. *Early Childhood Research Quarterly, 8(4),* 479–497.

Honig, A. S., & McCarron, P. A. (1988). Prosocial behaviors of handicapped and typical peers in an integrated preschool. *Early Child Development and Care, 33,* 113–125.

Hops, H., & Finch, M. (1985). Social competence and skill: A reassessment. In B. H. Schneider, K. H. Rubin, & J. E. Ledingham (Eds.), *Children's peer relations: Issues in assessment and intervention* (pp. 23–40). New York: Springer-Verlag.

Howes, C. (1988). Peer interaction of young children. *Monographs of the Society for Research in Child Development, 53(1).*

Howes, C., & Matheson, C. (1992). Sequences in the development of competent play with peers: Social and social pretend play. *Developmental Psychology, 28,* 961–974.

Howes, C., & Stewart, P. (1987). Child's play with adults, toys, and peers: An examination of family and child care influences. *Developmental Psychology, 23,* 423–430.

Hubbard, J. A., & Cillessen, A. H. N. (1993). *Social strategies and sociometric status within the context of social problem types.* Presentation at the biennial meeting of the Society for Research in Child Development, New Orleans. (ERIC Document Reproduction Service No. ED 358 954)

Hymel, S., Rubin, K. H., Rowden, L., & LeMare, L. (1990). Children's peer relationships: Longitudinal prediction of internalizing and externalizing problems from middle to late childhood. *Child Development, 61,* 2004–2021.

Hymel, S., Wagner, E., & Butler, L. (1990). Reputational bias: View from peer group. In S. Asher & J. Cole (Eds.), *Peer rejection in childhood* (pp. 156–188). New York: Cambridge University Press.

Kohn, M. (1977). *Social competence, symptoms, and underachievement in childhood: A longitudinal perspective.* Washington, DC: Winston.

Kupersmidt, J., Coie, J., & Dodge, K. (1990). Poor peer relationships and later disorder. In S. R. Asher & J. D. Coie (Eds.), *Peer rejection in childhood* (pp. 274–308). New York: Cambridge University Press.

Ladd, G. W., Price, J. M., & Hart, C. H. (1990). Preschoolers' behavioral orientations and patterns of peer contact: Predictive of peer status? In S. R. Asher & J. D. Coie (Eds.), *Peer rejection in childhood* (pp. 90–118). New York: Cambridge University Press.

LaGreca, A. M., & Santogrossi, D. A. (1980). Social skills training with elementary school students: A behavioral group approach. *Journal of Consulting and Clinical Psychology, 48,* 220–227.

LaGreca, A. M., & Stark, P. (1986). Naturalistic observation of children's social behavior. In P. S. Strain, M. J. Guralnick, & H. M. Walker (Eds.), *Children's social behavior: Development, assessment, and modification* (pp. 181–214). Orlando, FL: Academic Press.

Lochman, J. E., & Dodge, K. A. (1994). Social-cognitive processes of severely violent, moderately aggressive, and nonaggressive boys. *Journal of Consulting and Clinical Psychology, 62*(2), 366–374.

Lothman, D. J., Pianta, R. C., & Clarson, S. (1990). Mother–child interaction in children with epilepsy: Relations with child competence. *Journal of Epilepsy, 3*(3), 157–163.

Love, J. M. (1994, November). Indicators of problem behaviors and problems in early childhood. Presented at Conference on Indicators of Children's Well-Being, Rockville, MD.

Masten, A., Morison, P., & Pelligrini, D. (1985). A revised Class Play method of peer assessment. *Developmental Psychology, 3,* 523–533.

McConnell, S. R., & Odom, S. L. (1986). Sociometrics. In P. S. Strain, M. J. Guralnick, & H. M. Walker (Eds.), *Children's social behavior: Development, assessment, and modification* (pp. 215–284). Orlando, FL: Academic Press.

McConnell, S. R., Strain, P. S., Kerr, M. M., Stagg, V., Lenkner, D. A., & Lambert, D. L. (1984). An empirical definition of elementary school adjustment: Selection of target behaviors for a comprehensive treatment program. *Behavior Modification, 8*(4), 451–473.

Meisels, S. J., Atkins-Burnett, S., & Nicholson, J. (1995). *Assessment of social competence, adaptive behaviors, and approaches to learning in young children* (Working Papers Series, National Center for Education Statistics). Washington, DC: U.S. Department of Education, Office of Educational Research and Improvement.

Meisels, S. J., Jablon, J. R., Marsden, D. B., Dichtelmiller, M. L., Dorfman, A. B., & Steele, D. M. (1994). The Work Sampling System. Ann Arbor, MI: Rebus Planning Associates.

Mize, J., & Cox, R. A. (1990). Social knowledge and social competence: Number and quality of strategies as predictors of peer behavior. *The Journal of Genetic Psychology, 15*(1), 117–127.

Mize, J., & Ladd, G. W. (1988). Predicting preschoolers' peer behavior and status from their interpersonal strategies: A comparison of verbal and enacted responses to hypothetical social dilemmas. *Developmental Psychology, 24*(6), 782–788.

Oden, C., & Asher, S. R. (1977). Coaching children in social skills for friendship making. *Child Development, 48*, 495–506.

Page, R. M., Frey, J., Talbert, R., & Falk, C. (1992). Children's feelings of loneliness and social dissatisfaction: Relationship to measures of physical fitness and activity. *Journal of Teaching in Physical Education, 11*(3), 211–219.

Parkhurst, J. T., & Asher, S. R. (1992). Peer rejection in middle school: Subgroup differences in behavior, loneliness, and interpersonal concerns. *Developmental Psychology, 28*(2), 231–241.

Pekarik, E.G., Prinz, R. J., Liebert, D. E., Weintraub, S., & Neale, J. M. (1976). The Pupil Evaluation Inventory: A sociometric technique for assessing children's social behavior. *Journal of Abnormal Child Psychology, 4*, 83–97.

Pettit, G. S. (1992). Developmental theories. In V. B. Van Hasselt & M. Hersen (Eds.), *Handbook of social development: A lifespan perspective* (pp. 3–28). New York: Plenum Press.

Pianta, R. C., & Caldwell, C. B. (1990). Stability of externalizing symptoms from kindergarten to first grade and factors related to instability. *Development and Psychopathology, 2*, 247–258.

Pianta, R. C., & Castaldi, J. (1989). Stability of internalizing symptoms from kindergarten to first grade and factors related to instability. *Development and Psychopathology, 1*, 305–316.

Pianta, R. C., & Nimetz, S. L. (1991). Relationships between children and teachers: Associations with classroom and home behavior. *Journal of Applied Developmental Psychology, 12*, 379–393.

Reschly, D. J., & Gresham, F. M. (1981). *Use of social competence measures to facilitate parent and teacher involvement and nonbiased assessment.* Unpublished manuscript, Ames, IA: Iowa State University.

Reschly, D. J., Gresham, F. M., & Graham-Clay, S. L. (1985). *Multifactored non-biased assessment: Convergent and discriminant validity of social and cognitive measures with black and white regular and special education students: Final project report.* Washington, DC: Office of Special Education, U.S. Department of Education Grant. (ERIC Document Reproduction Service No. ED 252 034)

Roff, M., Sells, S. B., & Golden, M. M. (1972). *Social adjustment and personality development in children.* Minneapolis: University of Minnesota Press.

Rubin, K. H., LeMare, L. J., & Lollis, S. (1990). Social withdrawal in childhood: Developmental pathways to peer rejection. In S. R. Asher & J. D. Coie (Eds.), *Peer rejection in childhood* (pp. 217–252). New York: Cambridge University Press.

Rubin, K. H., & Rose-Krasnor, L. (1992). Interpersonal problem solving and social competence in children. In V. B. Van Hasselt & M. Hersen (Eds.), *Handbook of social development: A lifespan perspective* (pp. 283–323). New York: Plenum Press.

Rubin, K. H., & Ross, H. S. (1988). Commentary: Toward the study of social competence, social status, and social relations. In C. Howes, Peer interaction of young children. *Monographs of the Society for Research in Child Development, 53*(1), 79–87.

Schaefer, E. S., & Edgerton, M. (1983, August). *Unified model for academic competence, social adjustment, and psychopathology.* Paper presented at the annual convention of the American Psychological Association. (ERIC Document Reproduction Service No. ED 235 895)

Short, E. J. (1992). Cognitive, metacognitive, motivational, and affective differences among normally achieving, learning-disabled, and developmentally handicapped students: How much do they affect school achievement? *Journal of Clinical Child Psychology, 21*(3), 229–239.

Siperstein, G. N. (1992). Social competence: An important construct in mental retardation. *American Journal on Mental Retardation, 96*(4), iii–vi.

Skinner, E. A., & Belmont, M. J. (1993). Motivation in the classroom: Reciprocal effects of teacher behavior and student engagement across the school year. *Journal of Educational Psychology, 85*(4), 571–581.

Stipek, D., Feiler, R., Daniels, D., & Milburn, S. (1995). Effects of different instructional approaches on young children's achievement and motivation. *Child Development, 66,* 209–223.

Stipek, D. J., & Mason, T. C. (1987). Attributions, emotions, and behavior in the elementary school classroom. *Journal of Classroom Interaction, 22*(2), 1–5.

Strassberg, Z., Dodge, K. A., Pettit, G. S., & Bates, J. E. (1994). Spanking in the home and the children's subsequent aggression toward kindergarten peers. *Development and Psychopathology, 6,* 445–461.

Strayhorn, J. M., & Strain, P. S. (1986). Skills for preventive mental health. In P. S. Strain, M. J. Guralnick, & H. M. Walker (Eds.), *Children's social behavior: Development, assessment, and modification* (pp. 287–330). Orlando, FL: Academic Press.

Stuart, D. L., Gresham, F. M., & Elliott, S. N. (1991). Teacher ratings of social skills in popular and rejected males and females. *School Psychology Quarterly, 6*(1), 16–26.

Swanson, H. L., & Malone, S. (1992). Social skills and learning disabilities: A meta-analysis of the literature. *School Psychology Review, 21*(3), 427–443.

Swartz, J. P., & Walker, D. K. (1984). The relationship between teacher ratings of kindergarten classroom skills and second-grade achievement scores:

An analysis of gender differences. *Journal of School Psychology*, 22(2), 209–217.

Swick, K. J., & Hassell, T. (1988). *Parental efficacy and the development of social competence in young children*. Columbia: University of South Carolina. (ERIC Document Reproduction Service No. ED 306 031)

Turnure, J., & Zigler, E. (1964). Outerdirectedness in the problem solving of normal and retarded children. *Journal of Abnormal and Social Psychology*, 69, 427–436.

Ullman, C. A. (1957). Teachers, peers, and tests as predictors of adjustment. *Journal of Educational Psychology*, 48, 257–267.

Van Hasselt, V. B, Hersen, M., & Bellack, A. S. (1984). The relationship between assertion and sociometric status of children. *Behaviour Research and Therapy*, 22(6), 689–696.

Vaughn, S., Zaragoza, N., Hogan, A., & Walker, J. (1993). A four-year longitudinal investigation of the social skills and behavior problems of students with learning disabilities. *Journal of Learning Disabilities*, 26(6), 404–412.

Vitaro, F., Gagnon, C., & Tremblay, R. E. (1990). Predicting stable peer rejection from kindergarten to grade one. *Journal of Clinical Child Psychology*, 19(3), 257–264.

Vitaro, F., Tremblay, R. E., Gagnon, C., & Boivin, M. (1992). Peer rejection from kindergarten to grade 2: Outcomes, correlates, and prediction. *Merrill-Palmer Quarterly*, 38(3), 382–400.

Vitaro, F., Tremblay, R. E., Gagnon, C., & Pelletier, D. (1994). Predictive accuracy of behavioral and sociometric assessments of high risk kindergarten children. *Journal of Clinical Child Psychology*, 23(3), 272–282.

Volling, B. L., MacKinnon-Lewis, C., Rabiner, D., & Baradaran, L. (1993). Children's social competence and sociometric status: Further exploration of aggression, social withdrawal, and peer rejection. *Development and Psychopathology*, 5(3), 459–483.

Walker, H. M., & McConnell, S. R. (1988). Walker-McConnell Scale of Social Competence and School Adjustment. Austin, TX: PRO-ED.

Walker, H. M., Stieber, S., & Eisert, D. (1991). Teacher ratings of adolescent social skills: Psychometric characteristics and factorial replicability across age-grade ranges. *School Psychology Review*, 20(2), 301–314.

Weiss, B., Dodge, K. A., Bates, J. E., & Pettit, G. S. (1992). Some consequences of early harsh discipline: Child aggression and maladaptive social information processing style. *Child Development*, 63(6), 1321–1335.

Werner, E. E. (1990). Protective factors and individual resilience. In S. J. Meisels & J. P. Shonkoff (Eds.), *Handbook of early childhood intervention* (pp. 97–116). New York: Cambridge University Press.

Zill, N., & Peterson, J. L. (1986). Behavior Problems Index. Washington, DC: Child Trends.

CHAPTER 9

Evaluation and Parents of Young Children

Alice Sterling Honig

Leaders in the field of enrichment programs for young children and their families often have a difficult time when considering the pros and cons of program evaluation. Their major energies are focused on thinking through programmatic philosophy and implementing procedures to enhance children's development and learning careers. Whether and how to include families in assessment procedures in order to enhance the quality of service provision only recently has become a professional priority. Other planning decisions claim the attention of evaluators, such as how much and how often to do evaluation, how to choose instruments, and how to train testers, observers, and interviewers. Program directors and funding agencies have focused primarily on aspects of the technical and logistic dimensions of evaluation. Child-care staff and their professional organizations instead have emphasized the development of guidelines for developmentally appropriate curriculum (Bredekamp, 1987) and criticized the use of tests with young children (National Association for the Education of Young Children, 1988). Early childhood educators often are wary of the *value* of assessment, particularly readiness testing, in early childhood (Meisels, 1987). Parents as well as teachers need to understand the value of individually administered evaluation with full parent participation. Respect for parents as partners in evaluation procedures can galvanize parental cooperation with educational planning and ensure positive family participation in educational plans.

THE IMPORTANCE OF PARENT INVOLVEMENT
IN ASSESSMENT PROCEDURES

The critical importance of involving parents in *transdisciplinary evaluations* for children was emphasized by Public Law 99–457 (Simeonsson, 1988). This law extended the goals of PL 94–142, which actively mandated the design of assessments to screen, identify, and find appropriate placements for young children with disabilities. The challenge for early childhood educators of special needs children has been to carry out assessments that will result in placement in inclusive settings for optimal service provision. Collaborative teamwork and increased communication among specialists began to be viewed as more cost-effective and time-efficient, and more likely to provide families with an integrated and comprehensive picture of their children's strengths and areas of developmental delay. Thus, *transdisciplinary assessment* is a method of making the process of evaluation and identification of service provision "more meaningful to and empowering of parents and thus more useful to their children" (Bergen, 1994, p. 9). The goal of the transdisciplinary team is to integrate data obtained from each specialist who assesses the referred child, in order to formulate appropriate recommendations for services. The team meeting typically involves the assessors, educators, and parents of the referred child (Nuttall, Romero, & Kalesnik, 1992). However, parents may not be involved during the assessment procedures but only in the information-sharing and decision-making procedures subsequent to the assessments. Thus, even now, the concept of parents as indispensable participants who should be invited to be present during each assessment and who need to have the process and findings explained in an ongoing, clear fashion is not extensively implemented by early childhood personnel.

Particularly when infants are assessed, evaluation professionals do respect the crucial nature of parental participation. "Infant assessment requires that the examiner develop a good rapport with the mother (or father!) as well as with the baby. . . . It is important to explain the testing procedures thoroughly to the mother and to continue to explain them as the testing progresses" (Kamphaus, 1993, p. 88).

Systematic efforts to evaluate children for enrollment in early childhood enrichment and intervention programs require much professional decision making. Depending on the goals of the evaluation, the form and focus, intensity and extensiveness of the procedures, and the level of formality will vary (Honig, 1994). The "jargon" of evaluation and intervention personnel can be very confusing to parents. How can program personnel and families jointly understand and negotiate the evaluation process?

What aspects need to be explained in simpler terms so that families can participate more knowledgeably in assessment procedures?

Some assessment decisions are mandated by State Departments of Social Services who send families to specialists for particular "tests," without even requiring that parents be present during the testing procedures. Miscommunications occur, as described in this personal vignette.

A parent brought her 10-year-old child for mandated developmental evaluation. As a licensed psychologist, I was required to use an intelligence test to determine whether the child was eligible for services. The mother was bitter; she explained that she had left her daughter in the care of older family members for several years prior to bringing her child to this country. The child had been repeatedly raped by a grandparent. Why did the psychologist bother with an intelligence test? Her daughter needed emotional counseling! Yet, the principal had reported early school failure for this child, and only confirmation by developmental tests would pave the way to provision of special services for the child.

Professionals and parents need to be able to communicate freely so that evaluations serve the needs of families, as well as centers, schools, and state requirements (Greenspan & Meisels, 1995). This does not mean that parents will care to learn about split-half reliability or the fine points of construct versus content validity. However, they are deeply concerned about their children's development and learning. Significant participatory roles for parents entail providing them with information about evaluation. Below are presented some topic areas and factors that parents will need to know about in order to participate more effectively as consumers and/or as targets of evaluation in early childhood programs.

CHOICE OF EVALUATION MEASURES

Choice of evaluation measures may be determined more by impersonal agency or state rules than by needs perceived by family or early childhood educators. There is a bewildering proliferation of measures in early childhood. Whether parents, child-care facilities, or schools initiate a request for assessment, choice and timing of assessment procedures will need to involve families. This means that families must be given information and clear ideas about what assessments are being considered for children of different ages and stages of development and how those choices will be helpful to the child and the parents.

Screening versus Psychometric Measures

Many preschool enrichment programs are a first line of defense against the risk of later school failure for children from at-risk families. Parents may not be as concerned about how high children's IQs are, but they are concerned that their child might need particular targeted specialist services. Caregivers can share with parents their know-how in administering easy-to-learn screening tools, even if initial results confirm that a child needs further, more specialized assessment. Good screening instruments are like nets cast wide to catch children markedly in need of services. They do not give parents or teachers subtle insights into child difficulties. They do signal children acutely at risk for developing a learning problem or handicap and urgently needing educational intervention; they are cost-effective in terms of budget, space, and expertise required to learn them. The Denver Developmental Screening Test (DDST-R) (Frankenberg & Dodds, 1990) identifies a preschooler's functioning (in relation to the percentage of children of that age developing skills at a normal rate) in four sectors: personal-social, fine motor-adaptive, language, and gross motor. If the child fails two or more items in two or more of the four areas tested, then further, more refined psychometric tests, requiring lengthy administrations and expert examiners, may be needed. Provided with knowledge about such distinctions, parents who remain concerned about developmental delays although their youngster "passed" a screening test, may then urge program personnel to consider provision of more thorough psychometric testing.

Formal versus Informal Assessments

Parents need to become aware of the advantages *and* the disadvantages of choosing more formal, standardized assessments or more informal measures (Goodwin & Goodwin, 1993). They need to be aware that the theoretical orientation or philosophy of the program often determines the type of evaluation that is carried out. Child-care personnel must inform parents as fully as possible about center policies on assessment. Decisions will have to be made that depend on budget as well as programmatic constraints. How much time can staff spend, for example, on extensive written, in-depth running records of child–child or child–adult interactions if caregivers are not given time for elaborate record keeping?

Informal Assessments. If an early childhood educational program prefers to carry out informal assessments with young children, parents need to know the full implications of the ongoing and careful work of teachers in gathering materials. Care providers who are committed to informal assessments need to meet with parents and explain how records of children's interactions and responses are kept, how artwork is gathered, what checklists are used, and how dictated stories, interview data, and other portfolio entries are chosen as representative of the ongoing work of each child (Meisels & Steele, 1991). Parents will need to be informed of the mechanisms for case conferences that a child-care facility has put into place so that staff and parents and assessment personnel can all contribute their expertise in order to elucidate concerns, for example, with youngsters whose development is problematic (Gullo, 1994).

Formal Assessments. If formal assessments are preferred, then parents need to know whether assessments for specific areas of suspected delay will be used, such as the Illinois Test of Psycholinguistic Abilities (Kirk, McCarthy, & Kirk, 1968), which tests children on many aspects of language development; the Peabody Picture Vocabulary Test (Dunn & Dunn, 1981), which targets receptive language abilities only; or the Boehm Test of Basic Concepts (Boehm, 1986). Sometimes a more global test of intelligence and developmental level is required. Parents will need more elaborate explanations regarding formal tests such as Dial-R (Mardell-Czundowski & Goldenberg, 1983), Kaufman (Kaufman & Kaufman, 1983), McCarthy Scales of Children's Abilities (McCarthy, 1972), Stanford-Binet (Thornton, Hagen, & Sattler, 1986), or the WISC-R (Wechsler, 1990), each of which must be individually administered by a competent, highly trained specialist.

> Deeply anxious, a parent telephoned me because her 8-year-old son, unable to do even first-grade work, was now in third grade. Teachers in parent conferences in each of the two earlier grades had told her he was "just a little slow" in learning. She reported that she had never been invited to sit in on any preschool or school assessments. Frantically she exclaimed: "I will take out all my savings to pay for testing. Please see my child and me, and tell me exactly what the difficulties are and how I can help or what can be done."

Such parents want a trained tester. They want to be present during the assessment. They convey their desire for an assessment professional who will be skillful in working with the child and in explaining results and the implications of scores in uncomplicated ways. Only if the results of evaluations are clearly understandable to parents can they fully partici-pate in more realistic and appropriate planning for their young children's education. Some corporations that publish assessment instruments for young children also provide materials on how to share test results with parents (Psychological Corporation, 1980).

Criterion- versus Norm-Referenced Assessments. Teachers can help parents understand the differences between *types* of formal assessments that a school administers. Criterion-referenced assessments measure whether a child, for example, has achieved a particular program goal, still needs assistance, or has not yet shown signs of attaining a particular learning goal, such as color and shape recognition, or finding ways to resolve a social conflict peaceably with a peer. Unlike norm-referenced tests, which compare a child's performance with others, "criterion-referenced mea-sures de-emphasize distinctions between individual performances; rather, they indicate whether the individual has mastered the objectives that were tested . . . and [are used] for developmental screening, diagnostic evalua-tion, and instructional planning" (Wortham, 1995, p. 72).

Age-Appropriate Assessments

Parents need to know that different tests have been created especially for different age children. There are even assessments for the first minutes after birth as well as for preschoolers and for school-aged children. When an infant is born, in the first and fifth minute postbirth, the APGAR test (Apgar, 1975) is performed. Healthy respiration, color, muscle tone, heart rate, and strength of reflexive cry are assessed at two points for each category. Infants medically healthiest score from 8 to 10 points. During the early weeks of life, the Brazelton Neonatal Scales (Brazelton, 1984), which sample a newborn's reflexes and responses to tones, lights, and other stimuli, are administered while the parents observe along with the administrator. Brazelton reports that as he, the pediatrician, enlists par-ents to become more sophisticated noticers of the very earliest competen-cies of their newborns, they develop an appreciative pride in the baby's capacities, which is more likely to ensure optimal care after discharge from the hospital.

During the infant/toddler period, several psychometric tests are avail-able to assess how well the very young child is developing (Zero to Three, 1995). Unfortunately, the most psychometrically valid of the infant tests, the Bayley Scales of Infant Development (Bayley, 1994), are lengthy and expensive to administer. Another infancy test, the Cattell Infant Intelligence Scale, provides an easy-to-compute IQ score (Cattell, 1970) plus items at each month-age level. Parents attending a Cattell assessment can easily follow along and regard for themselves the progress of their baby on each item at each age level.

Assessment Measures for Atypical Children

Parents of special needs children particularly will need to know that there are specialized assessments created specifically to optimize the responses of children with disabilities, who may be unable to respond to items that require vision, hearing, or muscular coordinations. Some assessments, such as the Portage Classroom Curriculum Checklist, are strongly tied to intervention. For this checklist,"home-based instruction by the mother is based on assessment and instruction from a trained paraprofessional" (Nuttall et al., 1992, p. 298).

Multicultural Sensitivity in Assessment

Assessment measures need to be sensitive to differential strengths and areas of familiarity or unfamiliarity for children in minority families (Barona, 1991). Parents of minority children or bilingual children need to be informed that some assessment instruments have carefully included minority children proportionally in the norming group. The Battelle Developmental Inventory (Newborg, Stok, Wnek, Guidobaldi, & Svinicki, 1984) is so normed as well as curriculum based; it is also appropriate for young children with developmental delays.

Many assessment instruments have been translated so that they can be administered to children speaking languages other than English. Particularly, versions in Spanish are available. For example, 1974 marked the publication of a Spanish version of the Caldwell Cooperative Preschool Inventory (Caldwell & Bradley, 1984). Using this Inventory with inexpensive materials for a brief time period, a caregiver or parent assesses how well a child has achieved preschool learning goals, such as colors, shapes, body parts, and polar opposite words (e.g., loud vs. soft). Parents can learn this brief achievement test easily and might even offer to help staff by assessing preschoolers to add to teacher knowledge about specific domains of knowledge for each child. The standardization sample of this Inventory reported that middle-class youngsters at 4 years of age could respond correctly to as many items as 6-year-old children from lower socioeconomic families. Thus, the Caldwell Inventory is a sensitive, brief, and inexpensive achievement test; is easy to administer; and is easy for parents to interpret. Administered prior to and after a preschool enrichment experience, it provides a clear measure of what preschool children are learning.

Formative and Summative Evaluations

Formative Evaluations. Directors and staff need to explain to parents the importance of *ongoing, periodic evaluations.* These formative evaluations determine *how well children are progressing toward mastery of curricular objectives.* They also can provide feedback on how well program personnel are serving the particular needs of a young child. Ongoing assessment is vital, for example, to discover how well language learning is progressing as teachers work with a preschooler with language delays, or how well socialization encouragement is progressing for an aggressive or a very shy child.

Formative evaluations are crucial for determining whether a program is actually fulfilling its goals. Are teachers arranging the environment for active, hands-on learning? Are caregivers using daily routines, such as diapering time, for rich turn-taking talk and loving interactions with infants? Parents can be shown how to use easy-to-learn checklists, such as the Adult Behaviors in Caregiving (ABC) (Honig, 1983; Honig & Lally, 1988, 1989) in classrooms to check off specific teacher transactions every 2 minutes. While using such checklists, parents become empowered as facilitators of their own children's learning. They are participants in making decisions about where program changes are most needed, about areas of teaching that need a boost. Parents from the Family Development Research Program (FDRP) (Lally, Mangione, & Honig, 1988) used the ABC-3 Checklists (for teachers of older preschoolers) to assess kindergartens. Using the ABC-3 checklists to tally whenever teachers provided opportunities for learning fine or gross motor skills, Piagetian tasks, social games with peers, and language, parents felt they were in charge as effective decision makers about where their children could best be educated after graduation from the FDRP program center. Programs empower parents by teaching them to use checklists, such as the Early Childhood Environment Rating Scale (ECRS) (Harms & Clifford, 1980) or the ABC scales (Honig & Lally, 1981), themselves in order to assess early child-care environments and especially the quality of the interactions that teachers provide for young children.

A close partnership between curriculum and assessment enhances program options and effectiveness for children's development (McAfee & Leong, 1994). Parents may be particularly glad to learn about curricula that include built-in assessment tools and reflect carefully tailored choices. In preschool classrooms that promote the whole language approach, for example, assessments will be chosen to reflect the program's curricular philosophy (Cambourne & Turbell, 1990).

In the domain of enhancement of personal social skills, Shure (1992) created programs called "I Can Problem Solve" (ICPS) for teachers of young children. Along with the curricular scenarios for teachers, she provides assessment tools such as the What Happens Next game to use with each child. Armed with the children's responses, teachers can best work with each child in terms of boosting social problem-solving skills. Shure (1994) also created a parallel curriculum for parents to use with their young children. A self-evaluation checklist helps parents focus on how well they are doing in using ICPS techniques to promote young children's abilities to resolve everyday social conflicts with peers and adults.

When evaluation becomes an integral aspect of a program, then parents and teachers together have a stake in it. An important aspect of regular data gathering is that caregivers and staff become intimately involved in and responsive to whether or not programmatic innovations are actually producing desired effects. True, some programmatic innovations take time to implement and time before effects are seen. When caregivers themselves are observing, recording, and pondering the meaning of a child's lack of responsiveness or are becoming excited by child advances after worrisome delays, then evaluation becomes owned by the concerned adults. Their work makes a positive difference in young children's lives. An additional advantage is that when screening or assessments are done in an ongoing fashion, even children from isolated and poorly socialized environments become accustomed to the rules and procedures of "testing" that staff carries out in individualized loving and affirmative interactions with them.

Summative Evaluations. Most parents are familiar with summative evaluations as "grades" given at the end of a school year. Summative evaluations provide a clear confirmation of the effectiveness of the early learning program at the end of the program. Alternatively, they may provide discouraging evidence that a program has not been sufficiently tailored to meet the needs of a particular youngster. Retuning of intervention methods may be required as well as more attention to enlisting and training parents as teachers and tutors for the problems that are being addressed.

DATA COLLECTION

The Data Gatherers

Parents will be better consumers of assessment data when they are primed to ask about the testing skills of program personnel. When psychometric tests such as the Stanford-Binet are chosen as evaluation measures, the testers must be thoroughly trained and capable clinicians. They should be caring and intimate in relating to young children and deeply appreciative of a child's cooperation. Hastily trained or ill-prepared testers without knowledge of how to interact effectively with young children cannot be trusted to gather reliable and valid data despite the fact that they may have "learned" the rudiments of the items to be presented in a given battery of tests. Screening tests that are brief and easy to learn require less tester training.

Optimal testing of children by data gatherers is fervently to be desired. That means every child is well rested and well fed before being tested. Sometimes the testing person needs to break up a long series of tests over several days, or feed a youngster between tests, or take a break with toys in a playroom, or even take a walk around the block in the fresh air before continuing a battery of tests (Honig & Lally, 1989).

Degree of Data-Collection Obtrusiveness

Staff, boards of directors, and parents may differ on how intrusive assessment should be. Parents may object if children are removed frequently from classrooms for assessments, particularly when parents are not invited to be present.

When programs focus on supporting parents as their children's first teachers, then program evaluations may well focus on changes in parenting style and educational appropriateness. Suppose outside evaluators choose to carry out potentially stressful in-depth interviews with teen parents. A director serving the teen parents in a program providing infant/toddler child care plus classes for young mothers could feel anxious that overly intrusive inquiries will cause some of the teen parents to drop out of the program. That director may opt for using naturalistic observations of parent–child interactions rather than extensive interviews and questionnaires. Enhancing staff and parent observation skills is a highly desirable program goal (Cohen, Stern, & Balaban, 1983).

Caregivers can be quite effective in facilitating more appropriate child or parent behaviors when they respond empathically and supportively, contingent on their perceptive, unobtrusive observations. In a program where I was consultant, one teen mother would growl, "Shut up, you," as she changed her infant when ready to take him home after the child-care program and her own schooling in the same building were over for the day. As staff in this center continued to provide empathic supports and insights for the young mothers, caregiver modeling of gentleness with both mother and baby resulted in positive changes in maternal–infant interactions.

Ongoing versus Brief Samples of Assessments

Parents may want to be kept informed about the extensiveness of program record keeping. Some programs keep longitudinal running-record descriptions of children's interactions and progress. Others briefly sample children's progress from time to time. Parents often want to have a say in such decision making. They may prefer daily feedback, however brief, about their child's experiences in care.

SHARING RESEARCH "STORIES" WITH PARENTS

Where financial resources permit, an evaluation team may decide to enhance *external validity*, which means that findings can be generalized to larger groups, such as children of different ethnicity and/or family socioeconomic status. Large-scale projects, such as that of Whitebook, Howes, and Phillips (1989) on child-care staffing patterns and quality of care, collect data on geographically and ethnically representative families. Stability and quality of care were found significantly tied to staff salary and child development training. Sharing brief "stories" of such important research findings with parents will increase their knowledge about the role of evaluation in ensuring quality programming. When research findings are presented as "stories," even parents who are suspicious of research may find themselves fascinated by the information and concepts that research findings provide. An example of a research story could be findings from a New Orleans research study with low-income families. Parents who enjoyed their children, required chores of young children, read daily to children, kept their homes neat, and talked together at mealtimes, had children whom kindergarten teachers characterized as hard-working, with a sense of humor, persistent at school tasks, and amiable with peers (Swan & Stavros,1973). Parents also will find particularly reassuring research findings that show that all children go through some difficult phases, such as stranger anxiety toward the end of the first year, or oppositional behaviors during the "terrible 2s."

EVALUATION OF PROGRAM QUALITY AND CHILD OUTCOMES

When parents understand how strongly program quality is related to child outcomes, they themselves may advocate for regular ongoing assessments of program quality. Some evaluations make explicit the organization and structural components of a program. In residential nurseries in England, hierarchical characteristics of the institution affected child language outcome measures. The more rigidly caregivers were dependent on a director's decisions, the less competent the children were on the Reynell scales of receptive and expressive language. When caregivers were given more autonomy and flexibility in deciding their own daily schedules, the children's Reynell language scores were higher (Tizard, Cooperman, Joseph, & Tizard, 1972).

Many evaluators rightly set as the first priority the *measurement of the environment for children*. On paper, program goals and professed adherence to developmentally appropriate practices (Bredekamp, 1987) may look impressive, but it is imporant to ask whether program activities and interactions actually match the stated goals. Attention to such evaluations may prove significant over time. Primary school children in Trinidad who had attended a more definitively teacher-directed rather than child-centered preschool program had lower mean achievement scores and were less likely to tell important events to their teachers and to concentrate in class (Kutnick, 1994).

The way in which learning areas are structured, the movement of children from one activity to another, the amount of teacher-dominated versus child choice that is reflected in the ongoing daily activities may all be the focus of evaluation. Parents need to be alerted to the importance of factors such as provision of appropriate play materials and of nurturant and language-rich interactions during personal care routines, so that they as consumers of child care can better evaluate programs.

Focus on the Target Child

Many program evaluations focus exclusively on evaluating changes in the children served. Measures include achievement tests, on-task performance rates, positive or inappropriate socioemotional interactions (with peers and with adults), and cognitive competencies often defined as IQ or developmental scores on psychometric tests. In recent years there have been vigorous efforts to change from an emphasis on product-oriented test results to process-oriented evaluations of the ongoing work of the child, such as drawings and dictated stories. Genishi (1992) urges that such assessments are more naturally and conceptually linked to curriculum. Teachers may need to explain to parents the value of process-oriented assessments in comparison with letter grades, for example, with which parents are already familiar.

The High/Scope Child Observation Record (COR) (High/Scope, 1992; Schweinhart, 1993) for ages 2½ to 6 years is an assessment instrument designed for keeping anecdotal records of a child's behaviors initiated in regular program activities over several weeks or months. The observer completes this form by noting behaviors that best characterize the child's experiences in each of six general curriculum areas: initiative, social relations, creative representation, music and movement, language and literacy, and logic and mathematics. Programs that vigorously promote the use of portfolio assessments rather than grades need to hold workshops for parents where staff explains the reasons why portfolios are a valid and richly informative method of monitoring a young child's learning.

Some parents conceptualize evaluation primarily in terms of children's cognitive scores. Staff may want to explore why IQ scores may not be the best long-term measure of gains. For example, in the early evaluations of Head Start, minor intellectual gains were found that washed out by third grade. Yet the percentage of children whose medical problems were identified and remediated during the Head Start years was impressive as a measure of success. Over the years, program graduates were less likely to have a history of delinquency or a criminal record, and, for girls, were less likely to be teenage mothers (Schorr, 1988).

Parents may be unclear about the distinctions between short-term effects and long-term effects of enrichment efforts. For example, when staff model and teach positive interaction styles that nurture early learning, *vertical diffusion effects* may be found. That is, the younger siblings of the target child in a program may show even greater effects of program efforts.

Evaluations that test for effects immediately postintervention may miss both *positive sleeper effects and disappointing washout effects*. Long-term evidence of positive child self-esteem, fewer repeated school grades, less delinquency, and more attempts to complete a high school education may well convince parents that developmentally appropriate practices have valuable consequences, even though they may not at first seem comfortable in light of initial parental beliefs (Honig, 1989).

Sometimes evaluators find that there appears to be no difference between children in experimental (enriched) preschool programs and their controls. When parenting styles are taken into account, however, the positive effects of programs become clearer. Levenstein (1988) describes the difference between "hesitator" and "striver" mothers in her home visitation project. Both groups of mothers had babies and dropped out of school. But striver mothers subsequently went back for high school equivalency diplomas or enrolled in work/study programs. On a long-term basis, their children were not significantly affected by the 2-year mother–child home visitation (MCHV) program that brought books and toys to the toddlers' homes weekly. However, children of the hesitator mothers (who had not galvanized themselves toward either self- or family improvement) did significantly better than control youngsters even many years after their participation in the MCHV program. Similar 10-year results have been reported in the United Kingdom (Meadows & Cashdan, 1988).

Focus on Parents

Evaluation efforts focus primarily on parents when they, rather than the child, are the prime target of programmatic intervention. Home visitors provide insights, personal supports, information, books, developmentally appropriate toys, and social skills (such as positive discipline techniques) that support more effective parenting in at-risk families (Honig, 1979). Evaluation techniques need to be creatively conceived in order to confirm the impact of such efforts on child development. The fact that a parent knows how to reach out and find appropriate social services or is using a library regularly to find books to read with the child may be excellent outcome measures of the success of program. The current presence of a stable and positive fathering figure for a young child is a positive measure of the effectiveness of the program's impact on family. Significantly decreased rates of confirmed child abuse, several years after an at-risk famiy has completed participation in a parenting program, provide a sensitive measure of program effectiveness (Honig & Morin, 1996). Another excellent assessment tool is Caldwell's HOME Inventory, widely used nationally as a sensitive observation plus interview measure of positive family support for young children's optimal development (Caldwell & Bradley, 1984).

Standardized tests and measures are not the only way programs can assess their support for more effective parenting. The FDRP in Syracuse, New York (Lally et al., 1988) assessed change as positive when a mother was able to respond positively to the home visitor's expressed admiration for the child during a home visit, or when the mother was eating meals and talking with the child more frequently without the TV on at dinner time. Mothers reported still spanking but also giving reasons when they punished a child.

When paraprofessionals are trained to collect formative evaluation data after weekly home visits, frequent meetings may be necessary to make sure that no drift in *operational definitions* of observed or inquired items has occurred.

PARENTS AS OBSERVERS OF ASSESSMENT: A LEARNING OPPORTUNITY

Watching a home visitor carry out assessments sharpens a new parent's observational skills and heightens a parent's pleasure in recognizing budding new child abilities and in nurturing them. In a child-care facility, when parents are invited to be present for assessments, the *power of assessment as a further enrichment tool* can be marked. Parents sharpen their observation skills. They begin to value children's tries instead of just "perfect" or "correct" scores. Parents learn to model the genuine delight that a seasoned tester shows as she or he lures each young child into struggling with difficult problems and tasks on the cutting edge of learning. The parent learns how the Vygotskian "zone of proximal development" really works as the examiner assists the child in focusing on a task and supports a child's longer attention span and persistence at the task. *The importance of the adult as playmate and teaching companion* in the child's learning process is clearly modeled as a parent observes a skilled examiner assist the child to perform optimally. A seasoned examiner, even when working with a child who lags developmentally, will provide items that allow for clear-cut child success as she or he attempts to assess basal and ceiling scores for a psychometric test. The examiner rejoices verbally and with clapping gestures at the young child's competent behaviors. Parents learn from skilled evaluators how to become better "child watchers," how to appreciate small steps forward on the developmental ladders of learning (Honig, 1982), and how to develop patience and respect for the child's attempts to solve problems or answer difficult questions. They hone their ability to understand just where the child needs more sustained and helpful adult work toward new adventures in learning.

CONCLUSIONS

Flexibility and creativity in choice of assessments can enrich the lives of children rather than cause "test anxiety" to become entrenched early in a child's life. Child portfolios can be systematically gathered in ongoing evaluations, and evaluators can use both brief screening and more fine-tuned psychometric assessments judiciously. Well-chosen evaluations help program personnel more clearly to decide where their efforts need boosting and where their strengths are evident in working with children and families.

Parents need to be invited to become part of transciplinary teams from the initial planning stages through the assessment procedures and the group meetings where findings are evaluated and decision plans are uniquely tailored for a child. As parents sit in on assessment sessions where warm, intimate interactions take place between adult and child, they will find rich rewards in getting to know their own child better and getting to appreciate small but significant advances in their young child's learning. Participating adults will feel that they are "on top" of each individual child's learning patterns and abilities, so that they can uniquely individualize their personal goals and supportive interactions for each child.

REFERENCES

Apgar, V. (1975). A proposal for a new method of evaluation of a newborn infant. *Anesthesia and Analgesia, 32,* 260–267.

Barona, A. (1991). Assessment of multi-cultural preschool children In B. A. Bracken (Ed.), *The psychoeducational assessment of preschool children* (2nd ed.; pp. 379–391). Boston: Allyn & Bacon.

Bayley, N. (1994). *Bayley Scales of Infant Development–Second Edition.* San Antonio, TX: Psychological Corporation.

Bergen, D. (Ed.). (1994). *Assessment methods for infants and toddlers: Transdisciplinary team approaches.* New York: Teachers College Press.

Boehm, A. E. (1986). *Boehm Test of Basic Concepts: Preschool Version.* San Antonio, TX: Psychological Corporation.

Brazelton, T. B. (1984). *Neonatal Behavioral Assessment Scale* (2nd ed.). Philadelphia: Lippincott.

Bredekamp, S. (Ed.). (1987). *Developmentally appropriate practice in early childhood programs serving children from birth through age 8.* Washington, DC: National Association for the Education of Young Children.

Brigance, A. S. (1976). *Brigance Diagnostic Inventory of Basic Skills.* Woburn, MA: Curriculum Associates.

Caldwell, B. M. (1970). *The Cooperative Preschool Inventory.* Princeton, NJ: Educational Testing Services.

Caldwell, B. M., & Bradley, R. H. (1984). *Home observation for measurement of the environment* (rev. ed.). Little Rock: University of Arkansas.

Cambourne, B., & Turbell, J. (1990). Assessment in whole-language classrooms: Theory into practice. *The Elementary School Journal, 90,* 337–349.

Cattell, P. (1970). *Infant Intelligence Scale.* New York: Psychological Corporation.

Cohen, D., Stern, V., & Balaban, N. (1983). *Observing and recording the behavior of young children* (3rd ed.). New York: Teachers College Press.

Dunn, L. R., & Dunn, C. (1981). *Peabody Picture Vocabulary Test–Revised.* Circle Pines, MN: American Guidance Service.

Frankenberg, W. K., & Dodds, J. B. (1990). *DDST–11.* Denver, CO: Denver Developmental Materials.

Genishi, C. (1992). *Ways of assessing children and curriculum: Stories of early childhood practice.* New York: Teachers College Press.

Goodwin, W. L., & Goodwin, L. D. (1993). Young children and measurement: Standardized and nonstandardized instruments in early childhood education. In B. Spodek (Ed.), *Handbook of research on the education of young children* (pp. 441–463). New York: Macmillan.

Greenspan, S., & Meisels, S. (1995, February). A new vision for assessment. *Exceptional Parent, 25*(2), 23–25.

Gullo, D. F. (1994). *Understanding assessment and evaluation in early childhood education*. New York: Teachers College Press.

Harms, T., & Clifford, R. M. (1980). *Early Childhood Environment Rating Scale*. New York: Teachers College Press.

High/Scope. (1992). *Child Observation Record*. Ypsilanti, MI: High/Scope Educational Research Foundation.

Honig, A. S. (1979). *Parent involvement in early childhood education*. Washington, DC: National Association for the Education of Young Children.

Honig, A. S. (1982). *Playtime learning games for young children*. Syracuse, NY: Syracuse University Press.

Honig, A. S. (1983). Evaluation of infant/toddler intervention programs. In B. Spodek (Ed.), *Studies in educational evaluation* (Vol. 8, pp. 305–316). London: Pergamon Press.

Honig, A. S. (1989). Longitudinal effects of quality preschool programs. *Day Care and Early Education, 17*, 35–38.

Honig, A. S. (1994). Assessing the preparation of infant-toddler caregivers. In S. Reifel (Ed.), *Advances in early education and day care* (Vol. 6, pp. 107–151). Greenwich, CT: JAI Press.

Honig, A. S., & Lally, J. R. (1981). *Infant caregiving: A design for training*. Syracuse, NY: Syracuse University Press.

Honig, A. S., & Lally, J. R. (1988). Behavior profiles of experienced teachers of infants and toddlers. In A. S. Honig (Ed.), Optimizing early child care and education [Special Issue]. *Early Child Development and Care, 33*, 181–199.

Honig, A. S., & Lally, J. R. (1989). Effects of testing style on language scores of four-year-old low-income "control" children in an intervention project. *Early Child Development and Care, 41*, 195–211.

Honig, A. S., & Morin, C. (1996, August). *Longitudinal evaluation of a teen parents and babies program*. Poster presented at the 1996 convention of the American Psychological Association, Toronto, Canada.

Kamphaus, R. W. (1993). *Clinical assessment of children's intelligence*. Boston: Allyn & Bacon.

Kaufman, A. S., & Kaufman, N. L. (1983). *Kaufman Assessment Battery for Children*. Circle Pines, MN: American Guidance Service.

Kirk, S. A., , McCarthy, J. J., & Kirk, W. D. (1968). *Illinois Test of Psycholinguistic Abilities*. Urbana: University of Illinois Press.

Kutnick, P. (1994). Does preschool curriculum make a difference in primary school performance: Insights into the variety of preschool activities and their effects on school achievement and behavior in the Caribbean Island of Trinidad. *Early Child Development and Care, 103*, 27–42.

Lally, J. R., Mangione, P., & Honig, A. S. (1988). The Syracuse University Family Development Research Program: Long-range impact of an early intervention with low income children and their families. In D. Powell (Ed.), *Parent involvement as early childhood intervention: Emerging directions in theory, research, and practice* (pp. 79–104). Norwood, NJ: Ablex.

Levenstein, P. (1988). *The Mother–Child Home Program and the prevention of school disadvantage*. Columbus: Ohio State University Press.

Mardell-Czundowski, C. D., & Goldenberg, D. S. (1983). *Developmental Indicators for the Assessment of Learning–Revised*. Edison, NJ: Childcraft.

McAfee, O., & Leong, D. (1994). *Assessing and guiding young children's development and learning*. Boston: Allyn & Bacon.

McCarthy, D. A. (1972). *McCarthy Scales of Children's Abilities*. San Antonio, TX: Psychological Corporation.

Meadows, S., & Cashdan, A. (1988). *Helping children learn*. London: David Fulton.

Meisels, S. J. (1987). Uses and abuses of developmental screening and school readiness testing. *Young Children, 42*, 4–6, 68–73.

Meisels, S. J., & Steele, D. M. (1991). *The early childhood portfolio collection process*. Ann Arbor: University of Michigan, Center for Human Growth and Development.

National Association for the Education of Young Children. (1988). NAEYC position statement on standardized testing of young children 3 through 8 years of age. *Young Children, 43*(3), 42–47.

Newborg, J., Stok, J. R., Wnek, L., Guidobaldi, J., & Svinicki, J. (1984). *Battelle Developmental Inventory*. Allen, TX: Teaching Resources.

Nuttall, E. V., Romero, I., & Kalesnik, J. (1992). *Assessing and screening preschoolers: Psychological and educational dimensions*. Boston: Allyn & Bacon.

Psychological Corporation. (1980). *On telling parents about test results*. (Test Service Notebook 154). New York: Author.

Schorr, L. (1988). *Within our reach: Breaking the cycle of disadvantage*. New York: Anchor Doubleday.

Schweinhart, L. J. (1993). Observing young children in action: The key to early childhood assessment. *Young Children, 48*, 29–33.

Shure, M. (1992). *I can problem solve: An interpersonal cognitive problem-solving program* (Vol. 1–preschool; Vol. 2–kindergarten and primary grades; Vol. 3–elementary grades). Champaign, IL: Research Press.

Shure, M. (1994). *Raising a thinking child: Help your young child to resolve everyday conflicts and get along with others*. New York: Henry Holt.

Simeonsson, R. J. (1988). Unique characteristics of families with young handicapped children. In D. B. Bailey & R. J. Simeonsson (Eds.), *Family assessment in early intervention* (pp. 27–44). Columbus, OH: Merrill.

Swan, R. W., & Stavros, H. (1973). Child rearing practices associated with the development of cognitive skills of children in low socioeconomic areas. *Early Child Development and Care, 2*, 23–38.

Thornton, R. L., Hagen, E. P., & Sattler, J. M. (1986). *Stanford-Binet Intelligence Scale–Fourth Edition*. Riverside, CA: Riverside Publishing.

Tizard, B., Cooperman, O., Joseph, A., & Tizard, J. (1972). Environmental effects on language development: A study of young children in long-stay residential nurseries. *Child Development, 43*, 337–358.

Wechsler, D. (1990). *Manual for the Wechsler Intelligence Scale for Children–Revised*. San Antonio, TX: Psychological Corporation.

Whitebook, M., Howes, C., & Phillips, D. (1989). *Who cares: Child care and the quality of care in America* (Final report of the National Child Care Staffing Study). Oakland, CA: Child Care Employee Project.

Wortham, S. C. (1995). *Measurement and evaluation in early childhood education* (2nd ed.). Englewood Cliffs, NJ: Merrill.

Zero to Three. (1995). *Diagnostic classification of mental health and developmental disorders of infancy and early childhood (DC: 0–3)*. Washington, DC: National Center for Clinical Infant Programs.

CHAPTER 10

Evaluation in Early Childhood Education: A Look to the Future

Bernard Spodek and Olivia N. Saracho

In recent years the concern for evaluation in early childhood education and about the uses of various forms of evaluation in the field has increased. It is highly probable that this increased concern will continue. As a way of understanding the nature and appropriate uses of evaluation in early childhood education and as the basis for making a prognosis about the future, it is helpful to look at evaluation and its uses in early childhood education in the past and present.

EVALUATING PROGRAMS

Past

Program evaluation has been a part of early childhood education for at least a century, although early childhood educators have recognized its importance only in recent years. The history of program evaluation goes back to the time when the first new programs in early childhood education challenged older, more established ones. As progressive education came to the fore at the dawn of the twentieth century, the validity of the older Froebelian kindergartens was challenged. A committee of the International Kindergarten Union was established to evaluate the two approaches to kindergarten education and make a recommendation as to which was more valid. The committee included early childhood educators with various philosophic points of view.

Rather than arrive at a consensus as to what was worthwhile kinder-garten education — Froebelian kindergarten education or progressive kin-dergarten education — the committee presented three reports. One report philosophically validated Froebelian kindergarten education by affirming its basic principles; another validated the progressive kindergarten, also by affirming its principles; and a third sought a middle ground (Commit-tee of Nineteen, 1913). At that time, it seemed, what was considered a worthwhile kindergarten program was determined by the basic values, or philosophic point of view, that the individual espoused and the match between a program and that point of view.

Not too long after those reports were written, William Heard Kil-patrick (1916) critically examined the Froebelian kindergarten. His philo-sophic analysis found this program deficient, at least partly because it did not adhere to principles of child development that were part of the ration-ale for the kindergarten curriculum.

The Froebelian kindergarten was not the only early childhood pro-gram evaluated by Kilpatrick. The Montessori method was similarly eval-uated (Kilpatrick, 1914). Kilpatrick viewed Maria Montessori in a positive way, seeing her as an educator in the tradition of Rousseau, Pestallozzi, and Froebel. However, he questioned the depth of her contribution to education. His criticisms of her method came as a result of a comparison of Montessori's views about education with those of John Dewey. He felt that Montessori had a much narrower conception of education. Her focus on simple sensory experiences and her use of didactic materials were con-sidered too limiting.

While the demise of the Montessori movement in the United States in the late 1920s has been attributed to Kilpatrick's assessment of the Montes-sori method, it is doubtful if this is indeed the case. Kilpatrick's slim (72 pages) book appeared before the Montessori movement had gained any strength in the United States. As a matter of fact, the movement actually grew in the 15 years following its publication. A more plausible explana-tion for the demise of Montessori schools after 1929 suggests that it was a consequence of the stock market crash and the depression that followed. In this era, many individuals were forced to remove their children from private schools whose tuition they could no longer afford — and the Mon-tessori schools of the time were private.

Early childhood program evaluation in the first quarter of the twenti-eth century was based on a determination of the basic assumptions of the program and whether these basic assumptions were consistent with a particular view of childhood and education. This form of program evalua-tion changed drastically in the 1960s. The change can be attributed partly to advances in evaluation technology, with the creation of a number of different tests of development and achievement. However, the greater influence was probably the result of different theories of child development that had evolved over time.

The predominant view of human development up to the 1960s was that an individual's development was a function of genetic makeup. Development was posited as a process of unfolding; this was especially considered true in the years prior to a child's admission to first grade. Parents, for example, were admonished to leave children alone when it came to preparation for academics, since it was felt that nothing that happened to the child prior to initial instruction in academics could make a difference. This contrasts with the current view of emergent literacy, for example, which suggests that the language experiences a child receives in the years prior to formal instruction have a great impact on the outcomes of instruction (see Spodek & Saracho, 1993).

With the acceptance of a constructivist view of development, stimulated by the work of Hunt (1964), the belief developed in early childhood education that there can be significant consequences of programs at the preschool level — that early childhood education could influence children's development. If there can be consequences of these programs, then they can be evaluated in terms of program outcomes.

Starting with the experimental programs of the early 1960s and continuing with the Head Start program, the evaluation of program outcomes became important. One issue raised was which outcomes to evaluate. Since programs were expected to influence development, either short term or long term, then changes in development were to be considered as program outcomes. Cognitive development was considered a prime goal of these programs. Children from low-income families had higher rates of school failure. Deficiencies in the environments in which these children were raised were viewed as limiting these children's cognitive development. These programs were designed to provide children with experiences that would increase their levels of intelligence upon entry to school and thus increase their chances of school success.

To some extent the decision about what to evaluate also was influenced by what tests of the different developmental domains were available. Intelligence and academic achievement were valued, by both educators and policy makers. Since tests of intellectual development were available and children had not yet been taught academics, IQ tests were used to assess the new early childhood programs. The question to be asked by evaluation was: How much could a particular program boost IQ?

These evaluations, based on the use of IQ tests, soon led to disappointment with the programs since gains on IQ scores were not forthcoming for the Head Start programs (Westinghouse Learning Corporation, 1969).

Although early results of some of the experimental programs showed increased IQ scores for children at the completion of the programs, these gains soon faded. Initial questions that were raised regarding the efficacy of these programs were soon followed by questions about the appropriateness of the measures. Other measures soon were used that showed significant and long-lasting effects of these programs (Collins & Delaria, 1983; Lazar & Darlington, 1982).

Present

Early childhood education programs continue to be evaluated in the same ways as in the past. Most program evaluations look at outcome data. Judgments about what is a good program are made based on what program is effective. There continues to be a call for empirical studies of the effects of school curricula as a basis for their evaluation (Karweit, 1993).

While it is important to gather information regarding the effects of early childhood programs, care must be taken that the measures of a program's effectiveness be consistent with the nature of the program itself. Two decades ago a range of alternative program models were implemented as part of the Planned Variations of Head Start and Follow Through. All of the programs were evaluated with the same measures in the hope that the design would uncover the most effective program(s) from among those tested. Serious questions were raised, however, as to the fairness of the evaluation. It was suggested that the evaluation instruments used were more appropriate for some of the programs than for others (House, Glass, Mclean, & Walker, 1978). Schweinhart and Epstein (Chapter 3, this volume) suggest that any evaluation needs to be consistent with the nature of the educational program being evaluated.

Early childhood programs also are still being evaluated in terms of their adherence to philosophic principles. Over the past decade, the National Association for the Education of Young Children (NAEYC) has been disseminating a position statement regarding good educational practices for young children. The position statement contains guidelines for "developmentally appropriate practices" for early childhood education (Bredekamp, 1987). The guidelines presented are validated by reference to a variety of books about early childhood education, including some scholarly books containing research and theory, and textbooks and advocacy books describing what education should be. The volume also includes examples of good practices — practices that meet these guidelines — and poor practices — those that do not meet the guidelines.

These NAEYC guidelines have been used extensively to evaluate early childhood programs. They also have been extensively criticized. For one thing, while they represent themselves as rooted in developmental theory, they do not reflect any one theory. Although they refer to Piaget's work, what is reflected in the guidelines seems more maturationist oriented than constructivist oriented. In addition, the guidelines do not suggest that early childhood programs are culturally driven. The fact that these guidelines do not recommend or even suggest ways of modifying early childhood programs to respond to the diversity of the children served, has led to serious criticism (Kessler & Swadener, 1992; Mallory & New, 1994).

EVALUATING CHILDREN

Past

Just as programs for young children have been evaluated for a considerable time, so have young children themselves. Most of the early evaluations of children were to determine whether they were ready for school or for particular instruction within the school.

For many years, well into the 1960s, the field of early childhood education was driven by a maturationist theory of development. This suggested that the individual's development was determined by his or her genetic makeup. Educational programs, at best, could be responsive to each child's level of development and should follow that pattern of development. Education was not viewed as being able to influence development positively. However, it was felt that children could be frustrated and even "turned off" to school by prematurely being offered instruction before they were "ready." This notion of readiness led to the development of indices of development to be used to help match instruction to children's level of development, that is, to create developmentally appropriate programs.

Assessment of readiness was used often in reading instruction. The need for indicators of reading readiness goes back to the early 1930s. In a classic study of children who were successful in beginning reading, it was determined that the difference was the child's appropriate mental age. This was shown to be 6 years and 6 months (Morpel & Washburne, 1931).

Later, readiness to learn to read was seen as less determined by developmental maturity and more a matter of having acquired a level of competence. Spache and Spache (1969), for example, suggested that readiness to read required a level of visual ability, speech, listening ability, and social and emotional maturity. They also suggested that children needed to be interested in learning to read. The readiness tests that were developed during this period assessed children's abilities in these areas prior to beginning reading instruction.

Developmental readiness for school instruction still remained an area of concern. In 1965, Ilg and Ames published a set of readiness tests used by the Gesell Institute. They suggested that one of the biggest educational problems was the placement of children in grades beyond their developmental level. Using their tests, educators could assess which children were ready for school. Those who were not ready could delay admission to school until they arrived at the appropriate level of maturity. These tests are still used in schools today.

Both the particular test and the concept of withholding education from children until they achieve some level of developmental maturity have been criticized. The Gesell test, while a "high-stakes test," has been questioned as to its validity and its accuracy (Meisels, Steele, & Quinn-Leering, 1993). In addition, the notion of withholding early education from children who are judged to be "not ready" runs counter to our idea of educating such children at an earlier age, helping to "create readiness." This is the rationale for early education underlying the Head Start program as well as other programs for children with disabilities and those who might be at risk of future educational failure.

Present

Children are still evaluated by schools to determine their "readiness," often for kindergarten. While the schools may not deny kindergarten entry, the child may be enrolled in a "developmental kindergarten," with an additional year of kindergarten required before entrance into first grade. This continues to occur even though research evidence suggests there is no difference in achievement between those children who are enrolled in 2 years of kindergarten and comparable children who move on to first grade after 1 year of kindergarten (Shepard & Graue, 1993).

Children's learning continues to be evaluated as before—using achievement tests. However, a broader range of evaluation techniques are being developed and utilized in schools. The notion of authentic evaluation, that is, the evaluation of children's learning in context, is being increasingly used. Evaluation by observing children functioning in classroom settings as they use the knowledge they have gained in school, and collecting and assessing products of children's activities, as suggested by Doris Bergen (Chapter 6, this volume) and Dominic Gullo (Chapter 7), is being used increasingly by teachers.

Another form of evaluation of children that has been used increasingly in early childhood education in recent years is the evaluation of children's development and functioning to determine whether disabilities exist in a child. Preschool screening, the term used for the initial phase of this form of evaluation, is being suggested for all children well in advance of their entrance to school. The screening process identifies those children who might need additional schooling prior to the typical entrance into school. If screening identifies a potential disability, then a more in-depth assessment is made to determine whether a disability does exist and its extent. At that point, a recommendation usually is made as to whether the child should be placed in an early childhood special education program or, in many cases, a program for at-risk children.

A wide range of screening and assessment instruments, including standardized and informal tests, are available to identify children with disabilities. In addition, various observation techniques are used. The technique that is most appropriate depends on the particular child and the context in which the child can be assessed (for a description of screening and assessment instruments, see Spodek & Saracho, 1994).

EVALUATION IN EARLY CHILDHOOD EDUCATION: THE FUTURE

Given the reasons for increased interest in evaluation noted in the Introduction—the increasing number of children enrolled in early childhood programs, the increased public expenditure for such programs, and the desires of educators, policy makers, and parents to know more about the programs and the children enrolled—one should expect a continuing high level of interest in the evaluation of early childhood programs as well as the children in those programs. Done appropriately, such evaluations would serve various constituencies—educators, policy makers, and parents.

It can be expected that early childhood programs continually will be evaluated according to the worth of the programs themselves as well as to their effectiveness. The worth of a program depends on the degree to which it is valued. The NAEYC guidelines suggest that one measure of worth is developmental appropriateness. Others need to be identified as well. These would include the knowledge that children gain in the program and the degree to which this knowledge serves children in society. Programs also need to be evaluated in terms of how well they serve constituencies—children from different linguistic, cultural, and ethnic groups as well as children with varied abilities and disabilities. Discussion is going on currently regarding a revision of NAEYC's developmentally appropriate practices guidelines. It is hoped that a revision will reflect these other bases for evaluation and will lead to a variety of programs being judged as appropriate for young children in different contexts.

Young children will continue to be assessed. Program outcomes are judged this way as is children's achievement. The concern is that the assessment be appropriate for children and for the program itself. The use of standardized tests for assessment has the danger of influencing the curriculum, often narrowing it to reflect only what is being tested. There is also the danger that children will be prepared for the test by relying on rote learning rather than on gaining meaning (Shepard, 1991). While standardized tests are not bad in themselves, they need to be used appropriately. William and Laura Goodwin (Chapter 5, this volume) raise issues about the appropriate use of standardized tests. These guidelines, along with those provided by Meisels and colleagues (1993), can help educators make appropriate use of tests. In addition, the tests themselves should meet the standards set by the American Psychological Association, the American Educational Research Association, and the National Council on Measurement in Education (1985).

Standardized tests represent a limited form of evaluation. They take children's knowledge out of context and require performance in an extremely artificial situation. There are an increasing number of alternative ways of evaluating young children. Portfolios of children's products and observations of children's ability to function in real situations also should be used. Even in screening children prior to entrance into early childhood programs, alternative ways of collecting information should be used.

Standardized tests are used in school to evaluate academic achievement. We also need to expand the range of evaluation instruments we use to reflect the range of program outcomes we value. Most programs in early childhood education see social competence as a valued outcome, yet it seldom is evaluated. Atkins-Burnett, Nicholson, and Meisels (Chapter 8, this volume) review the research on the assessment of social competence. They provide suggestions that might help educators better evaluate this realm of learning in young children.

While evaluation will continue to be a concern in early childhood education, evaluation done wisely and carefully can lessen the danger to programs, to children, and to teachers. It also can help to improve the quality of early childhood programs we provide.

REFERENCES

American Psychological Association, American Educational Research Association, & National Council on Measurement in Education. (1985). *Standards for educational and psychological testing.* Washington, DC: American Psychological Association.

Bredekamp, S. (Ed). (1987). *Developmentally appropriate practice in early childhood programs serving children from birth through age 8.* Washington, DC: National Association for the Education of Young Children.

Collins, R. C., & Delaria, D. (1983). Head Start research: A new chapter. *Children Today, 12*(4), 15–19.

Committee of Nineteen. (1913). *The kindergarten*. Boston: Houghton Mifflin.

House, E. R., Glass, G. V., Mclean, L. D., & Walker, D. F. (1978). No simple answers: Critique of the Follow Through evaluation. *Harvard Educational Review, 48*, 128–160.

Hunt, J. McV. (1964). *Intelligence and experience*. New York: Ronald Press.

Ilg, F. L., & Ames, L. B. (1965). *School readiness: Behavioral tests used at the Gesell Institute*. New York: Harper & Row.

Karweit, N. (1993). Effective preschool and kindergarten programs for students at risk. In B. Spodek (Ed.), *Handbook of research on the education of young children* (pp. 385–411). New York: Macmillan.

Kessler, S., & Swadener, B. B. (1992). *Reconceptualizing the early childhood curriculum*. New York: Teachers College Press.

Kilpatrick, W. H. (1914). *The Montessori system examined*. Boston: Houghton Mifflin.

Kilpatrick, W. H. (1916). *Froebel's kindergarten principles critically examined*. New York: Macmillan.

Lazar, I., & Darlington, R. (1982). *Lasting effects of early education*. Monographs of the Society for Research in Child Development, 47(2–3, Serial 195).

Mallory, B. L., & New, R. S. (1994). *Diversity and developmentally appropriate practices: Challenges for early childhood education*. New York: Teachers College Press.

Meisels, S. J., Steele, D. M., & Quinn-Leering, K. (1993). Testing, tracking, and retaining young children: An analysis of research and social policy. In B. Spodek (Ed.), *Handbook of research on the education of young children* (pp. 279–292). New York: Macmillan.

Morpel, M. V., & Washburne, C. (1931). When should children begin to read? *Elementary School Journal, 31*, 496–508.

Shepard, L. A. (1991). The influence of standardized tests on the early childhood curriculum, teachers, and children. In B. Spodek & O. N. Saracho (Eds.), *Yearbook in early childhood education: Vol. 2. Issues in early childhood curriculum* (pp. 166–189). New York: Teachers College Press.

Shepard, L. A., & Graue, M. E. (1993). The morass of school readiness screening: Research on test use and test validity. In B. Spodek (Ed.), *Handbook of research on the education of young children* (pp. 293–305). New York: Macmillan.

Spache, G. D., & Spache, E. B. (1969). *Reading in the elementary school*. Boston: Allyn & Bacon.

Spodek, B., & Saracho, O. N. (1993). *Yearbook in early childhood education: Vol. 4. Language and literacy in early childhood education*. New York: Teachers College Press.

Spodek, B., & Saracho, O. N. (1994). *Dealing with individual differences in the early childhood classroom*. New York: Longman

Westinghouse Learning Corporation. (1969). *The impact of Head Start: An evaluation of the effects of Head Start on children's cognitive and affective development*. (ERIC Document Reproduction Service No. ED 036 321)

About the Editors and the Contributors

Sally Atkins-Burnett is a doctoral student in early childhood special education at the University of Michigan. She earned her master's degree at Boston College and has taught regular and special education at both the preschool and elementary level. Her research interests include families with young children, inclusion, and young children's social development. She is currently involved with the Early Childhood Longitudinal Study, funded by the National Center for Educational Statistics.

Doris Bergen is Professor and Chair of the Department of Educational Psychology at Miami University. She has been a preschool and primary teacher and a university teacher of early childhood education, child and lifespan development, research and assessment, and educational psychology. Her research interests include play, social, and humor development of young children. She also has studied cross-cultural early childhood practices and beliefs and the effects of adult facilitation on the play of children with developmental delays. Her most recent book is *Assessment Methods for Infants and Toddlers: Transdisciplinary Team Approaches* (Teachers College Press).

Tony Bertram is Senior Research Fellow and Deputy Director of the Center for Early Childhood Research at Worcester College of Higher Education in England. He is Assistant Director of the research project, "Effective Early Learning: An Action Plan for Change," and is President of the European Early Childhood Education Research Association. He taught in first and primary schools prior to working in higher education. His research interests include early childhood teacher training, admission of children to school, and men in early childhood education.

Laurie Bozzi is a doctoral student in the Department of Human Development and Psychology at the Harvard Graduate School of Education. Her primary interest is early childhood development. Much of her work is focused on understanding the diverse educational beliefs, settings, and practices of child-care providers. She also is currently studying the social and moral development of young children by analyzing their personal narratives.

Ann S. Epstein is a Senior Research Associate at the High/Scope Educational Research Foundation. She has evaluated the effectiveness of educational programs for children from infancy through adolescence and their families. She also has conducted research on effective teacher-training practices in early childhood education. Her most recent publications include *Models of Early Childhood Education* and *Training for Quality: Improving Early Childhood Education Programs Through Systematic Inservice Training*. She received her Ph.D. in developmental psychology from the University of Michigan.

Bruce Fuller is Associate Professor of Comparative Policy at Harvard University. His work focuses on how family and educational policies affect households and early schooling organizations. Professor Fuller, trained as a sociologist, has been evaluating how federal and state policies have shaped the availability and quality of preschool programs in rich and poor communities. His forthcoming book, with Susan Holloway, is *Through My Own Eyes: Mothers' Views of Work and Child Rearing in Diverse Cultures of Poverty*.

Laura D. Goodwin received her Ph. D. in research methodology, evaluation, and measurement at the University of Colorado, Boulder. After 6 years at the University's Health Sciences Center, she joined the faculty of the University of Colorado at Denver. She is now Professor and Associate Dean there and is also a Presidential Teaching Scholar for the University of Colorado system. She teaches courses in statistics, measurement, and research methods. She has published extensively, often on methodological issues, in both nursing and education journals. Her most recent book (with William L. Goodwin) is *Understanding Quantitative and Qualitative Research in Early Childhood Education* (Teachers College Press).

William L. Goodwin received his Ph.D. in educational psychology at the University of Wisconsin. He was an AERA-USOE Postdoctoral Fellow in Early Childhood Education at Harvard University's Laboratory of Human Development and a Fellow in the USOE Leadership Training Institute for Early Childhood Education. He has been a professor at the University of Colorado at Denver and Coordinator of the Educational Psychology Division, where he teaches courses in early childhood education, educational psychology, measurement, and research methodology. His previous publications include books and articles in both educational psychology and early childhood education. His most recent book (with Laura D. Goodwin) is *Understanding Quantitative and Qualitative Research in Early Childhood Education* (Teachers College Press).

Dominic F. Gullo is Professor of Early Childhood Education and Associate Dean for Academic Affairs at the University of Wisconsin–Milwaukee. He received his doctorate from Indiana University in the Interdisciplinary Doctoral Program on Young Children. Before becoming a professor, he taught in public school kindergartens and prekindergartens and in Head Start. His most current book is *Understanding Assessment and Evaluation in Early Childhood Education* (Teachers College Press). He is Co-Principal Investigator of the Milwaukee Early Schooling Initiative Project.

Susan D. Holloway is currently Visiting Associate Professor in the Department of Human Development and Psychology at the Harvard Graduate School of Education. She is interested in the education and socialization of young children within family and early childhood education settings. Her most recent research examines cultural variation in American parents' views about child rearing, with a focus on the developmental implications and applications to child-care policy. She also is conducting studies of teachers' beliefs and practices in Japanese kindergartens and elementary schools.

Alice Sterling Honig is Professor Emerita of Child Development at Syracuse University. She is the author of over 200 articles and chapters and many books, including *Parent Involvement in Early Childhood Education* (NAEYC), *Playtime Learning Games for Young Children* (Syracuse University Press), and *Infant Caregiving: A Design for Training* (Syracuse University Press, with J. R. Lally). She has consulted with numerous child-care projects and in 1994 received the Chancellor's Citation for Excellence in Academic Achievement at Syracuse University where she has conducted a national workshop on infant/toddler caregiving.

Samuel J. Meisels is Professor and Research Scientist at the University of Michigan School of Education. He has taught preschool, kindergarten, and first grade. He was also a professor in the Department of Child Study at Tufts University where he served as director of the Eliot-Pearson Children's School. Dr. Meisels was selected in 1985 as the Mary Switzer Distinguished Fellow in Handicapped Research at the National Institute of Handicapped Research, U. S. Department of Education. He has published more than 100 articles, books, and monographs on early childhood development, assessment, and early childhood special education. His current research concerns the development of a comprehensive performance assessment for preschool–grade 5 (*The Work Sampling System*) and assessments for use in the Early Childhood Longitudinal Study.

Julie Nicholson is a doctoral student in early childhood at the University of Michigan. She is a former preschool and kindergarten teacher. She has a master's degree in early childhood from the University of Michigan and is completing a master's degree in developmental psychology at San Francisco State University. Her research interests include the relationship between children's emergent literacy and their social development, and the use of technology in early childhood education. She is currently working on the Early Childhood Longitudinal Study.

Christine Pascal holds the Chair in Early Childhood Education at Worcester College of Higher Education in England. She is currently the director of "Effective Early Learning: An Action Plan for Change," a national research project. From 1991–1994 she was National President of the British Association of Early Childhood Education and is now Vice-President. She taught in infant schools in Birmingham, and was a member of the RSA Start Right Inquiry into Early Learning and is currently a member of the Labor Party Early Years Inquiry. She is a co-founder of the European Early Childhood Education Research Association and has worked with the association at the local, national, and international level to raise the status and quality of education for young children.

Arthur J. Reynolds is Assistant Professor in the School of Social Work at the University of Wisconsin–Madison. He is conducting a longitudinal study of the effects of extended childhood intervention on social competence in high school. His research interests include poverty and child development, program evaluation, educational achievement, and quantitative methods.

Olivia N. Saracho is Professor of Education in the Department of Curriculum and Instruction at the University of Maryland. Her areas of scholarship include cognitive style, teaching, and teacher education in early childhood education. Dr. Saracho's most recent books are *Right from the Start: Teaching Children Ages Three Through Eight* (Allyn & Bacon), *Dealing with Individual Differences in the Early Childhood Classroom* (Longman), both with Bernard Spodek, and *Foundations of Early Childhood Education* (Allyn & Bacon) with Bernard Spodek and Michael J. Davis. She is also editor, with Roy Evans, of *Early Childhood Teacher Education: An International Perspective* (Gordon & Breach). Dr. Saracho is co-editor of the Yearbook in Early Childhood Education Series (Teachers College Press).

Lawrence J. Schweinhart is a researcher and speaker for educational leadership and decision makers throughout the United States. He chairs the research division of the High/Scope Educational Research Foundation in Ypsilanti, Michigan. He is the author of *Significant Benefits: The High/Scope Perry Preschool Study Through Age 27* and related studies. He received his Ph.D. in education from Indiana University, specializing in the development of young children. He has taught fourth and seventh grades, and he and his wife have raised two children beyond childhood.

Bernard Spodek is Professor of Early Childhood Education at the University of Illinois. He received his doctorate from Teachers College, Columbia University. His research and scholarly interests are in the areas of curriculum, teaching, and teacher education in early childhood education. Dr. Spodek's most recent books are *Right from the Start: Teaching Children Ages Three Through Eight* (Allyn & Bacon), *Dealing with Individual Differences in the Early Childhood Classroom* (Longman), both with Olivia N. Saracho, *Handbook of Research on the Education of Young Children* (Macmillan), and *Foundations of Early Childhood Education* (Allyn & Bacon) with Olivia N. Saracho and Michael J. Davis. Bernard Spodek is co-editor of the Yearbook in Early Childhood Education Series (Teachers College Press).

Herbert J. Walberg is Research Professor of Education at the University of Illinois at Chicago. He was awarded his Ph. D. in educational psychology by the university and formerly taught at Harvard University. He has written and edited more than 50 books and contributed more than 380 articles to educational and psychological journals. He is editor of *Evaluating Educational Performance* and co-editor of the *International Encyclopedia of Educational Evaluation*. He frequently serves a program design advisor and evaluator of educational programs.

Index

NAMES

213

SUBJECTS